MARVEL KNIGHTS
HULK

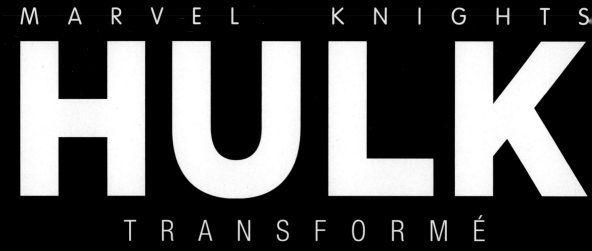

MARVEL KNIGHTS
HULK
TRANSFORMÉ

WRITER
JOE KEATINGE

ARTIST
PIOTR KOWALSKI

COLOR ARTIST
NICK FILARDI

LETTERER
VC'S CLAYTON COWLES

COVER ARTISTS
PIOTR KOWALSKI & NICK FILARDI

ASSISTANT EDITOR
JON MOISAN

EDITOR
BILL ROSEMANN

COLLECTION EDITOR: SARAH BRUNSTAD **ASSOCIATE MANAGING EDITOR:** ALEX STARBUCK
EDITORS, SPECIAL PROJECTS: MARK D. BEAZLEY & JENNIFER GRÜNWALD **SENIOR EDITOR, SPECIAL PROJECTS:** JEFF YOUNGQUIST
SVP PRINT, SALES & MARKETING: DAVID GABRIEL **BOOK DESIGNER:** RODOLFO MURAGUCHI

EDITOR IN CHIEF: AXEL ALONSO **CHIEF CREATIVE OFFICER:** JOE QUESADA
PUBLISHER: DAN BUCKLEY **EXECUTIVE PRODUCER:** ALAN FINE

MARVEL KNIGHTS: HULK — TRANSFORMÉ. Contains material originally published in magazine form as MARVEL KNIGHTS: HULK #1-4 and HULK #1. First printing 2014. ISBN# 978-0-7851-8406-5. Published by MARVEL WORLDWIDE, INC., a subsidiary of MARVEL ENTERTAINMENT, LLC. OFFICE OF PUBLICATION: 135 West 50th Street, New York, NY 10020. Copyright © 1962, 2013 and 2014 Marvel Characters, Inc. All rights reserved. All characters featured in this issue and the distinctive names and likenesses thereof, and all related indicia are trademarks of Marvel Characters, Inc. No similarity between any of the names, characters, persons, and/or institutions in this magazine with those of any living or dead person or institution is intended, and any such similarity which may exist is purely coincidental. **Printed in Canada.** ALAN FINE, EVP - Office of the President, Marvel Worldwide, Inc. and EVP & CMO Marvel Characters B.V.; DAN BUCKLEY, Publisher & President - Print, Animation & Digital Divisions; JOE QUESADA, Chief Creative Officer; TOM BREVOORT, SVP of Publishing; DAVID BOGART, SVP of Operations & Procurement, Publishing; C.B. CEBULSKI, SVP of Creator & Content Development; DAVID GABRIEL, SVP Print, Sales & Marketing; JIM O'KEEFE, VP of Operations & Logistics; DAN CARR, Executive Director of Publishing Technology; SUSAN CRESPI, Editorial Operations Manager; ALEX MORALES, Publishing Operations Manager; STAN LEE, Chairman Emeritus. For information regarding advertising in Marvel Comics or on Marvel.com, please contact Niza Disla, Director of Marvel Partnerships, at ndisla@marvel.com. For Marvel subscription inquiries, please call 800-217-9158. **Manufactured between 3/28/2014 and 5/5/2014 by SOLISCO PRINTERS, SCOTT, QC, CANADA.**

10 9 8 7 6 5 4 3 2 1

1

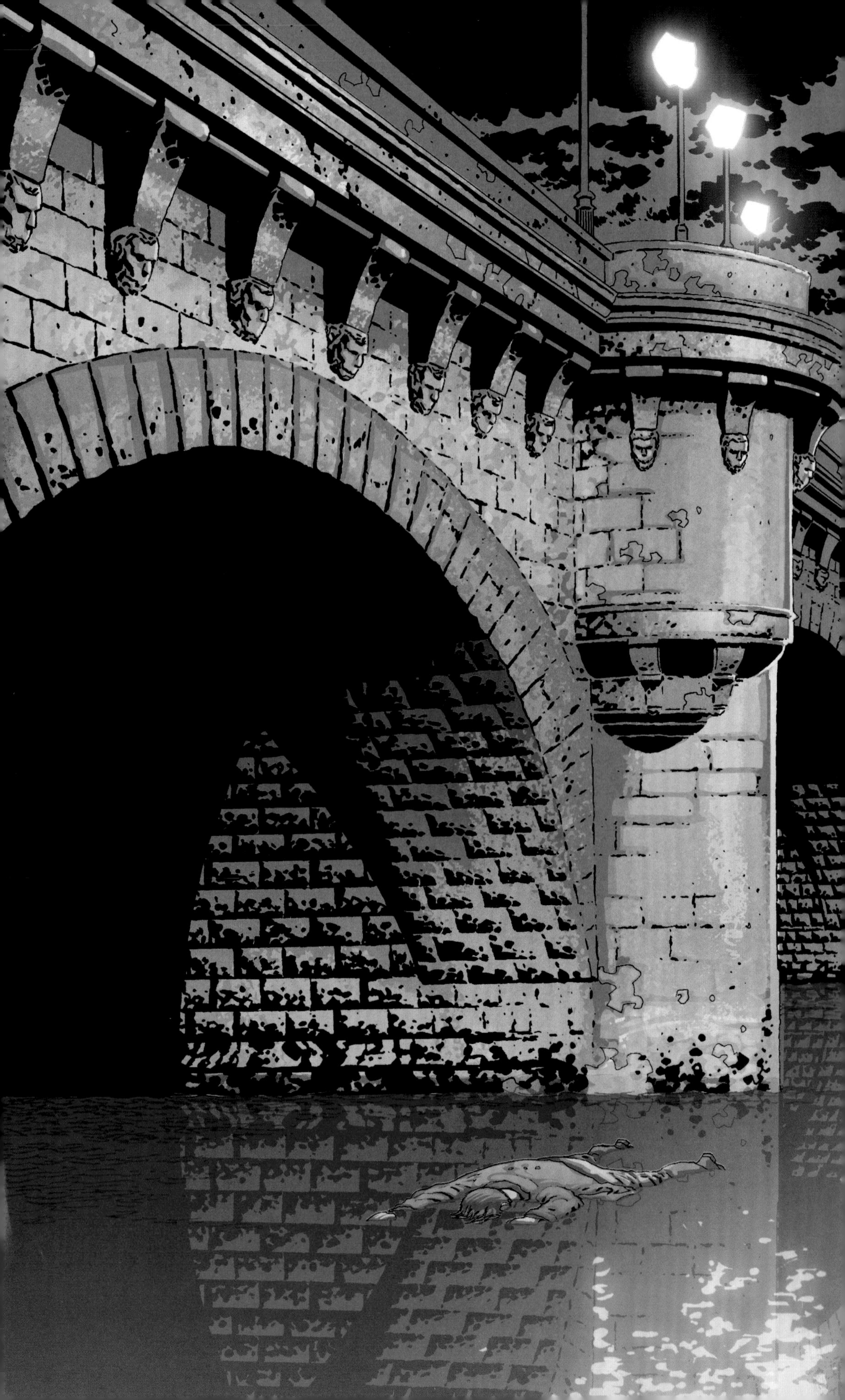

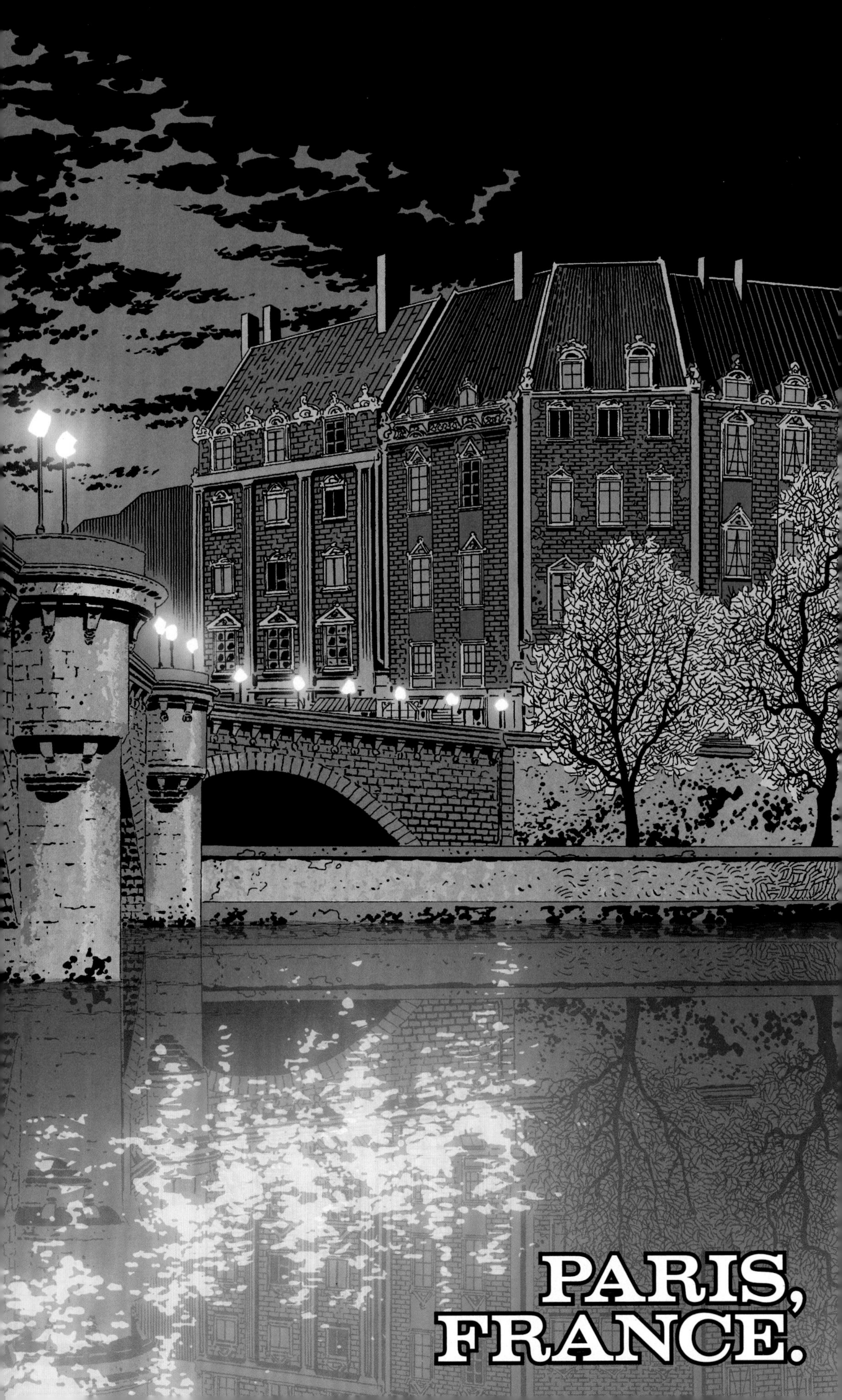
PARIS, FRANCE.

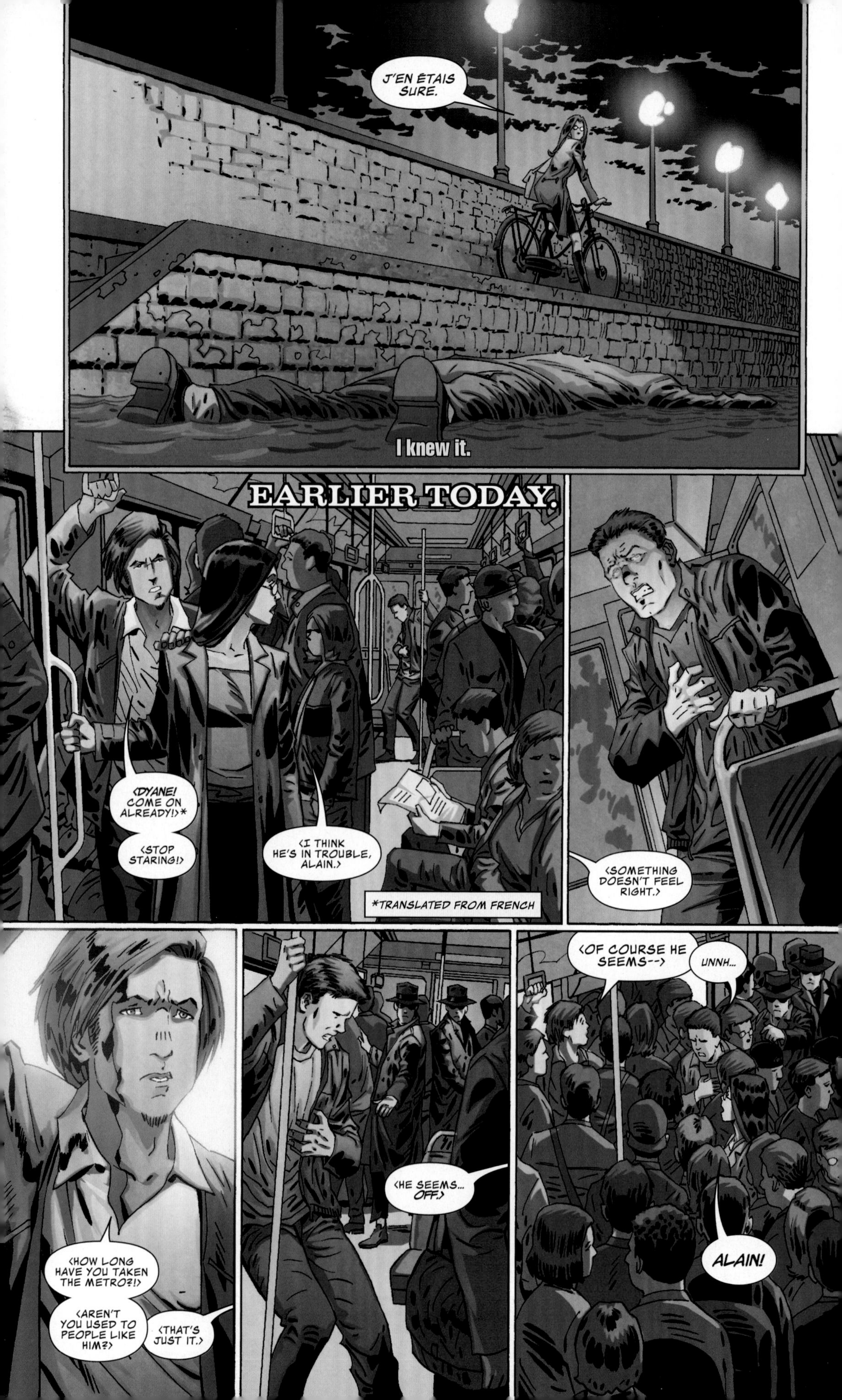
J'EN ÉTAIS SURE.
I knew it.
EARLIER TODAY.
<DYANE! COME ON ALREADY!>*
<STOP STARING!>
<I THINK HE'S IN TROUBLE, ALAIN.>
*TRANSLATED FROM FRENCH
<SOMETHING DOESN'T FEEL RIGHT.>
<HOW LONG HAVE YOU TAKEN THE METRO?!>
<AREN'T YOU USED TO PEOPLE LIKE HIM?>
<THAT'S JUST IT.>
<HE SEEMS... OFF.>
<OF COURSE HE SEEMS-->
UNNH...
ALAIN!

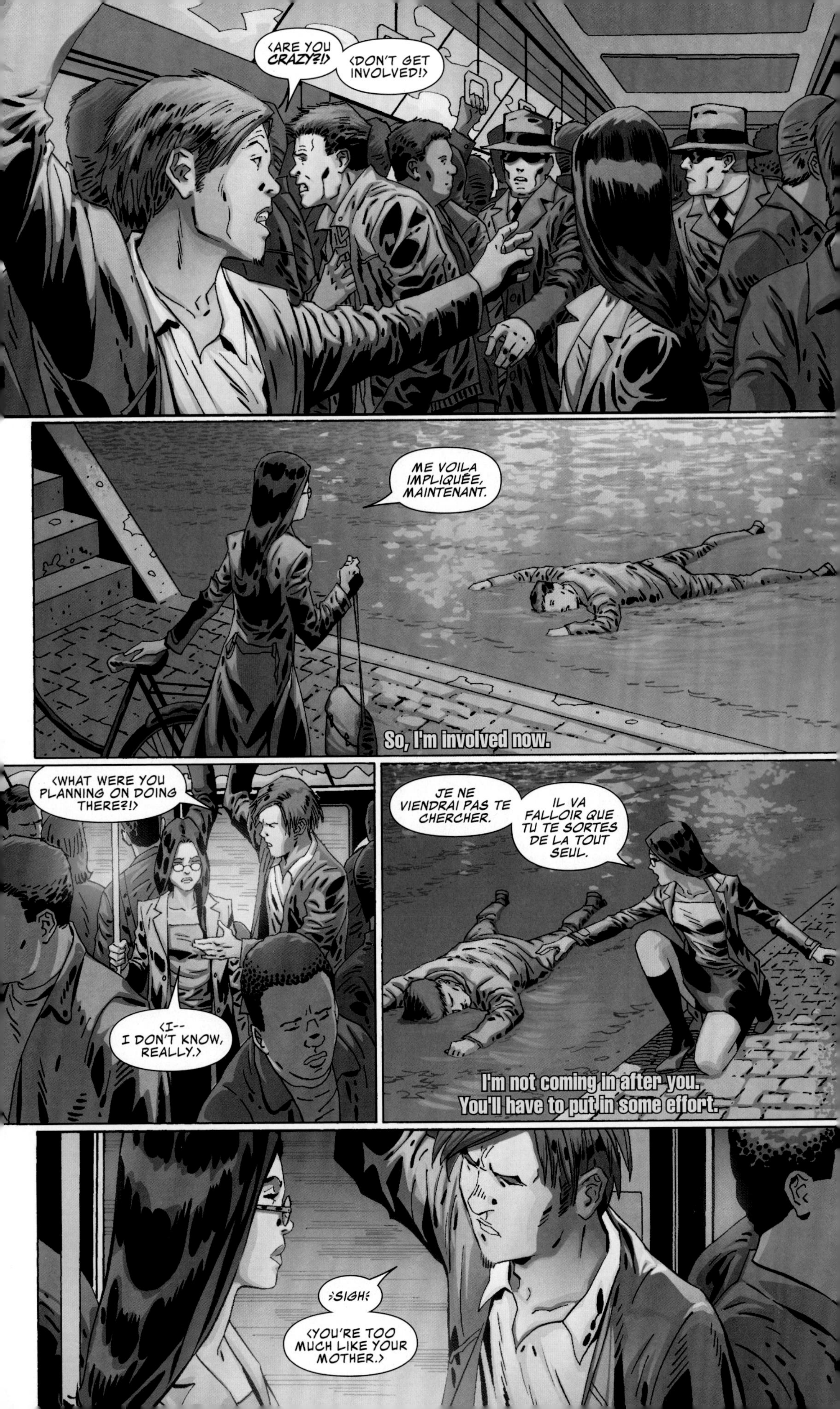

‹ARE YOU CRAZY?!›
‹DON'T GET INVOLVED!›
ME VOILA IMPLIQUÉE, MAINTENANT.
So, I'm involved now.
‹WHAT WERE YOU PLANNING ON DOING THERE?!›
‹I-- I DON'T KNOW, REALLY.›
JE NE VIENDRAI PAS TE CHERCHER.
IL VA FALLOIR QUE TU TE SORTES DE LA TOUT SEUL.
I'm not coming in after you. You'll have to put in some effort.
›SIGH‹
‹YOU'RE TOO MUCH LIKE YOUR MOTHER.›

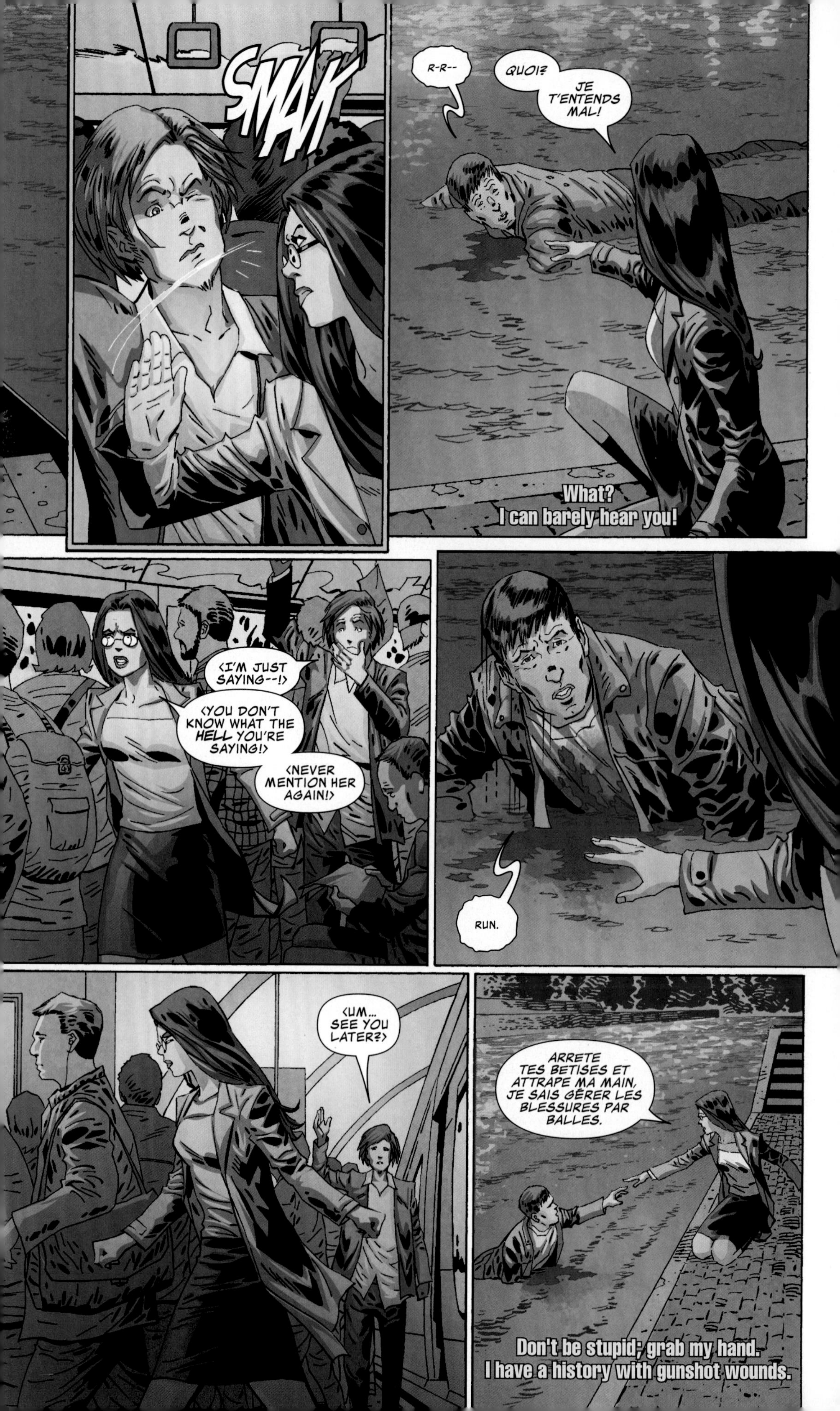
SMAK
R-R--
QUOI? JE T'ENTENDS MAL!
What? I can barely hear you!
<I'M JUST SAYING--!>
<YOU DON'T KNOW WHAT THE HELL YOU'RE SAYING!>
<NEVER MENTION HER AGAIN!>
RUN.
<UM... SEE YOU LATER?>
ARRETE TES BETISES ET ATTRAPE MA MAIN, JE SAIS GÉRER LES BLESSURES PAR BALLES.
Don't be stupid; grab my hand. I have a history with gunshot wounds.

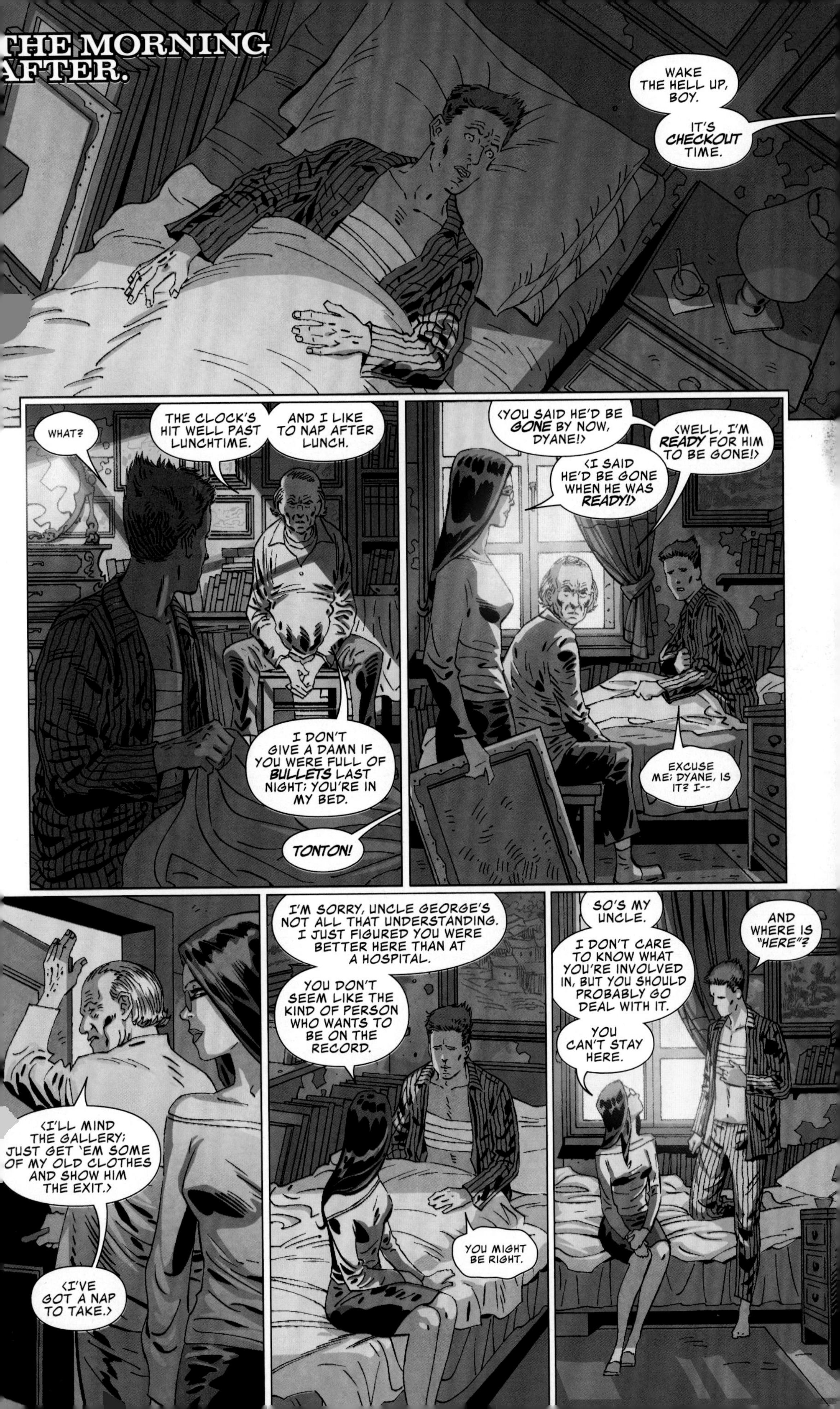
THE MORNING AFTER.
WAKE THE HELL UP, BOY.
IT'S CHECKOUT TIME.
WHAT?
THE CLOCK'S HIT WELL PAST LUNCHTIME.
AND I LIKE TO NAP AFTER LUNCH.
I DON'T GIVE A DAMN IF YOU WERE FULL OF BULLETS LAST NIGHT; YOU'RE IN MY BED.
TONTON!
<YOU SAID HE'D BE GONE BY NOW, DYANE!>
<I SAID HE'D BE GONE WHEN HE WAS READY!>
<WELL, I'M READY FOR HIM TO BE GONE!>
EXCUSE ME; DYANE, IS IT? I--
<I'LL MIND THE GALLERY; JUST GET 'EM SOME OF MY OLD CLOTHES AND SHOW HIM THE EXIT.>
<I'VE GOT A NAP TO TAKE.>
I'M SORRY, UNCLE GEORGE'S NOT ALL THAT UNDERSTANDING. I JUST FIGURED YOU WERE BETTER HERE THAN AT A HOSPITAL.
YOU DON'T SEEM LIKE THE KIND OF PERSON WHO WANTS TO BE ON THE RECORD.
YOU MIGHT BE RIGHT.
SO'S MY UNCLE.
I DON'T CARE TO KNOW WHAT YOU'RE INVOLVED IN, BUT YOU SHOULD PROBABLY GO DEAL WITH IT.
YOU CAN'T STAY HERE.
AND WHERE IS "HERE"?

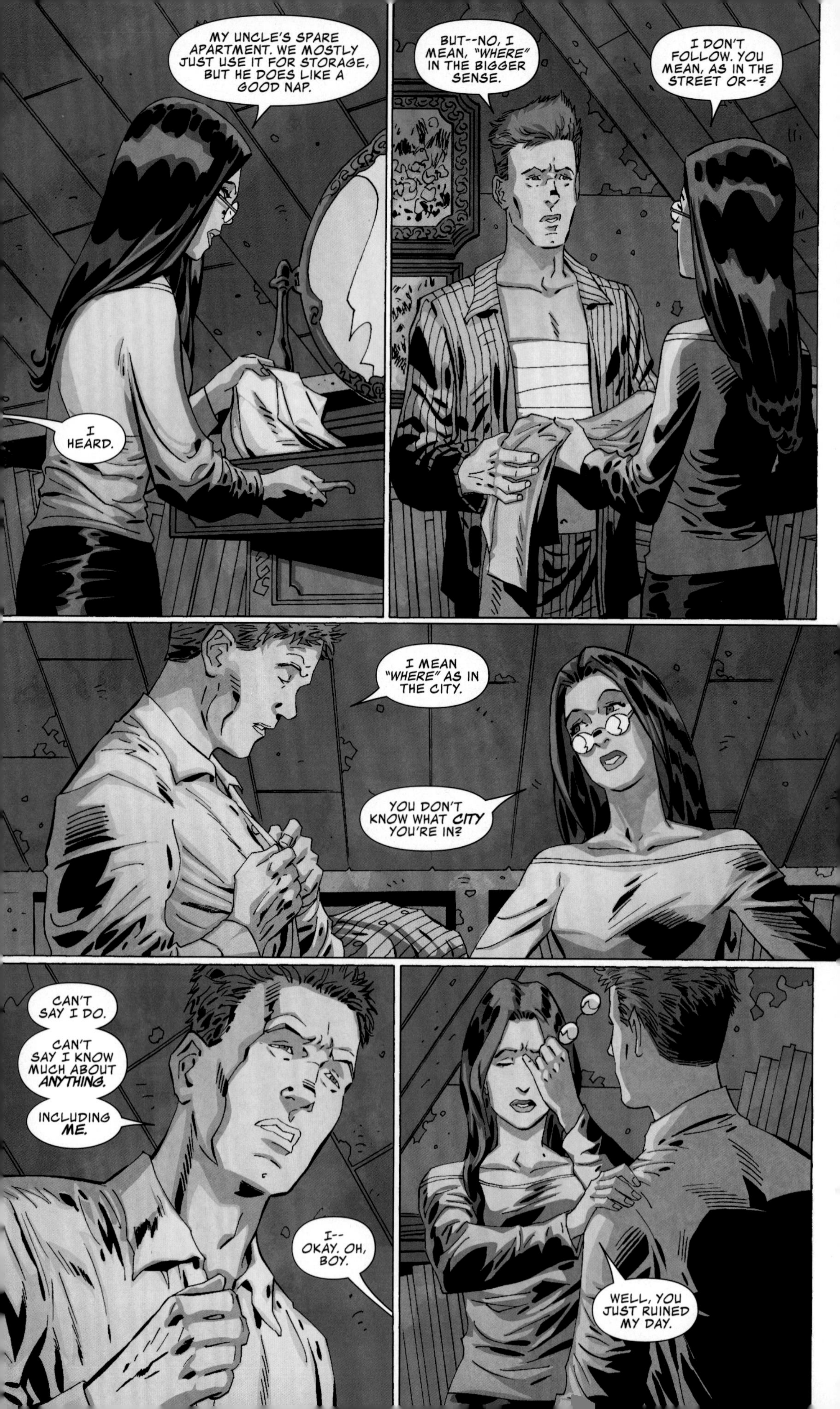

MY UNCLE'S SPARE APARTMENT. WE MOSTLY JUST USE IT FOR STORAGE, BUT HE DOES LIKE A GOOD NAP.
I HEARD.
BUT--NO, I MEAN, "WHERE" IN THE BIGGER SENSE.
I DON'T FOLLOW. YOU MEAN, AS IN THE STREET OR--?
I MEAN "WHERE" AS IN THE CITY.
YOU DON'T KNOW WHAT CITY YOU'RE IN?
CAN'T SAY I DO.
CAN'T SAY I KNOW MUCH ABOUT ANYTHING.
INCLUDING ME.
I-- OKAY. OH, BOY.
WELL, YOU JUST RUINED MY DAY.

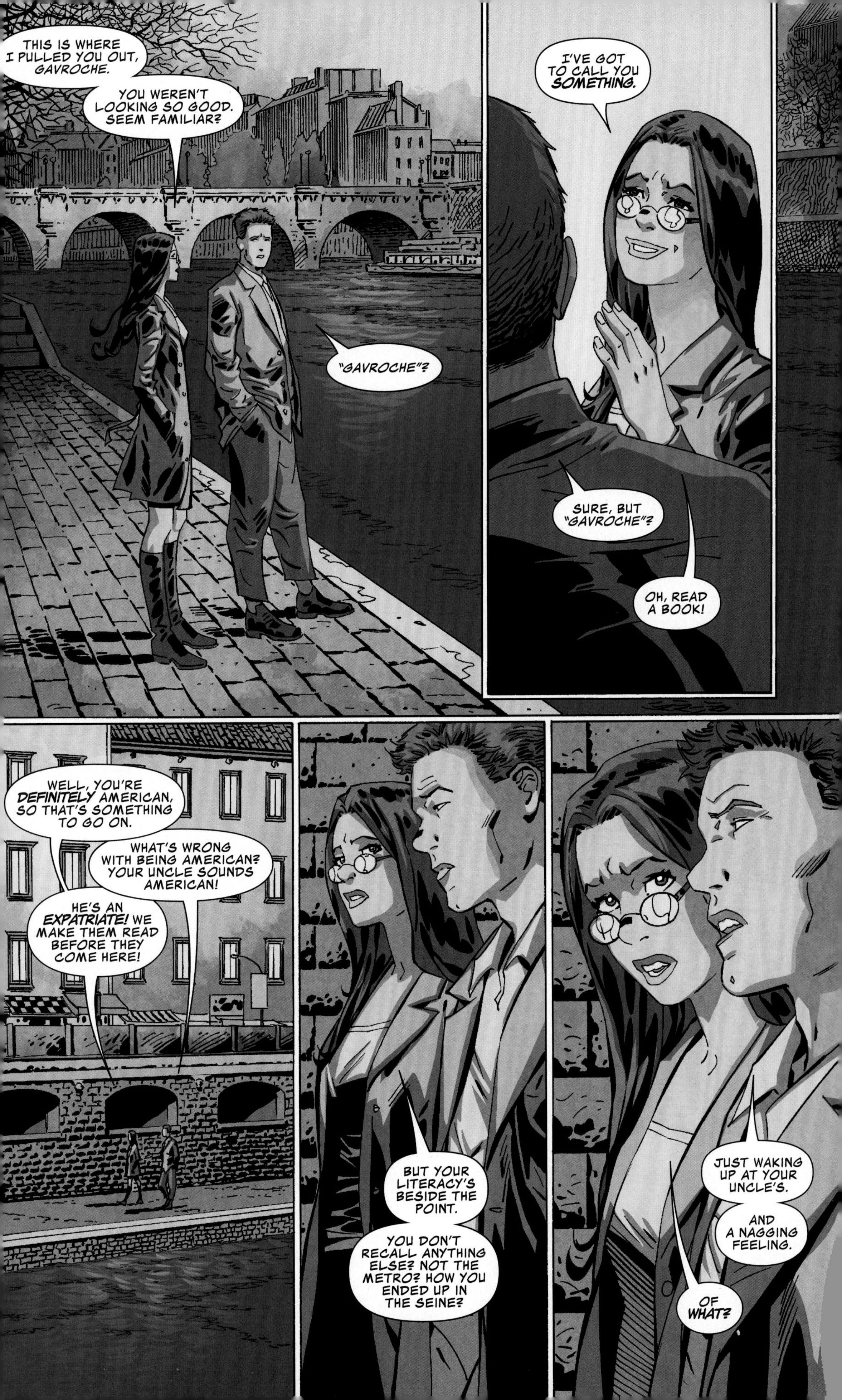
THIS IS WHERE I PULLED YOU OUT, GAVROCHE.
YOU WEREN'T LOOKING SO GOOD. SEEM FAMILIAR?
"GAVROCHE"?
I'VE GOT TO CALL YOU SOMETHING.
SURE, BUT "GAVROCHE"?
OH, READ A BOOK!
WELL, YOU'RE DEFINITELY AMERICAN, SO THAT'S SOMETHING TO GO ON.
WHAT'S WRONG WITH BEING AMERICAN? YOUR UNCLE SOUNDS AMERICAN!
HE'S AN EXPATRIATE! WE MAKE THEM READ BEFORE THEY COME HERE!
BUT YOUR LITERACY'S BESIDE THE POINT.
YOU DON'T RECALL ANYTHING ELSE? NOT THE METRO? HOW YOU ENDED UP IN THE SEINE?
JUST WAKING UP AT YOUR UNCLE'S.
AND A NAGGING FEELING.
OF WHAT?

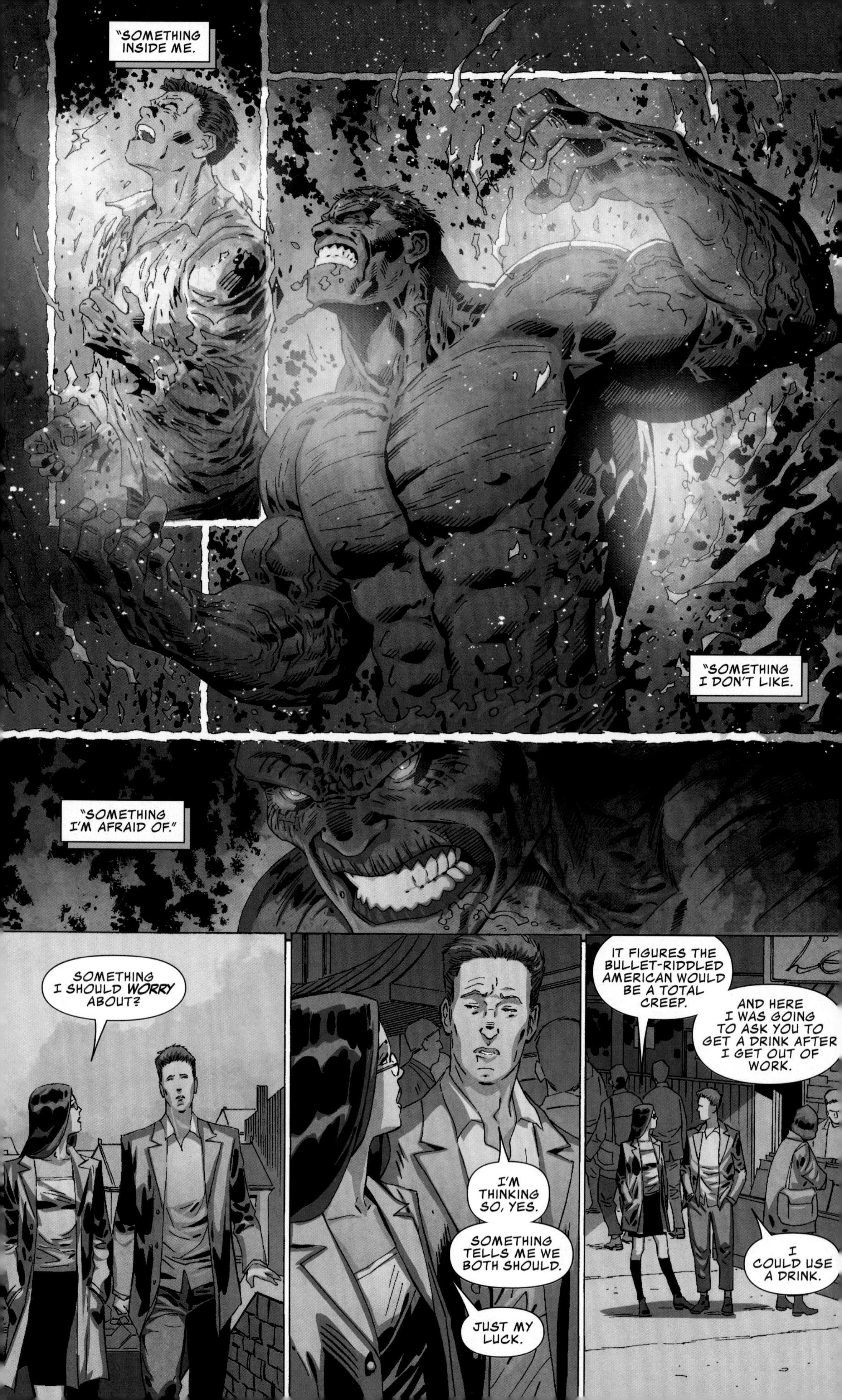
"SOMETHING INSIDE ME.
"SOMETHING I DON'T LIKE.
"SOMETHING I'M AFRAID OF."
SOMETHING I SHOULD WORRY ABOUT?
I'M THINKING SO, YES.
SOMETHING TELLS ME WE BOTH SHOULD.
JUST MY LUCK.
IT FIGURES THE BULLET-RIDDLED AMERICAN WOULD BE A TOTAL CREEP.
AND HERE I WAS GOING TO ASK YOU TO GET A DRINK AFTER I GET OUT OF WORK.
I COULD USE A DRINK.

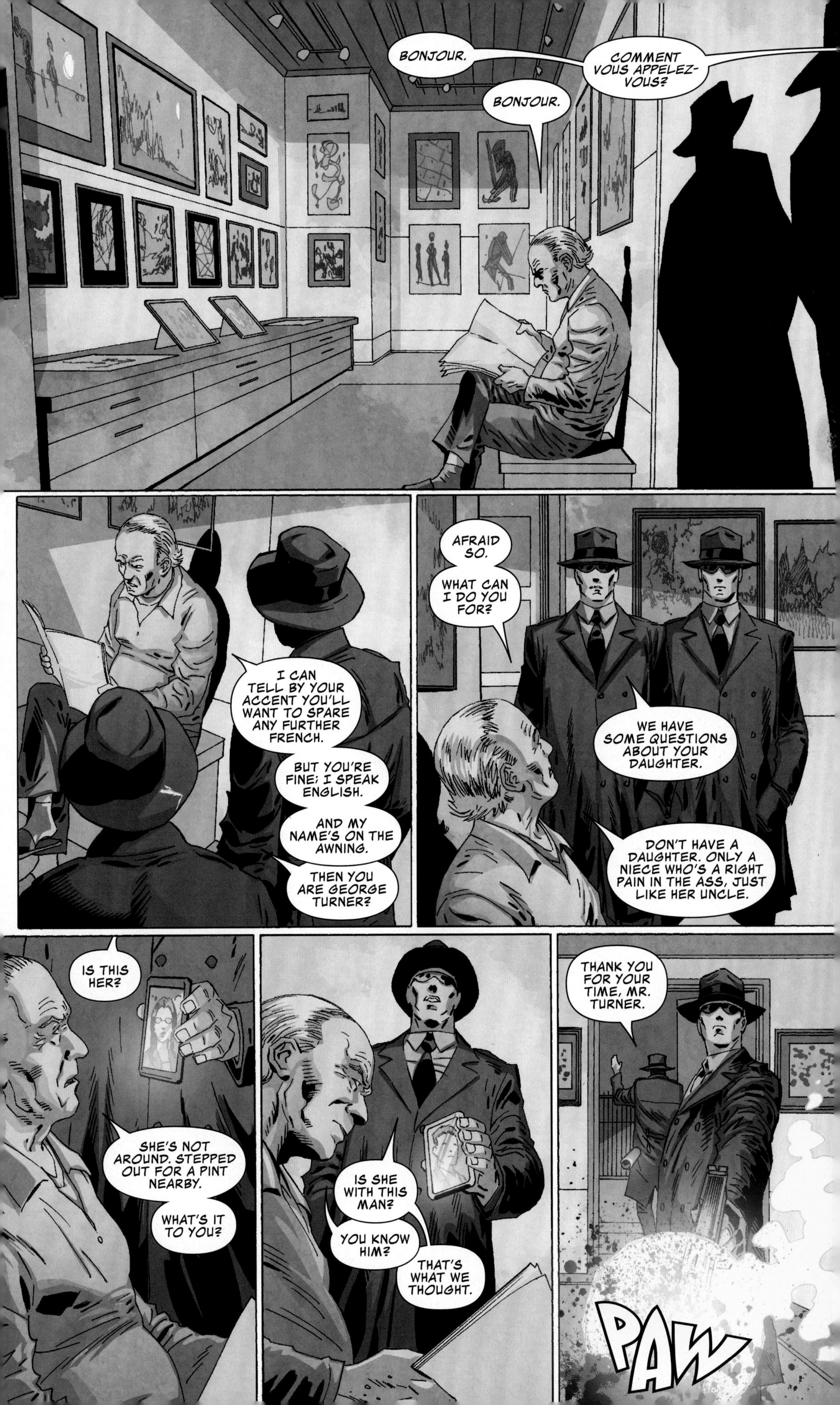
BONJOUR.
COMMENT VOUS APPELEZ-VOUS?
BONJOUR.
I CAN TELL BY YOUR ACCENT YOU'LL WANT TO SPARE ANY FURTHER FRENCH.
BUT YOU'RE FINE; I SPEAK ENGLISH.
AND MY NAME'S ON THE AWNING.
THEN YOU ARE GEORGE TURNER?
AFRAID SO.
WHAT CAN I DO YOU FOR?
WE HAVE SOME QUESTIONS ABOUT YOUR DAUGHTER.
DON'T HAVE A DAUGHTER. ONLY A NIECE WHO'S A RIGHT PAIN IN THE ASS, JUST LIKE HER UNCLE.
IS THIS HER?
SHE'S NOT AROUND. STEPPED OUT FOR A PINT NEARBY.
WHAT'S IT TO YOU?
IS SHE WITH THIS MAN?
YOU KNOW HIM?
THAT'S WHAT WE THOUGHT.
THANK YOU FOR YOUR TIME, MR. TURNER.
PAW

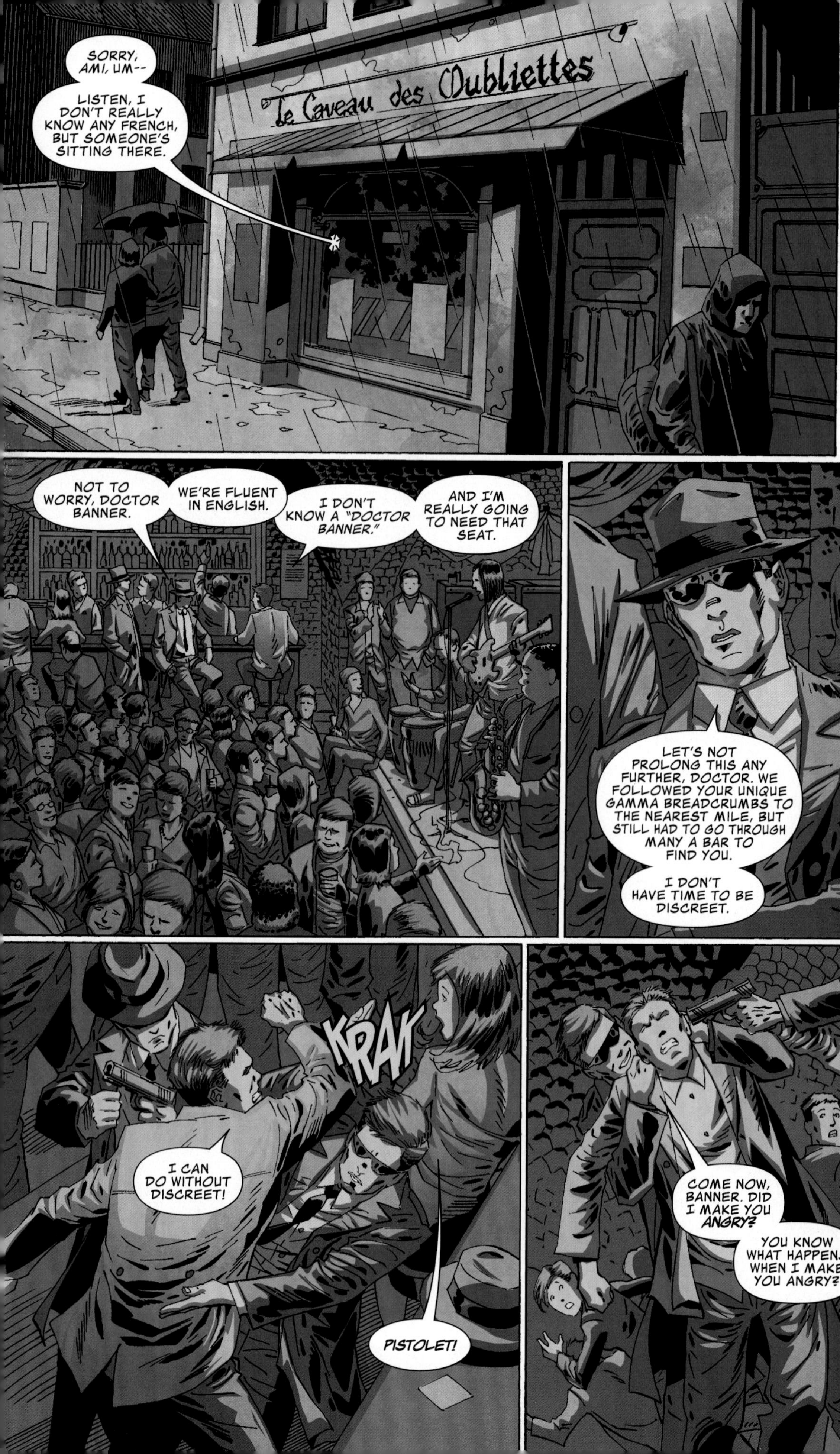

SORRY, AMI, UM--
LISTEN, I DON'T REALLY KNOW ANY FRENCH, BUT SOMEONE'S SITTING THERE.
Le Caveau des Oubliettes
NOT TO WORRY, DOCTOR BANNER.
WE'RE FLUENT IN ENGLISH.
I DON'T KNOW A "DOCTOR BANNER."
AND I'M REALLY GOING TO NEED THAT SEAT.
LET'S NOT PROLONG THIS ANY FURTHER, DOCTOR. WE FOLLOWED YOUR UNIQUE GAMMA BREADCRUMBS TO THE NEAREST MILE, BUT STILL HAD TO GO THROUGH MANY A BAR TO FIND YOU.
I DON'T HAVE TIME TO BE DISCREET.
KRAK
I CAN DO WITHOUT DISCREET!
PISTOLET!
COME NOW, BANNER. DID I MAKE YOU ANGRY?
YOU KNOW WHAT HAPPENS WHEN I MAKE YOU ANGRY?

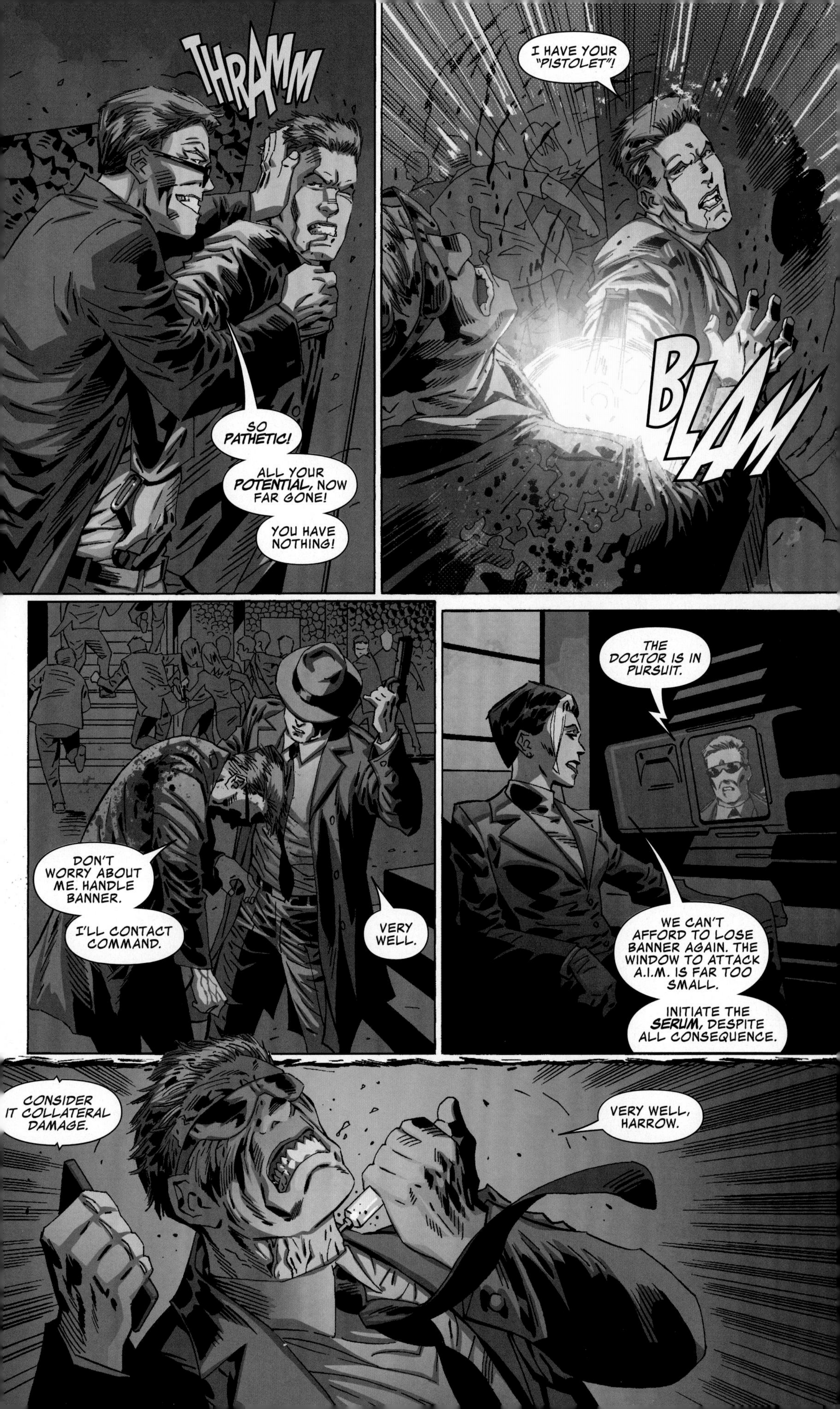
THRAMM
SO PATHETIC!
ALL YOUR POTENTIAL, NOW FAR GONE!
YOU HAVE NOTHING!
I HAVE YOUR "PISTOLET"!
BLAM
DON'T WORRY ABOUT ME. HANDLE BANNER.
I'LL CONTACT COMMAND.
VERY WELL.
THE DOCTOR IS IN PURSUIT.
WE CAN'T AFFORD TO LOSE BANNER AGAIN. THE WINDOW TO ATTACK A.I.M. IS FAR TOO SMALL.
INITIATE THE SERUM, DESPITE ALL CONSEQUENCE.
CONSIDER IT COLLATERAL DAMAGE.
VERY WELL, HARROW.

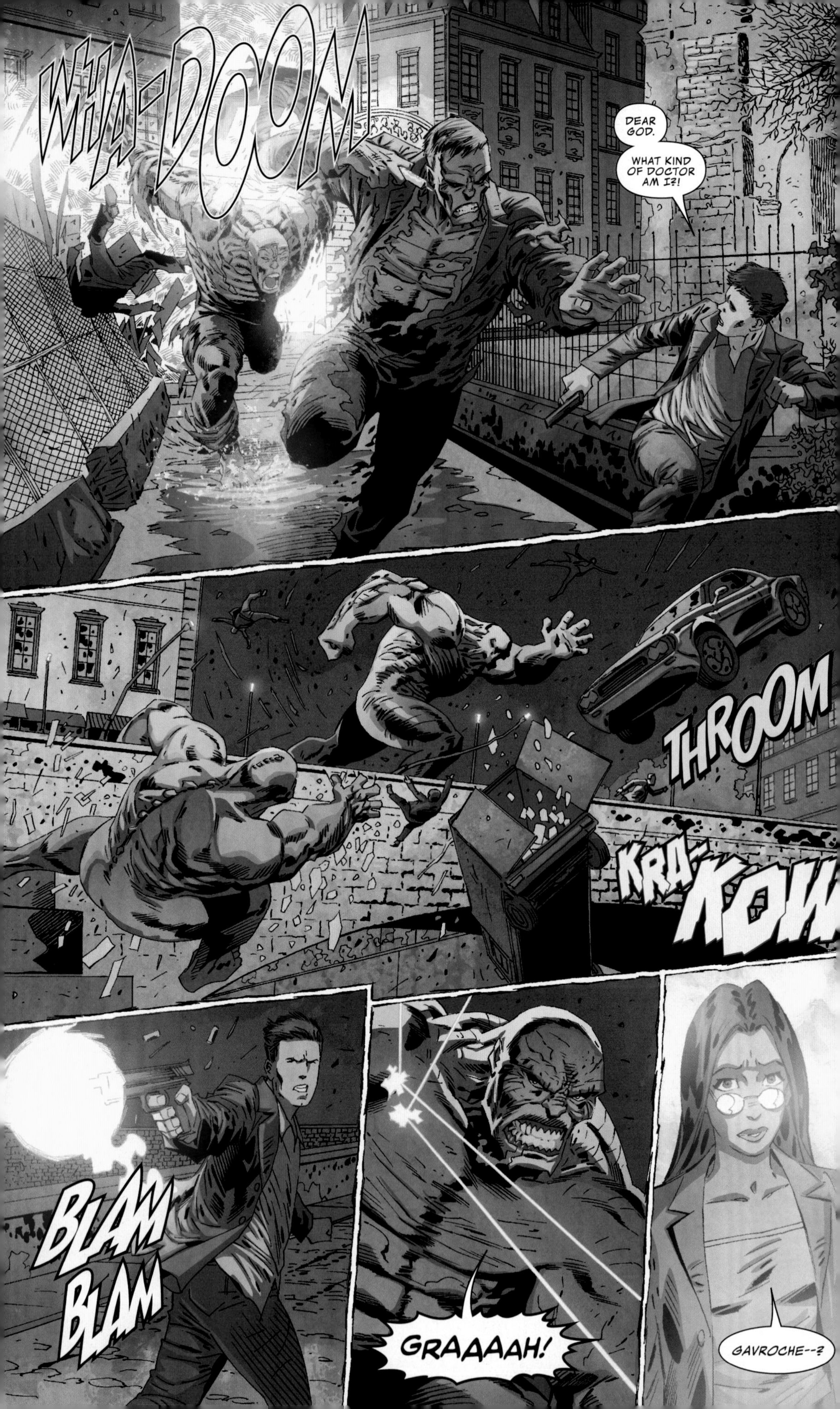
WHA-DOOM
DEAR GOD.
WHAT KIND OF DOCTOR AM I?!
THROOM
KRA-KOW
BLAM BLAM
GRAAAAH!
GAVROCHE--?

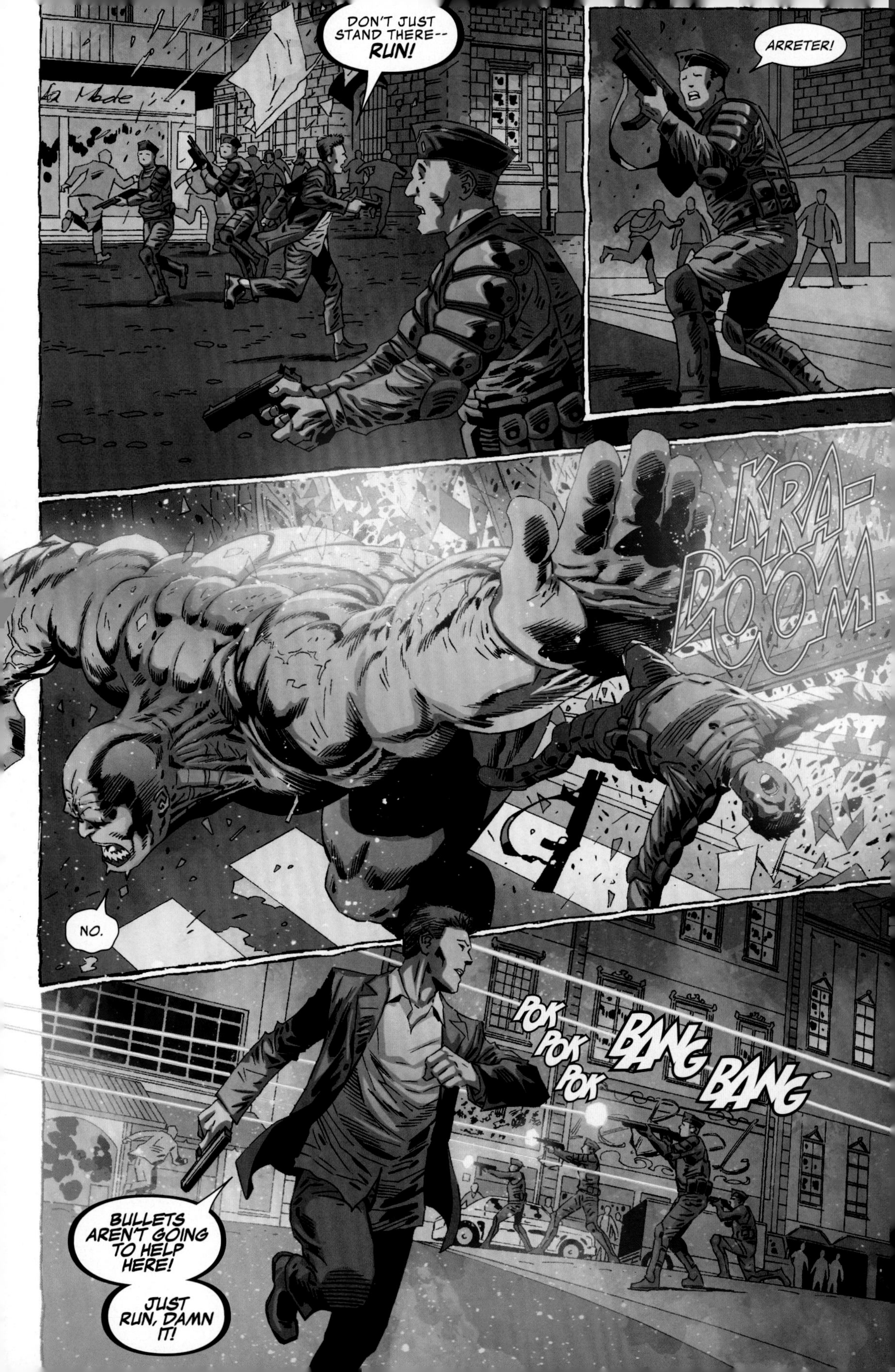
DON'T JUST STAND THERE-- RUN!
ARRETER!
KRA-DOOM
NO.
POK POK POK
BANG BANG
BULLETS AREN'T GOING TO HELP HERE!
JUST RUN, DAMN IT!

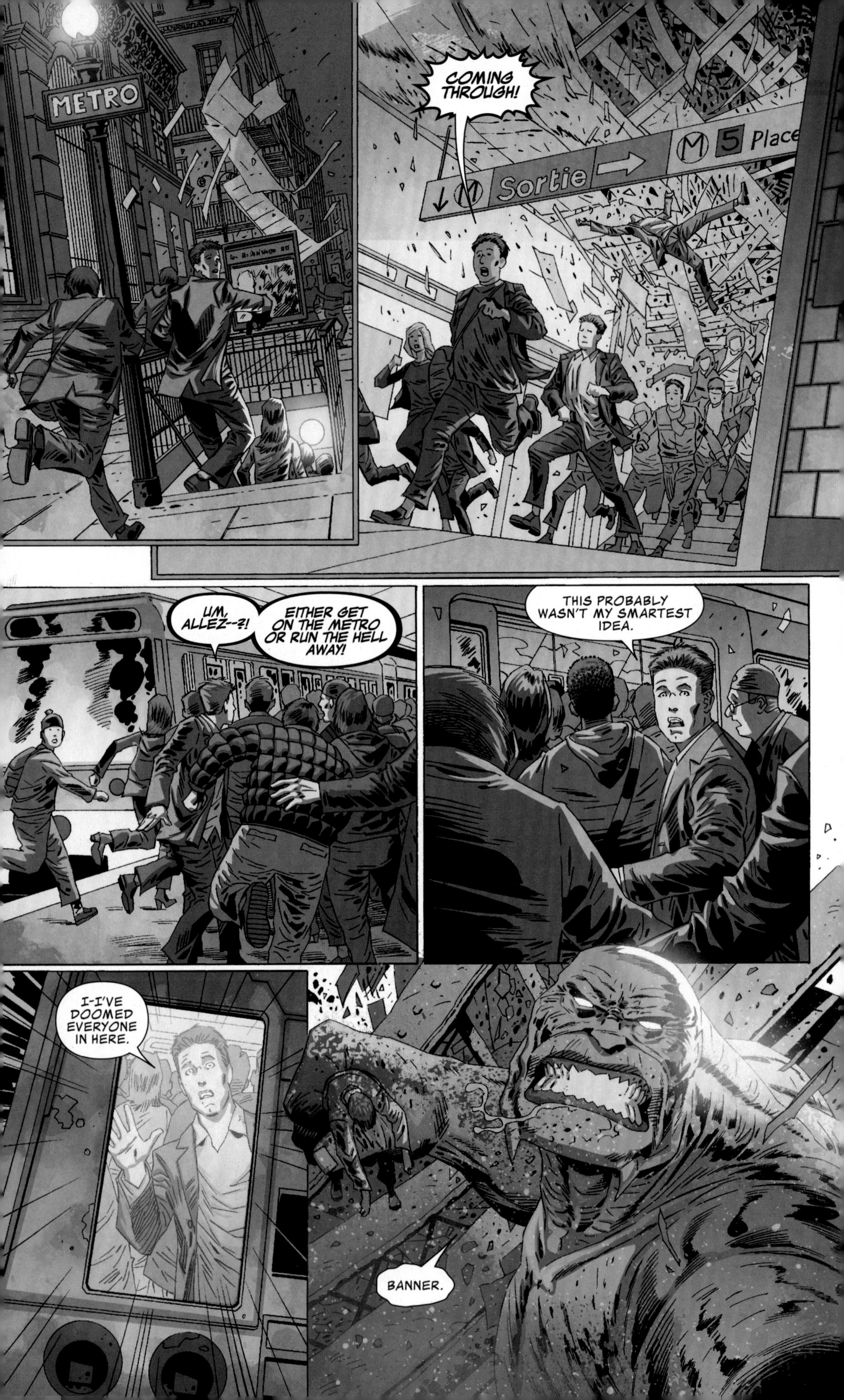
METRO
COMING THROUGH!
Sortie
Place
UM, ALLEZ--?!
EITHER GET ON THE METRO OR RUN THE HELL AWAY!
THIS PROBABLY WASN'T MY SMARTEST IDEA.
I-I'VE DOOMED EVERYONE IN HERE.
BANNER.

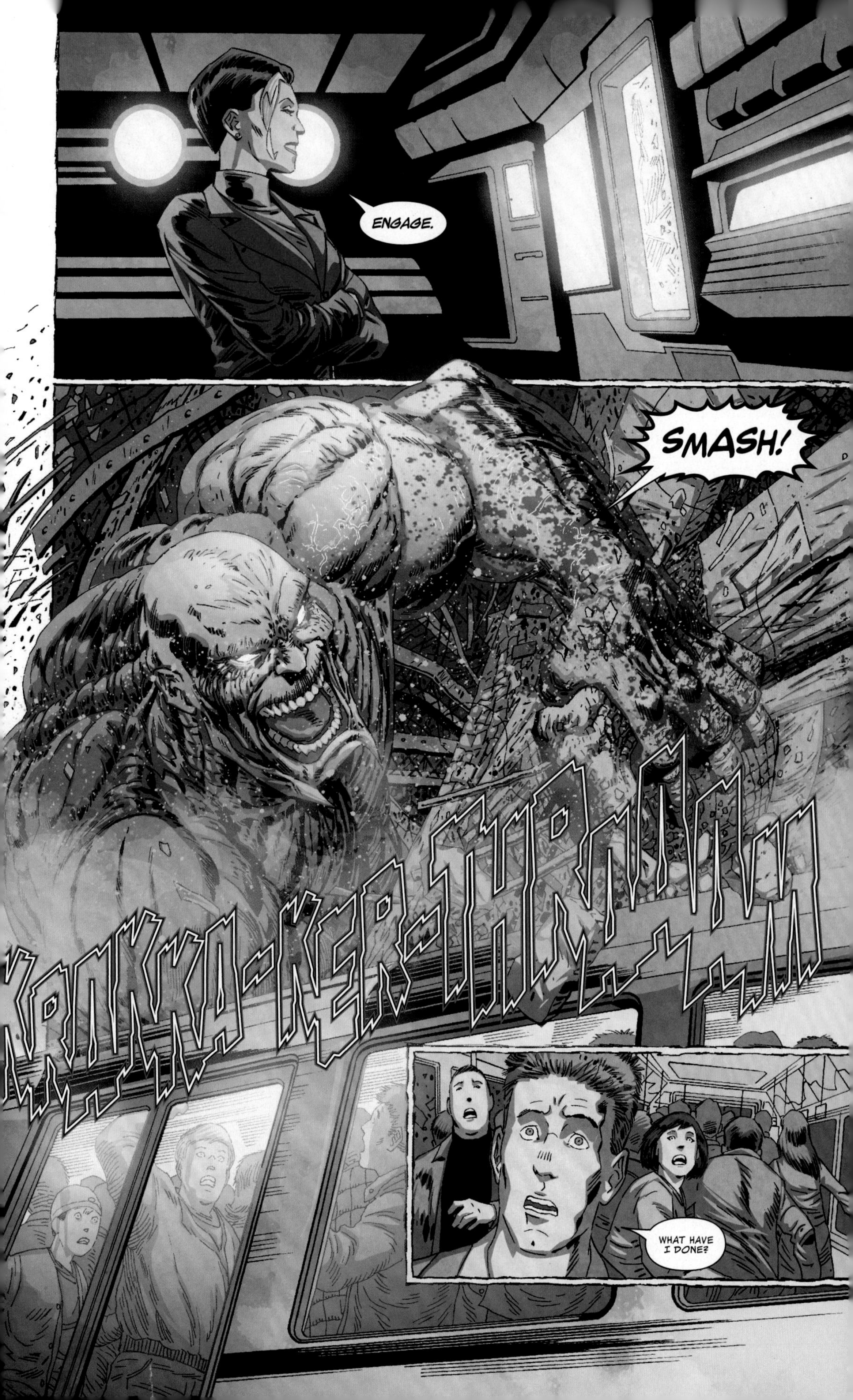

ENGAGE.
SMASH!
KRAKKA-KER-THRAAAM
WHAT HAVE I DONE?

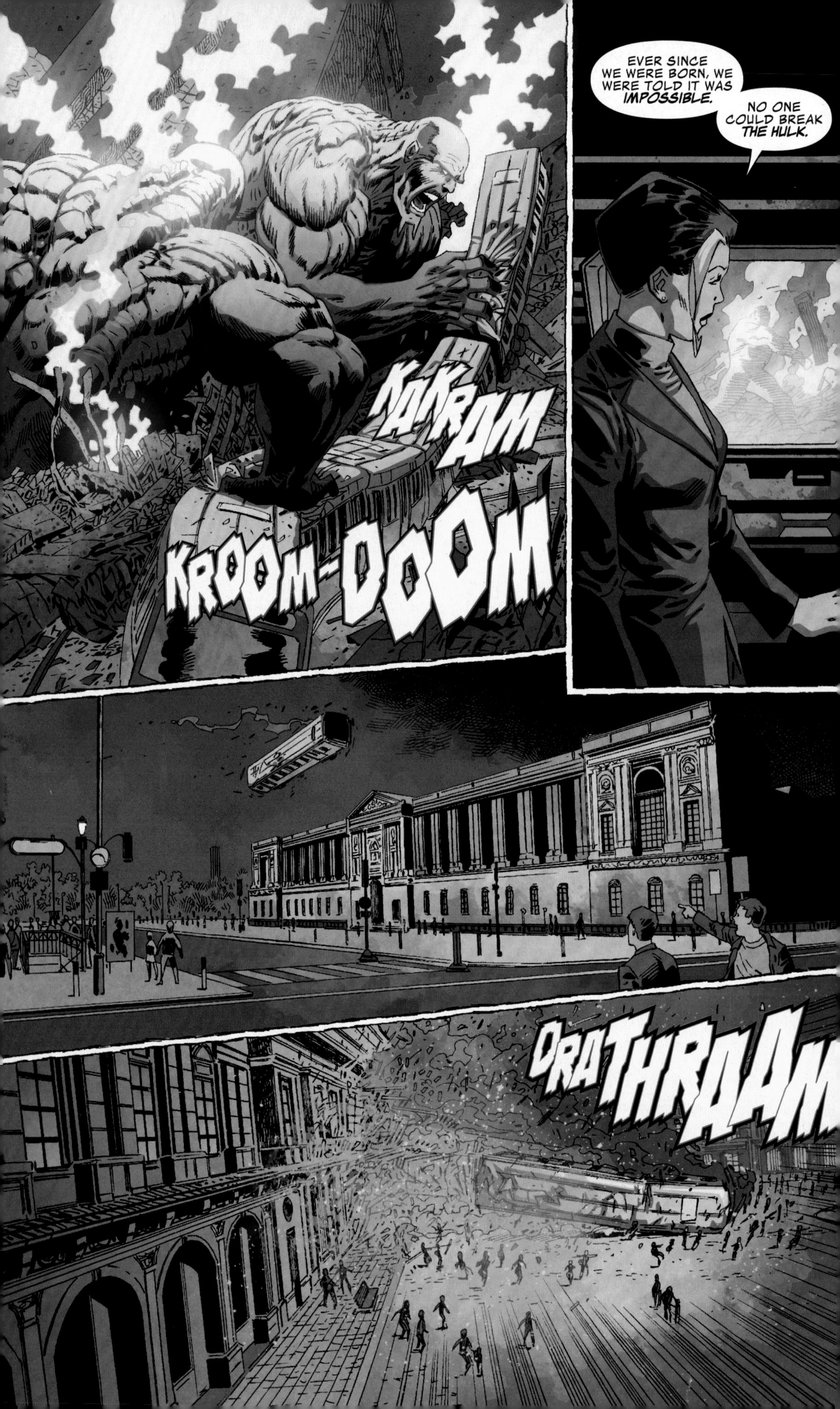
KAKRAM
KROOM-DOOM
EVER SINCE WE WERE BORN, WE WERE TOLD IT WAS IMPOSSIBLE.
NO ONE COULD BREAK THE HULK.
ORATHRAAM

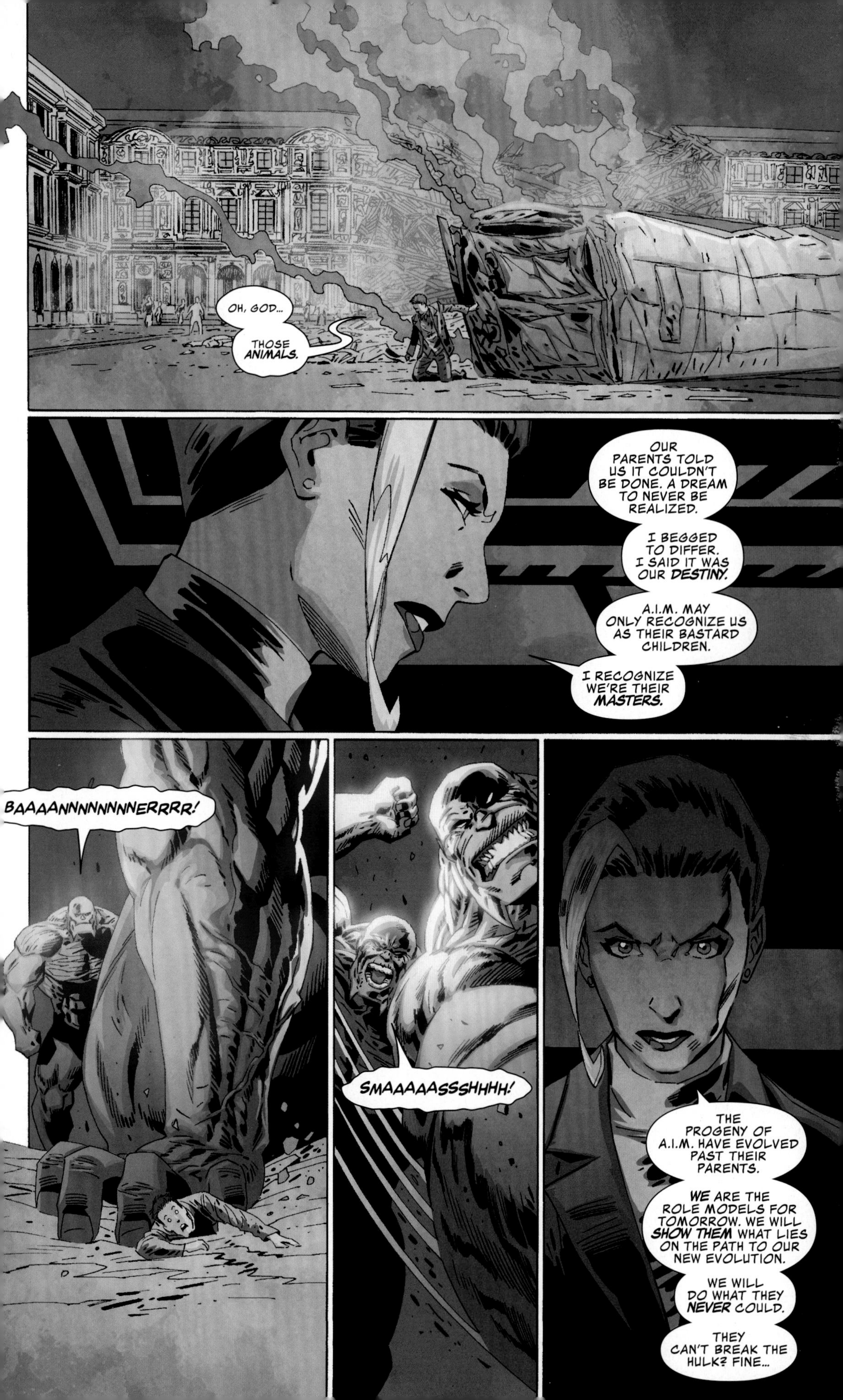
OH, GOD...
THOSE ANIMALS.
OUR PARENTS TOLD US IT COULDN'T BE DONE. A DREAM TO NEVER BE REALIZED.
I BEGGED TO DIFFER. I SAID IT WAS OUR DESTINY.
A.I.M. MAY ONLY RECOGNIZE US AS THEIR BASTARD CHILDREN.
I RECOGNIZE WE'RE THEIR MASTERS.
BAAAANNNNNNNERRRR!
SMAAAAASSHHHH!
THE PROGENY OF A.I.M. HAVE EVOLVED PAST THEIR PARENTS.
WE ARE THE ROLE MODELS FOR TOMORROW. WE WILL SHOW THEM WHAT LIES ON THE PATH TO OUR NEW EVOLUTION.
WE WILL DO WHAT THEY NEVER COULD.
THEY CAN'T BREAK THE HULK? FINE...

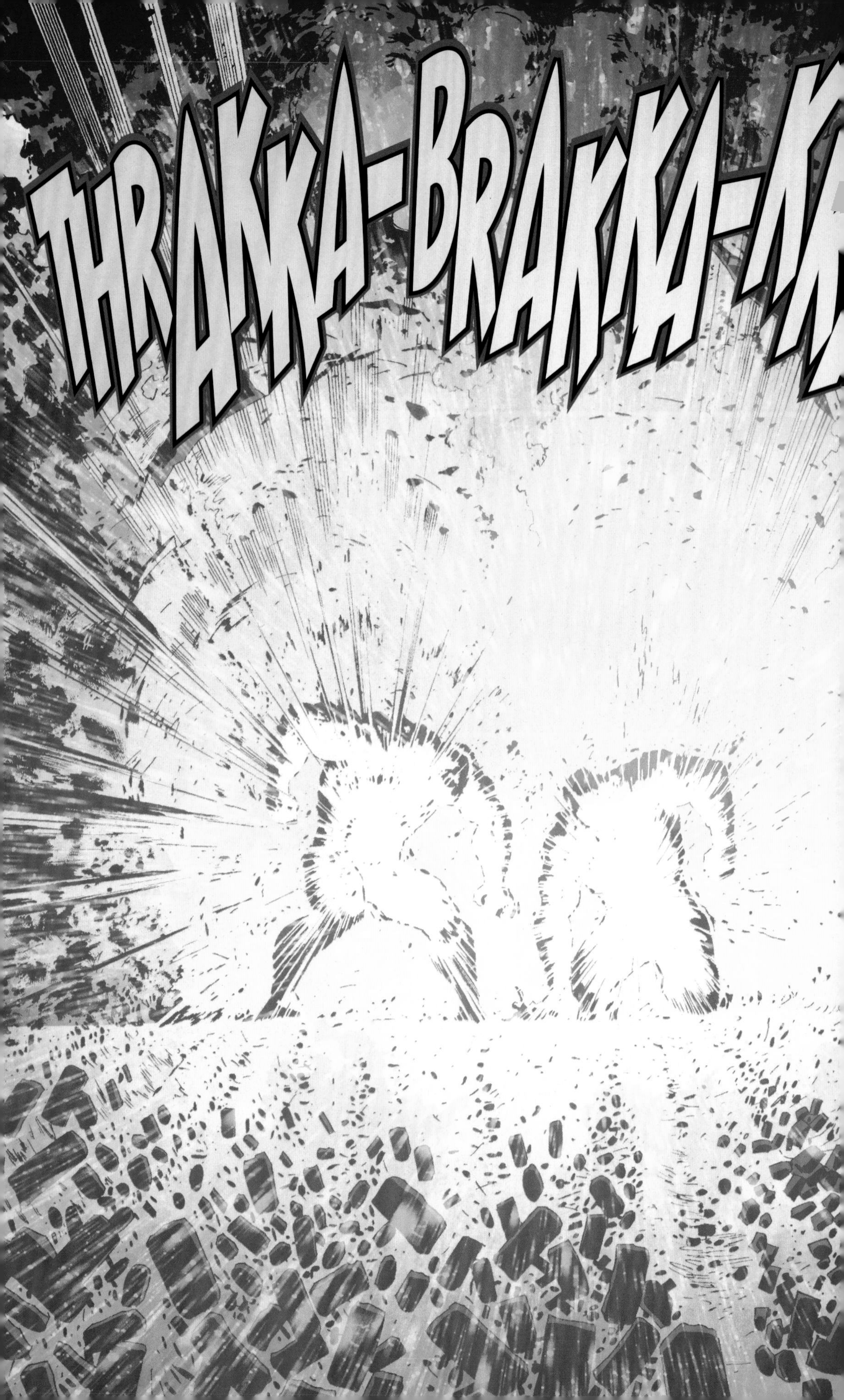
THRAKKA-BRAKKA-

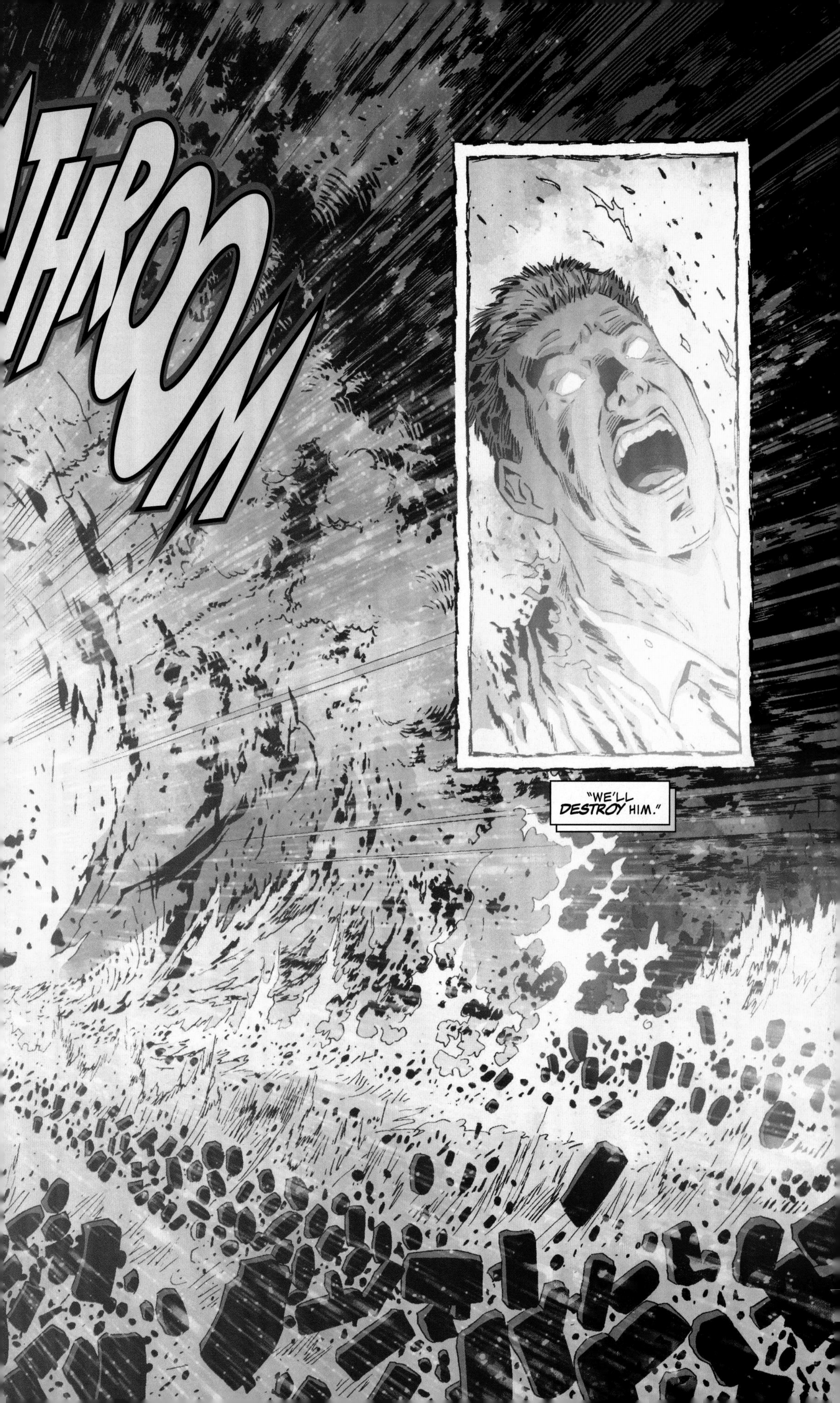
THROOM
"WE'LL DESTROY HIM."

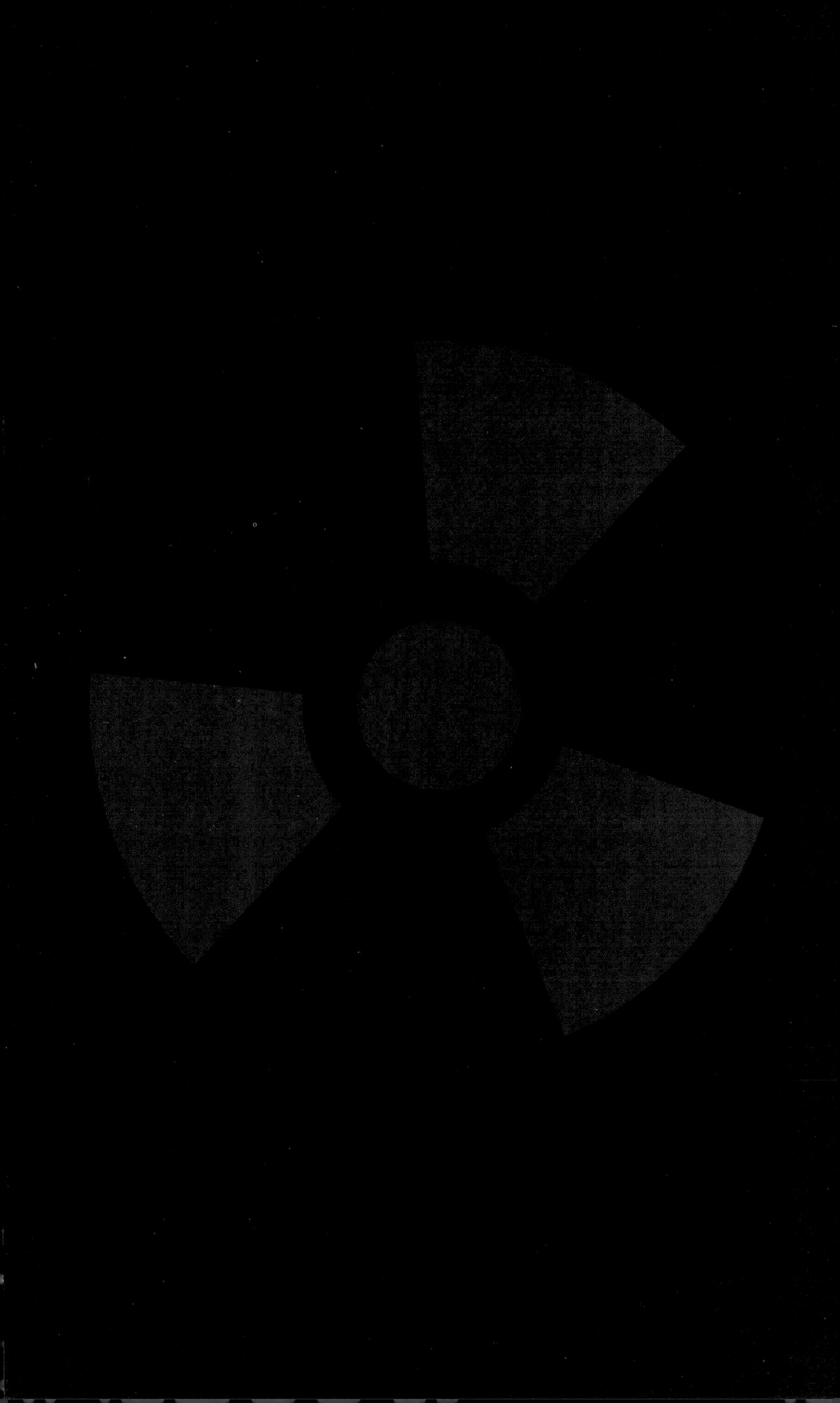

2

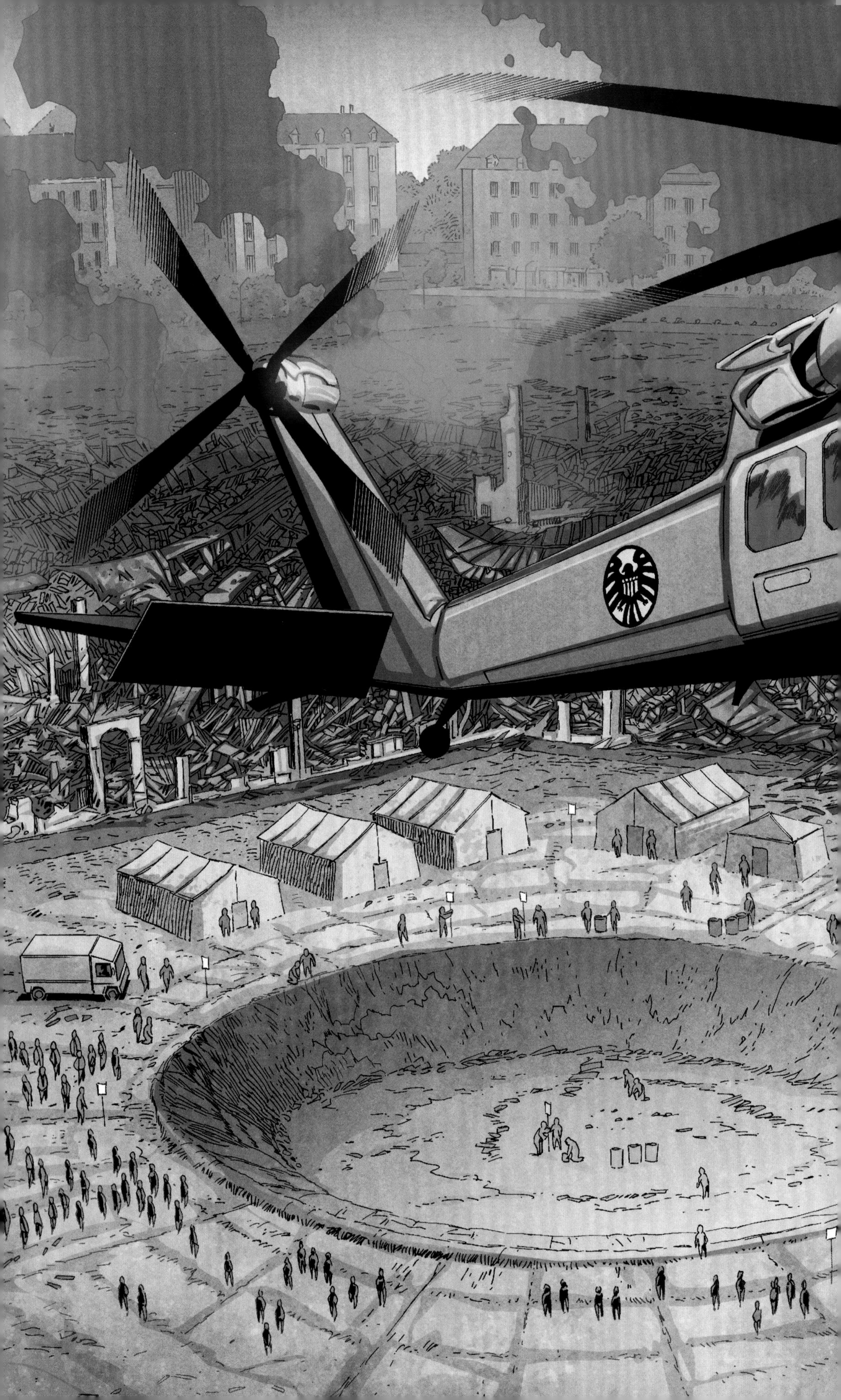

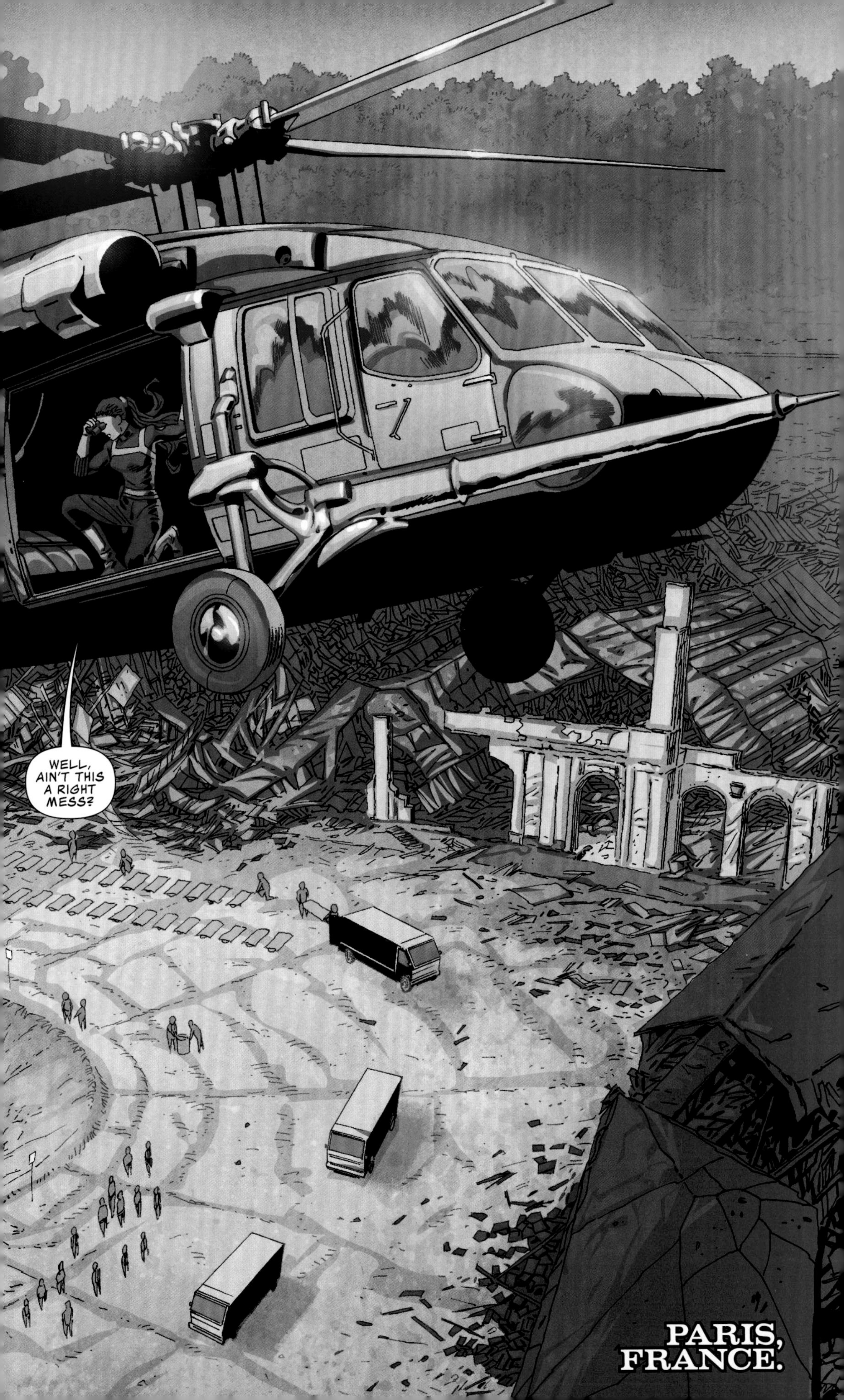
WELL, AIN'T THIS A RIGHT MESS?
PARIS, FRANCE.

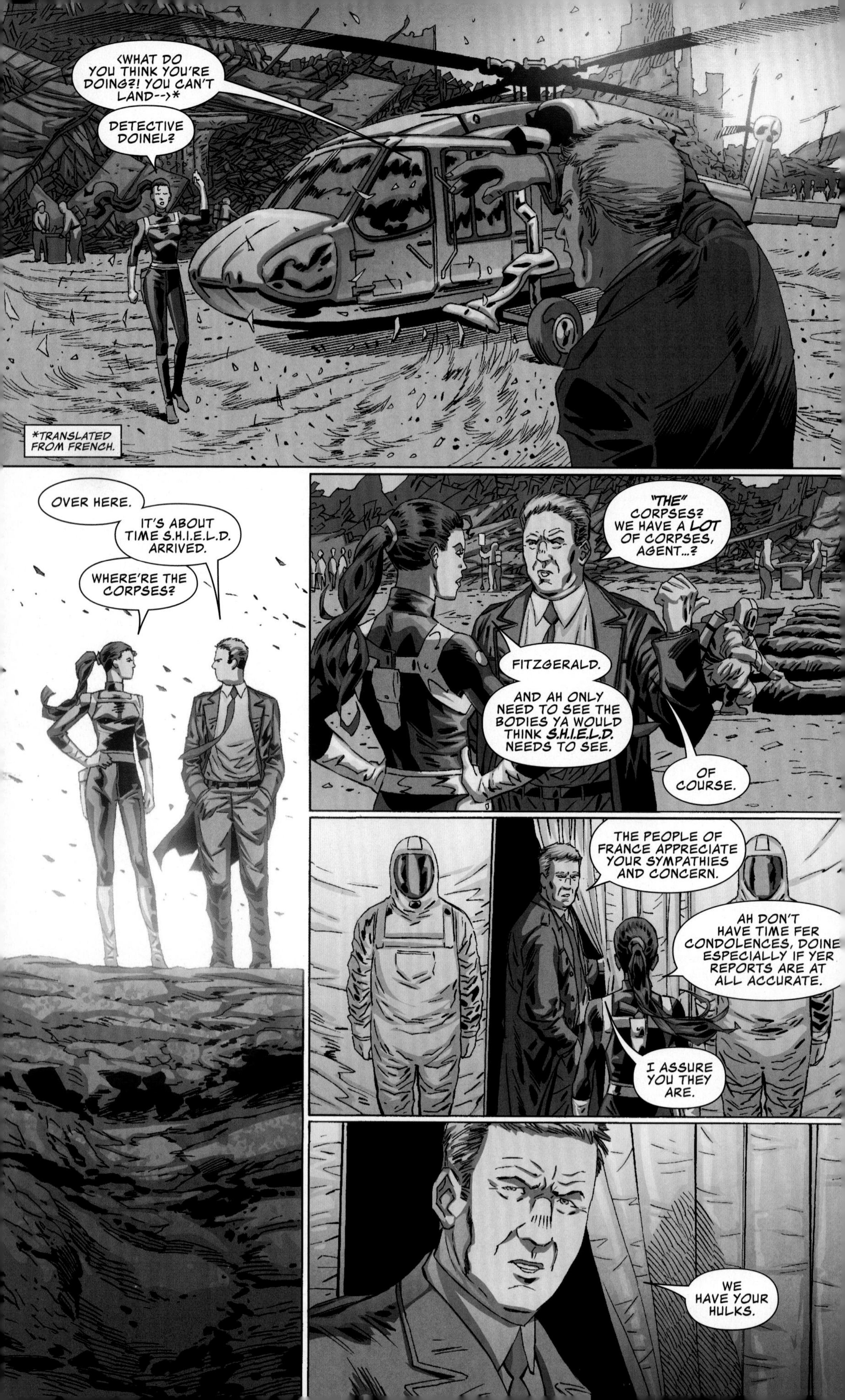
<WHAT DO YOU THINK YOU'RE DOING?! YOU CAN'T LAND-->*
DETECTIVE DOINEL?
*TRANSLATED FROM FRENCH.
OVER HERE.
IT'S ABOUT TIME S.H.I.E.L.D. ARRIVED.
WHERE'RE THE CORPSES?
"THE" CORPSES? WE HAVE A LOT OF CORPSES, AGENT...?
FITZGERALD.
AND AH ONLY NEED TO SEE THE BODIES YA WOULD THINK S.H.I.E.L.D. NEEDS TO SEE.
OF COURSE.
THE PEOPLE OF FRANCE APPRECIATE YOUR SYMPATHIES AND CONCERN.
AH DON'T HAVE TIME FER CONDOLENCES, DOINEL, ESPECIALLY IF YER REPORTS ARE AT ALL ACCURATE.
I ASSURE YOU THEY ARE.
WE HAVE YOUR HULKS.

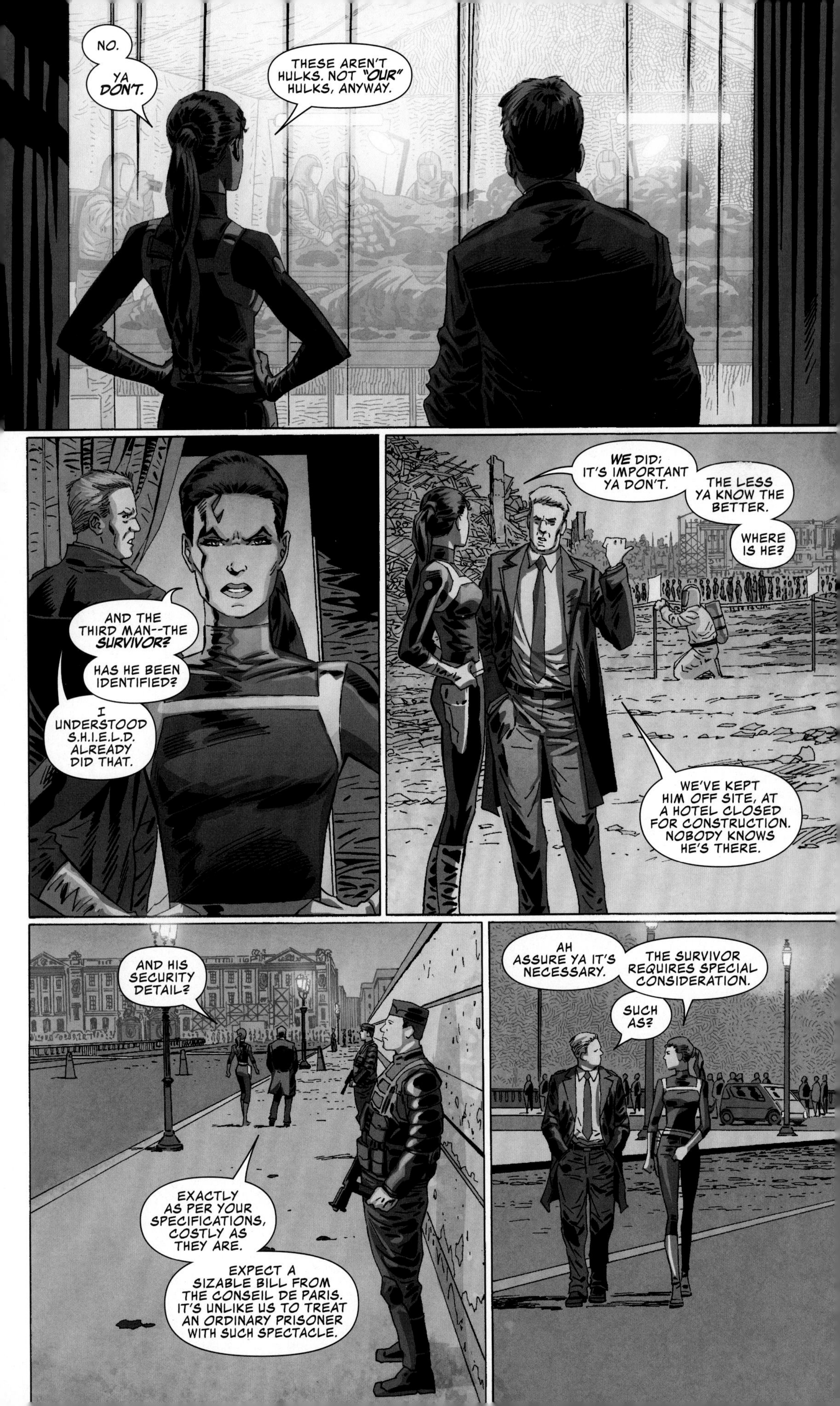
NO.
YA DON'T.
THESE AREN'T HULKS. NOT "OUR" HULKS, ANYWAY.
AND THE THIRD MAN--THE SURVIVOR?
HAS HE BEEN IDENTIFIED?
I UNDERSTOOD S.H.I.E.L.D. ALREADY DID THAT.
WE DID; IT'S IMPORTANT YA DON'T.
THE LESS YA KNOW THE BETTER.
WHERE IS HE?
WE'VE KEPT HIM OFF SITE, AT A HOTEL CLOSED FOR CONSTRUCTION. NOBODY KNOWS HE'S THERE.
AND HIS SECURITY DETAIL?
EXACTLY AS PER YOUR SPECIFICATIONS, COSTLY AS THEY ARE.
EXPECT A SIZABLE BILL FROM THE CONSEIL DE PARIS. IT'S UNLIKE US TO TREAT AN ORDINARY PRISONER WITH SUCH SPECTACLE.
AH ASSURE YA IT'S NECESSARY.
THE SURVIVOR REQUIRES SPECIAL CONSIDERATION.
SUCH AS?

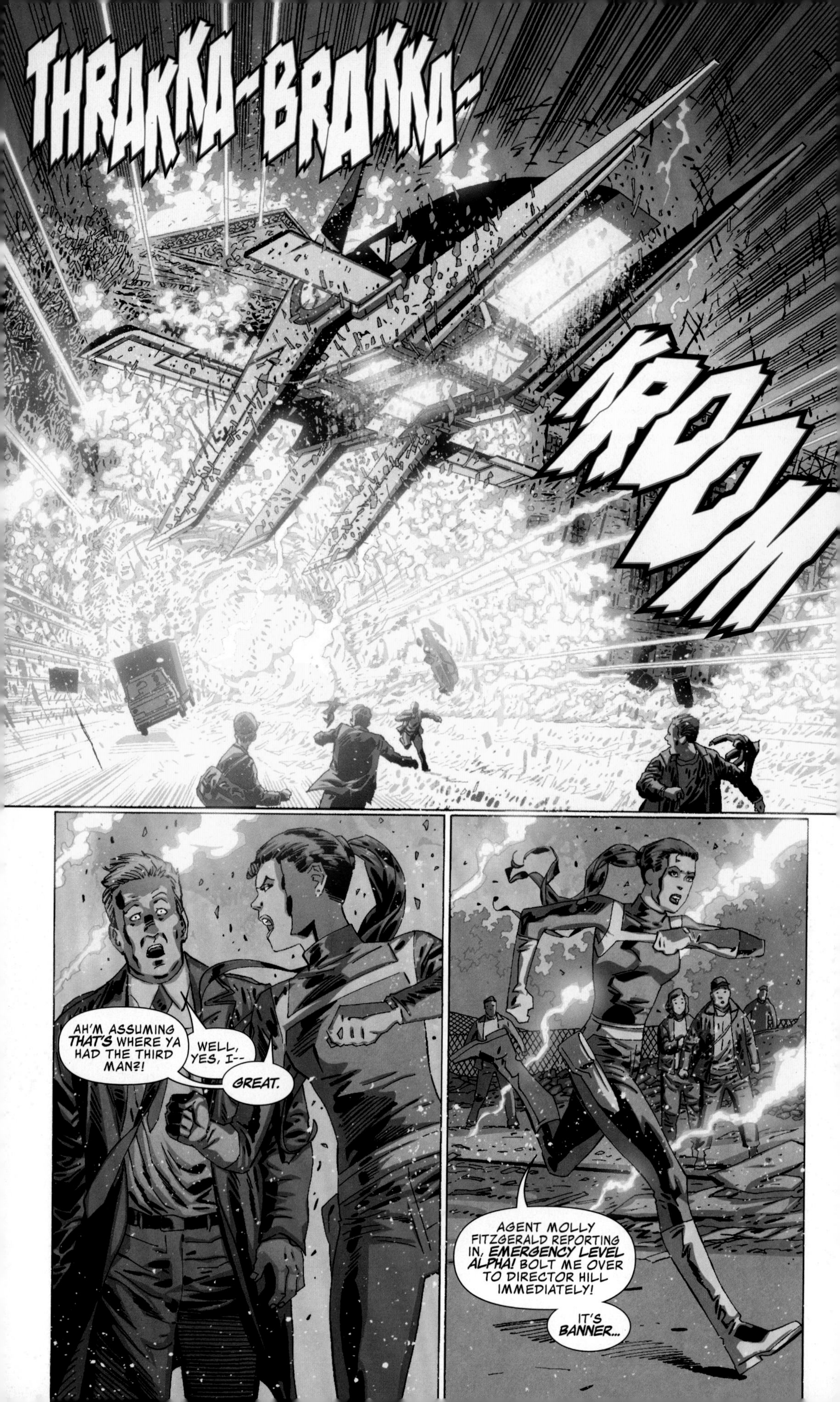
THRAKKA-BRAKKA-
KROOM
AH'M ASSUMING THAT'S WHERE YA HAD THE THIRD MAN?!
WELL, YES, I--
GREAT.
AGENT MOLLY FITZGERALD REPORTING IN, EMERGENCY LEVEL ALPHA! BOLT ME OVER TO DIRECTOR HILL IMMEDIATELY!
IT'S BANNER...

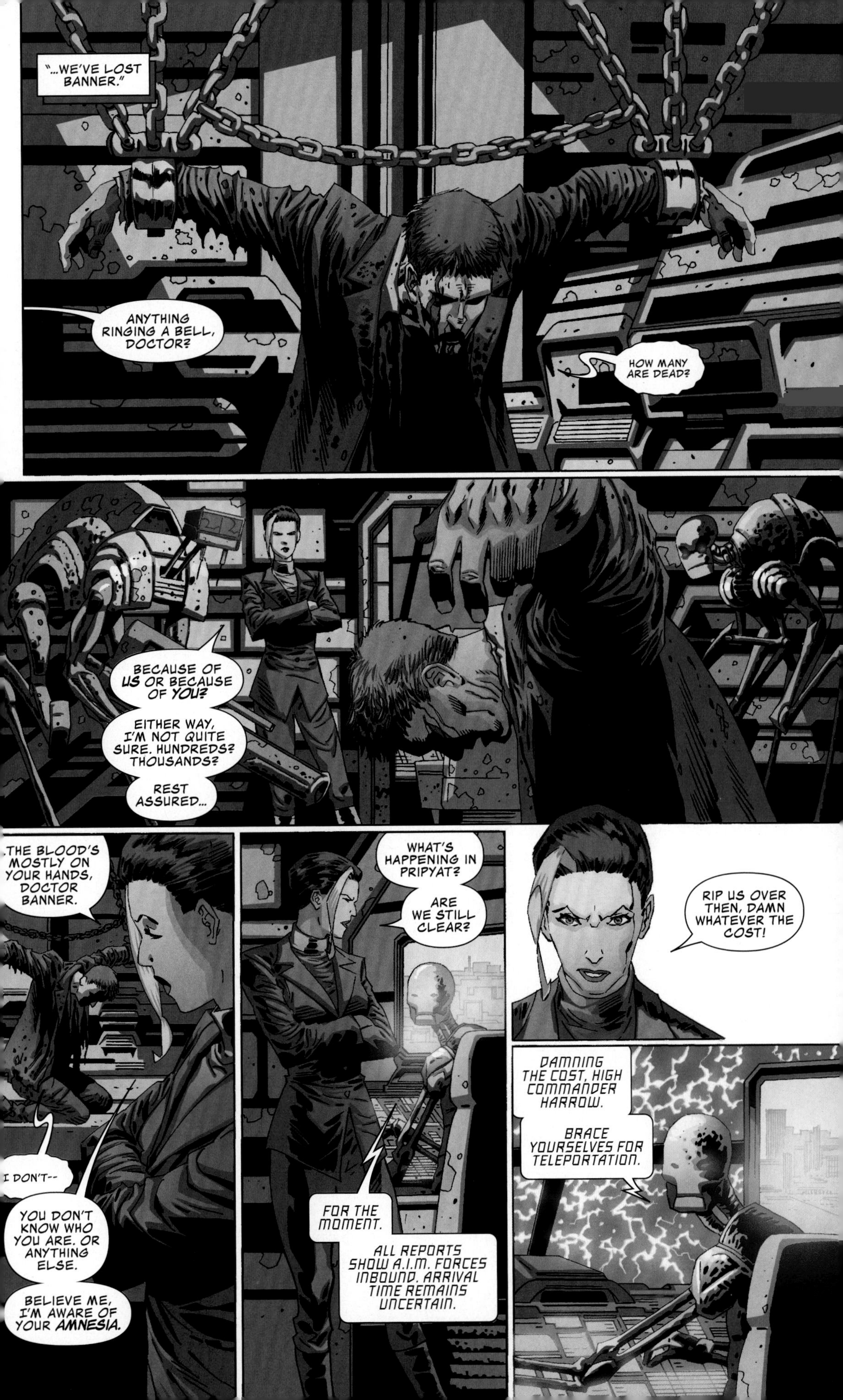
"...WE'VE LOST BANNER."
ANYTHING RINGING A BELL, DOCTOR?
HOW MANY ARE DEAD?
BECAUSE OF US OR BECAUSE OF YOU?
EITHER WAY, I'M NOT QUITE SURE. HUNDREDS? THOUSANDS?
REST ASSURED...
...THE BLOOD'S MOSTLY ON YOUR HANDS, DOCTOR BANNER.
I DON'T--
YOU DON'T KNOW WHO YOU ARE. OR ANYTHING ELSE.
BELIEVE ME, I'M AWARE OF YOUR AMNESIA.
WHAT'S HAPPENING IN PRIPYAT?
ARE WE STILL CLEAR?
FOR THE MOMENT.
ALL REPORTS SHOW A.I.M. FORCES INBOUND. ARRIVAL TIME REMAINS UNCERTAIN.
RIP US OVER THEN, DAMN WHATEVER THE COST!
DAMNING THE COST, HIGH COMMANDER HARROW.
BRACE YOURSELVES FOR TELEPORTATION.

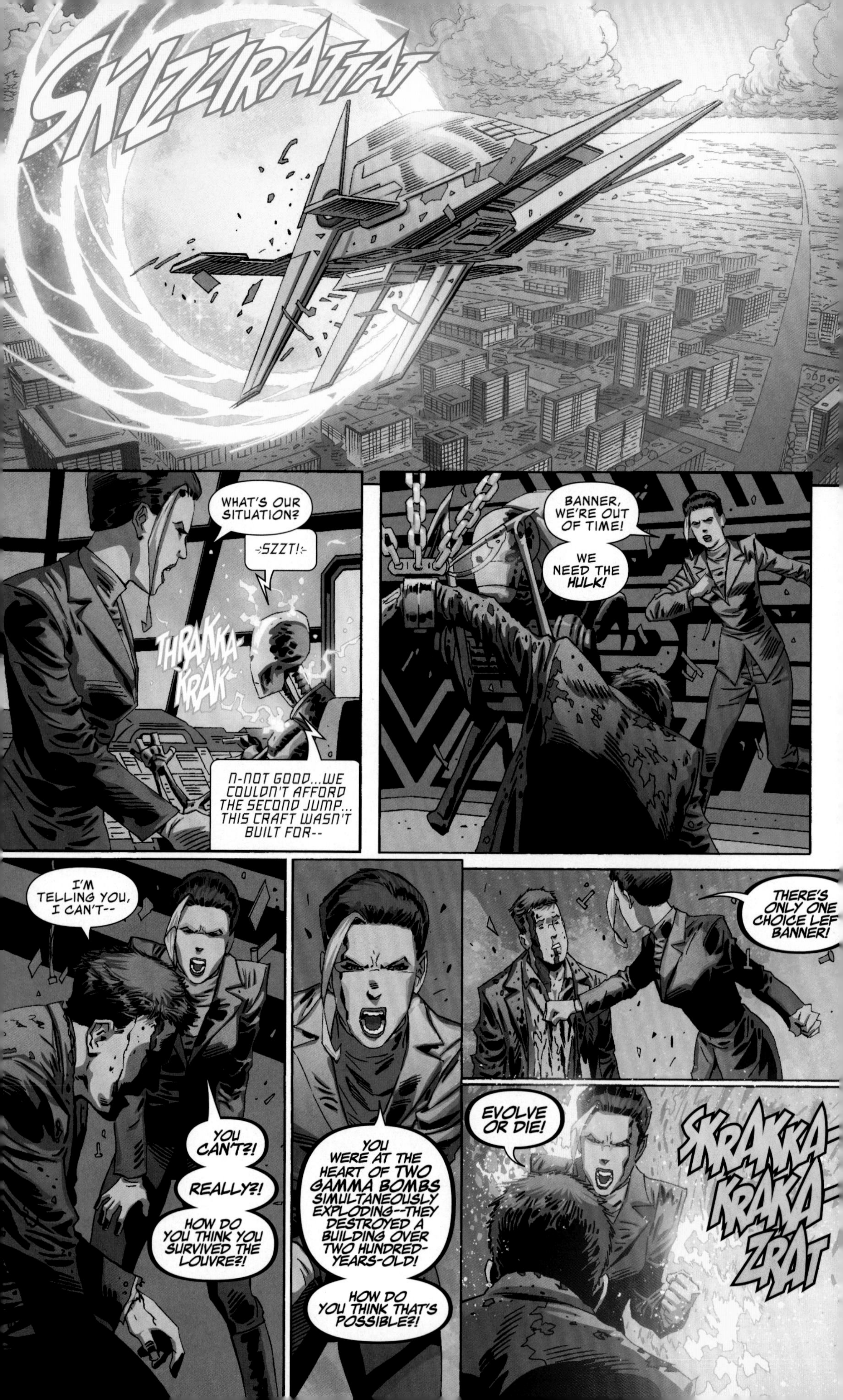
SKIZZRATTAT
WHAT'S OUR SITUATION?
-SZZT!-
THRAKKA-KRAK
N-NOT GOOD...WE COULDN'T AFFORD THE SECOND JUMP... THIS CRAFT WASN'T BUILT FOR--
BANNER, WE'RE OUT OF TIME!
WE NEED THE HULK!
I'M TELLING YOU, I CAN'T--
YOU CAN'T?!
REALLY?!
HOW DO YOU THINK YOU SURVIVED THE LOUVRE?!
YOU WERE AT THE HEART OF TWO GAMMA BOMBS SIMULTANEOUSLY EXPLODING--THEY DESTROYED A BUILDING OVER TWO HUNDRED-YEARS-OLD!
HOW DO YOU THINK THAT'S POSSIBLE?!
THERE'S ONLY ONE CHOICE LEF BANNER!
EVOLVE OR DIE!
SKRAKKA KRAKA ZRAT

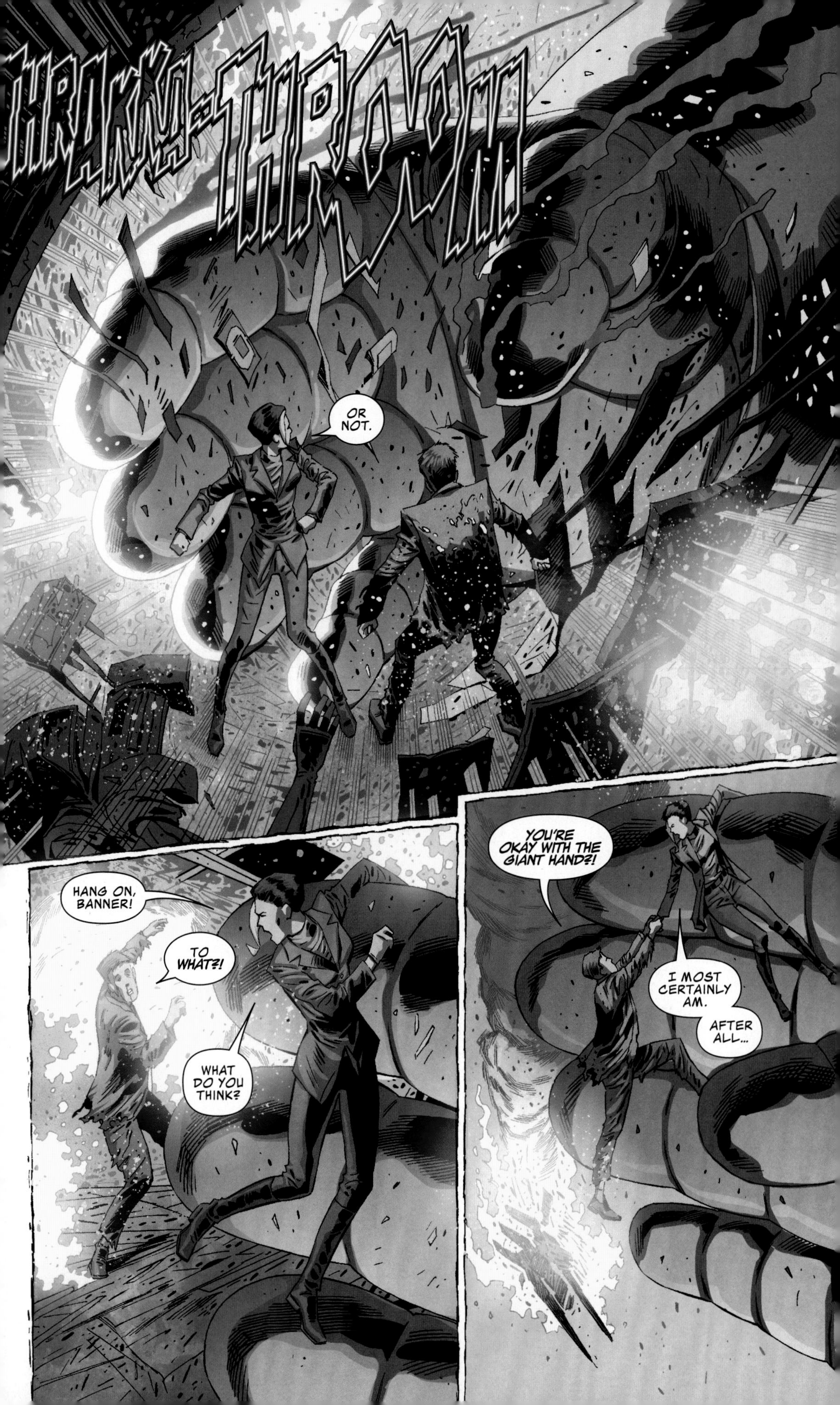

HRAKKA-THROOOM
OR NOT.
HANG ON, BANNER!
TO WHAT?!
WHAT DO YOU THINK?
YOU'RE OKAY WITH THE GIANT HAND?!
I MOST CERTAINLY AM.
AFTER ALL...

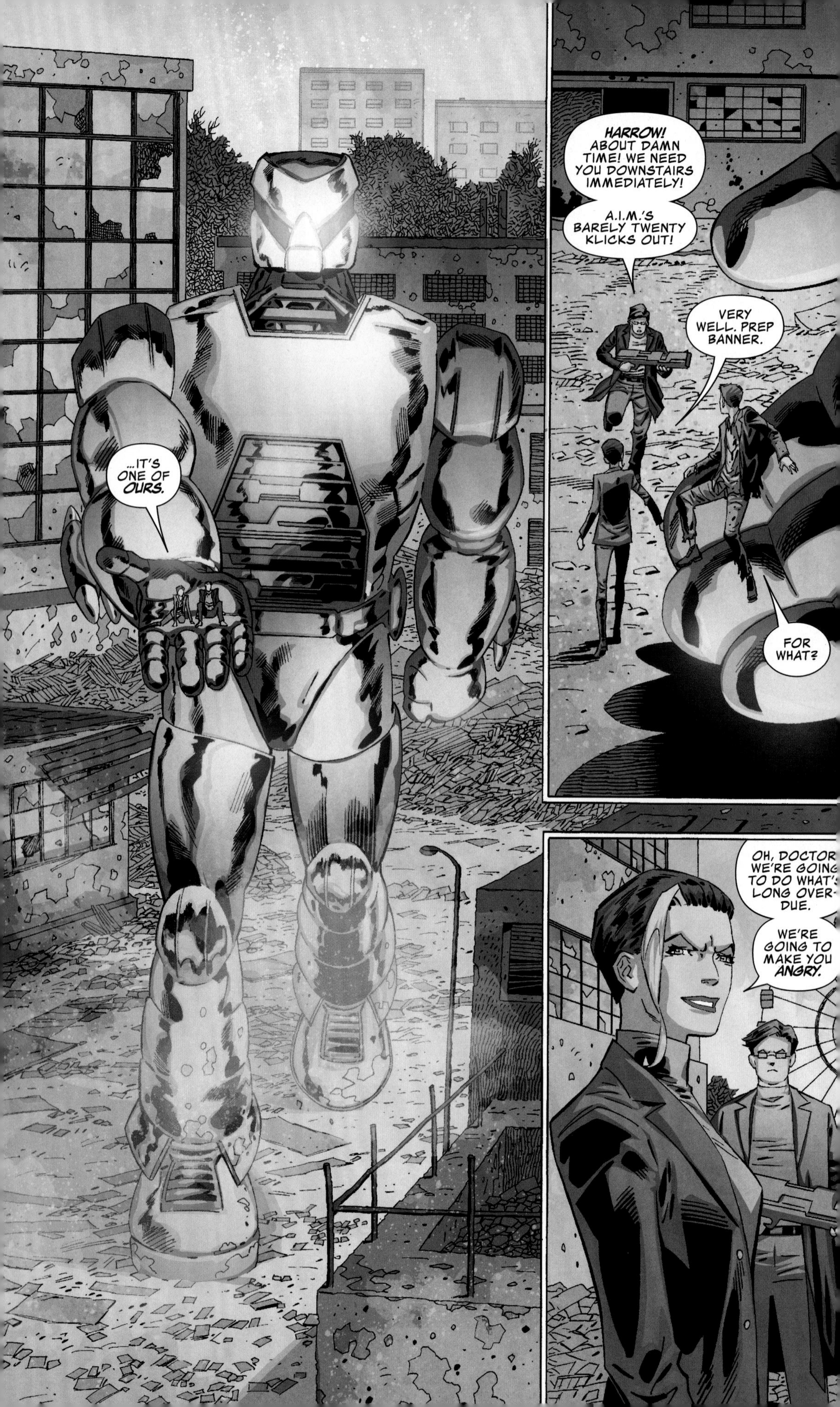

...IT'S ONE OF OURS.
HARROW! ABOUT DAMN TIME! WE NEED YOU DOWNSTAIRS IMMEDIATELY!
A.I.M.'S BARELY TWENTY KLICKS OUT!
VERY WELL. PREP BANNER.
FOR WHAT?
OH, DOCTOR WE'RE GOING TO DO WHAT'S LONG OVERDUE.
WE'RE GOING TO MAKE YOU ANGRY.

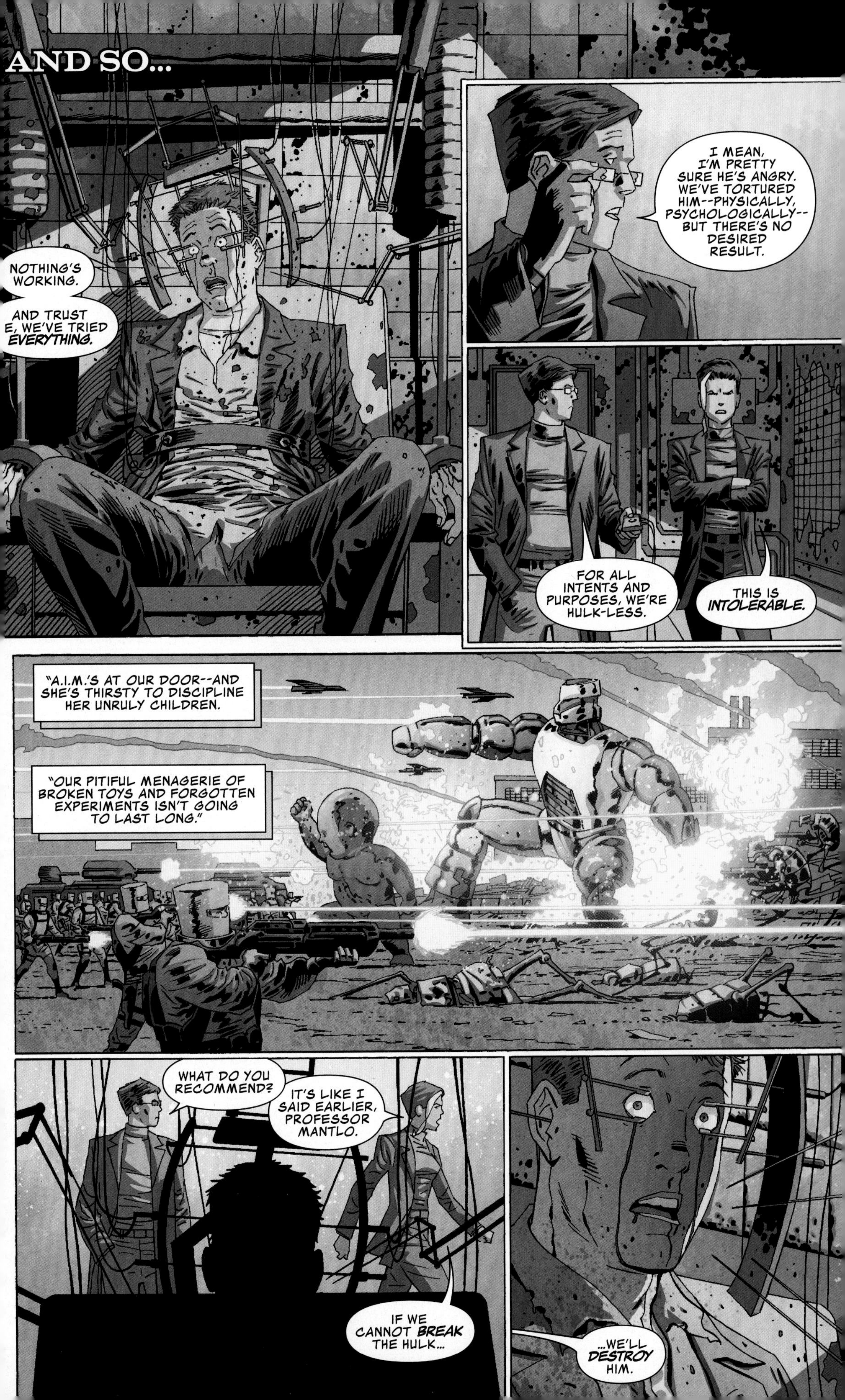
AND SO...
I MEAN, I'M PRETTY SURE HE'S ANGRY. WE'VE TORTURED HIM--PHYSICALLY, PSYCHOLOGICALLY--BUT THERE'S NO DESIRED RESULT.
NOTHING'S WORKING.
AND TRUST E, WE'VE TRIED *EVERYTHING.*
FOR ALL INTENTS AND PURPOSES, WE'RE HULK-LESS.
THIS IS *INTOLERABLE.*
"A.I.M.'S AT OUR DOOR--AND SHE'S THIRSTY TO DISCIPLINE HER UNRULY CHILDREN.
"OUR PITIFUL MENAGERIE OF BROKEN TOYS AND FORGOTTEN EXPERIMENTS ISN'T GOING TO LAST LONG."
WHAT DO YOU RECOMMEND?
IT'S LIKE I SAID EARLIER, PROFESSOR MANTLO.
IF WE CANNOT *BREAK* THE HULK...
...WE'LL *DESTROY* HIM.

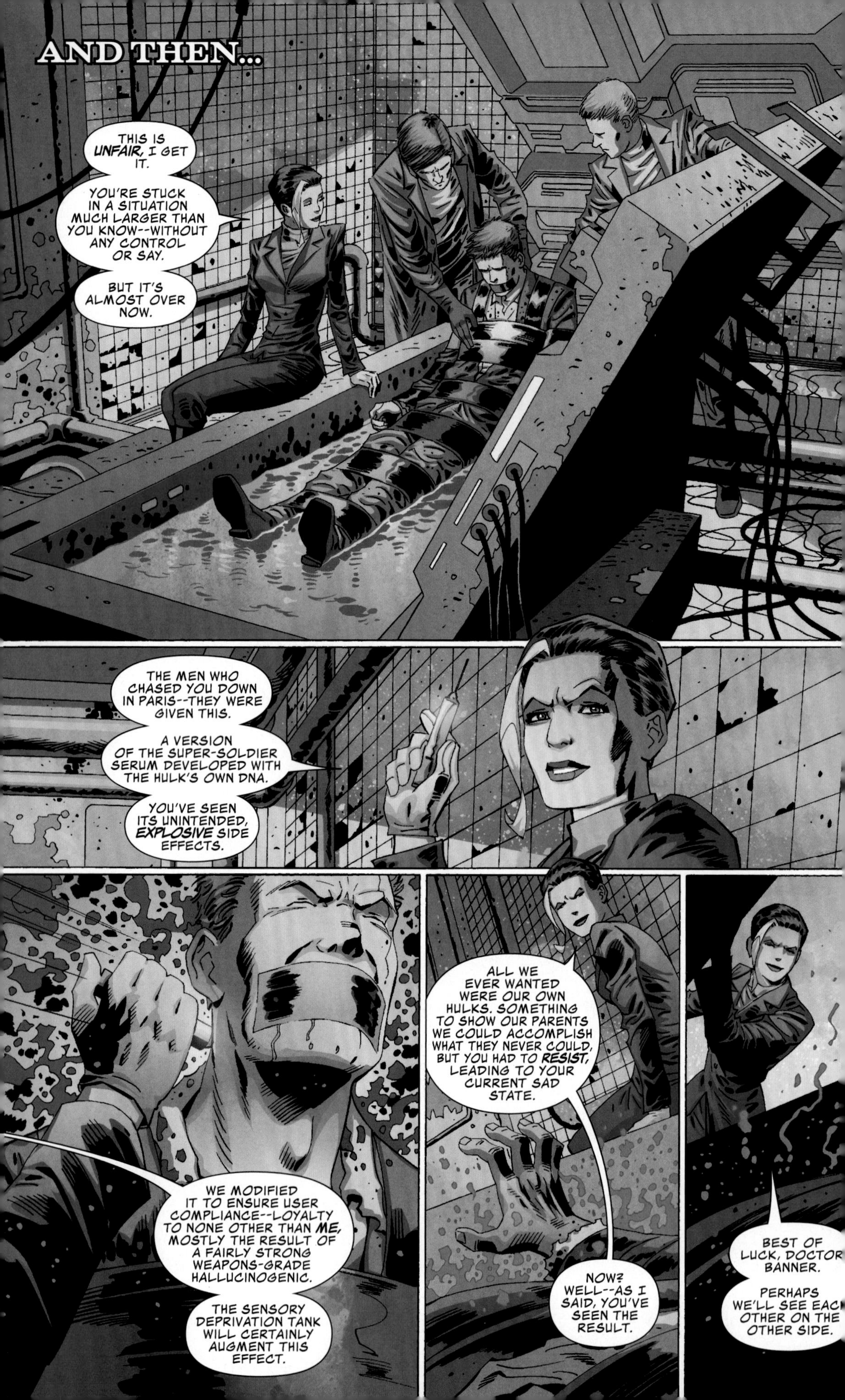
AND THEN...
THIS IS UNFAIR, I GET IT.
YOU'RE STUCK IN A SITUATION MUCH LARGER THAN YOU KNOW--WITHOUT ANY CONTROL OR SAY.
BUT IT'S ALMOST OVER NOW.
THE MEN WHO CHASED YOU DOWN IN PARIS--THEY WERE GIVEN THIS.
A VERSION OF THE SUPER-SOLDIER SERUM DEVELOPED WITH THE HULK'S OWN DNA.
YOU'VE SEEN ITS UNINTENDED, EXPLOSIVE SIDE EFFECTS.
WE MODIFIED IT TO ENSURE USER COMPLIANCE--LOYALTY TO NONE OTHER THAN ME, MOSTLY THE RESULT OF A FAIRLY STRONG WEAPONS-GRADE HALLUCINOGENIC.
THE SENSORY DEPRIVATION TANK WILL CERTAINLY AUGMENT THIS EFFECT.
ALL WE EVER WANTED WERE OUR OWN HULKS. SOMETHING TO SHOW OUR PARENTS WE COULD ACCOMPLISH WHAT THEY NEVER COULD, BUT YOU HAD TO RESIST, LEADING TO YOUR CURRENT SAD STATE.
NOW? WELL--AS I SAID, YOU'VE SEEN THE RESULT.
BEST OF LUCK, DOCTOR BANNER.
PERHAPS WE'LL SEE EACH OTHER ON THE OTHER SIDE.

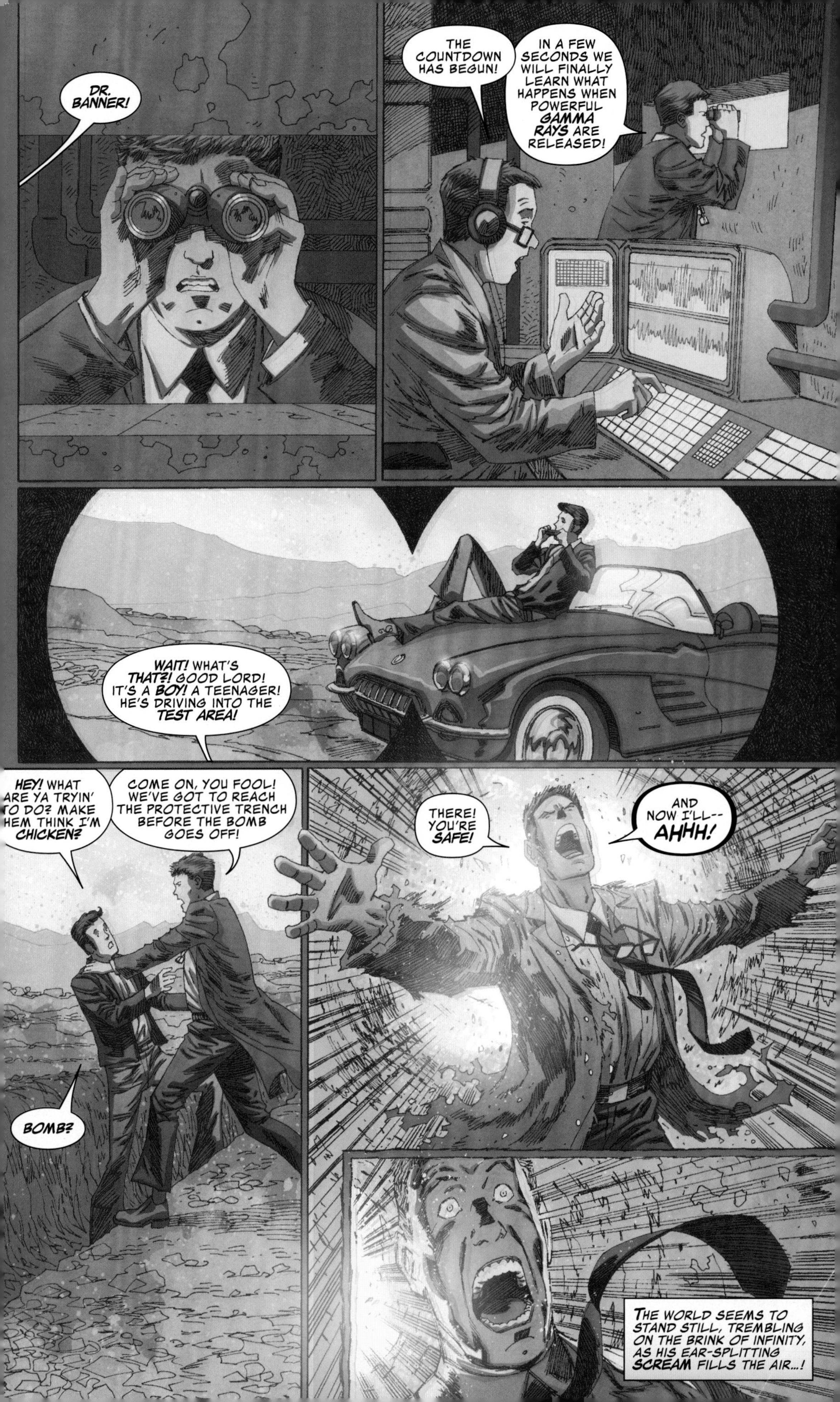
DR. BANNER!
THE COUNTDOWN HAS BEGUN!
IN A FEW SECONDS WE WILL FINALLY LEARN WHAT HAPPENS WHEN POWERFUL GAMMA RAYS ARE RELEASED!
WAIT! WHAT'S THAT?! GOOD LORD! IT'S A BOY! A TEENAGER! HE'S DRIVING INTO THE TEST AREA!
HEY! WHAT ARE YA TRYIN' TO DO? MAKE THEM THINK I'M CHICKEN?
COME ON, YOU FOOL! WE'VE GOT TO REACH THE PROTECTIVE TRENCH BEFORE THE BOMB GOES OFF!
BOMB?
THERE! YOU'RE SAFE!
AND NOW I'LL-- AHHH!
THE WORLD SEEMS TO STAND STILL, TREMBLING ON THE BRINK OF INFINITY, AS HIS EAR-SPLITTING SCREAM FILLS THE AIR...!

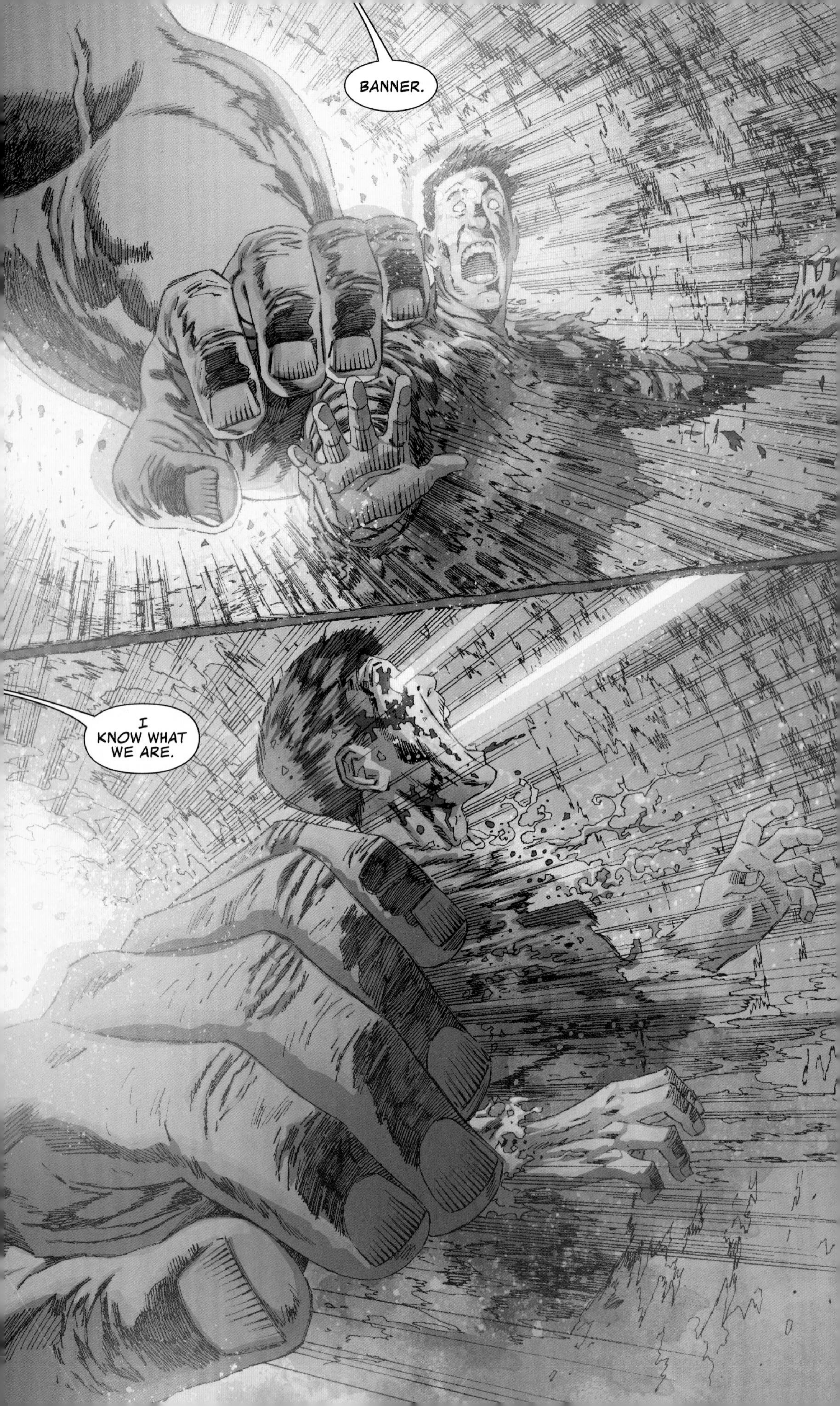
BANNER.
I KNOW WHAT WE ARE.

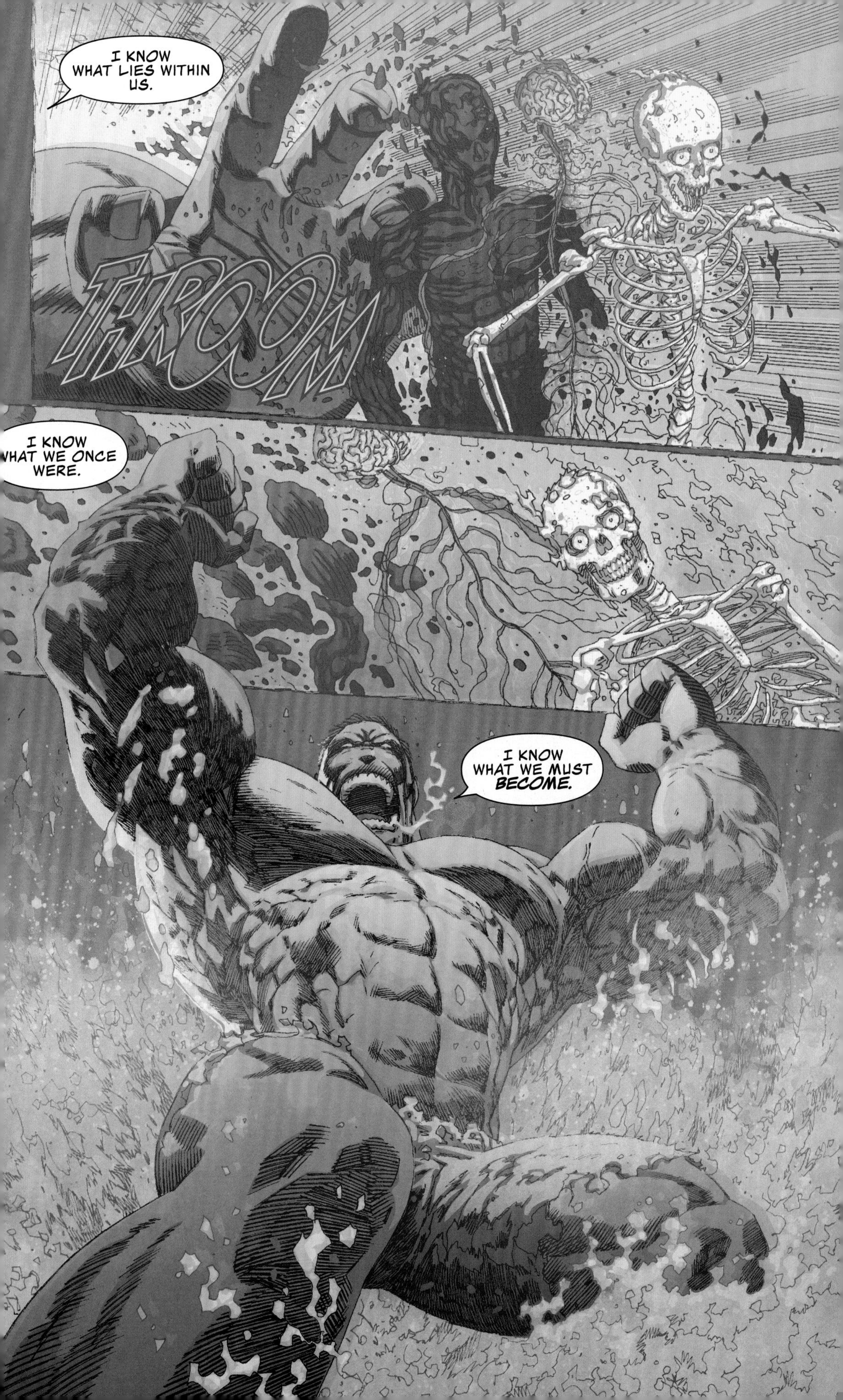
I KNOW WHAT LIES WITHIN US.
THROOM
I KNOW WHAT WE ONCE WERE.
I KNOW WHAT WE MUST BECOME.

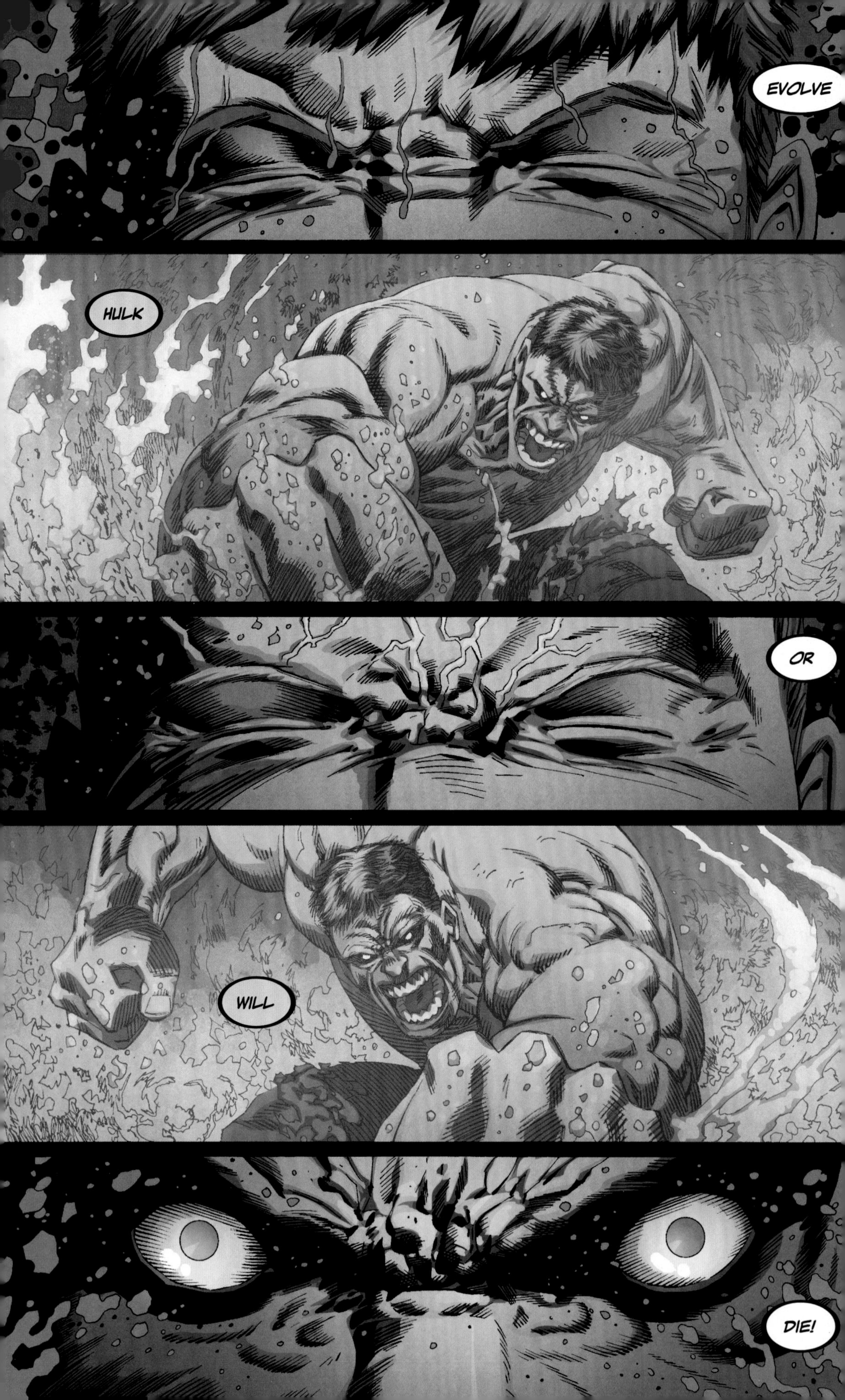
EVOLVE
HULK
OR
WILL
DIE!

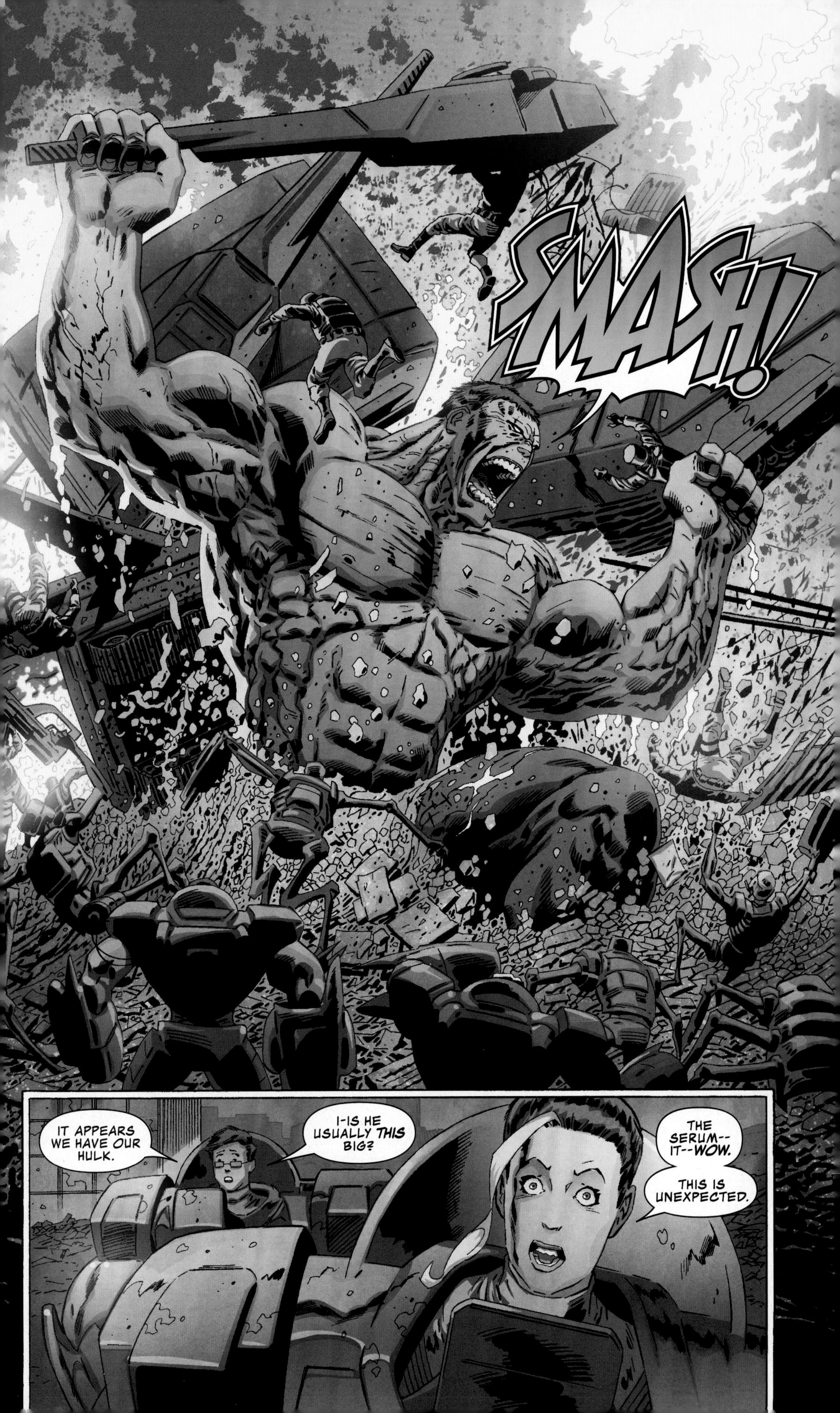
SMASH!
IT APPEARS WE HAVE OUR HULK.
I-IS HE USUALLY THIS BIG?
THE SERUM-- IT--WOW.
THIS IS UNEXPECTED.

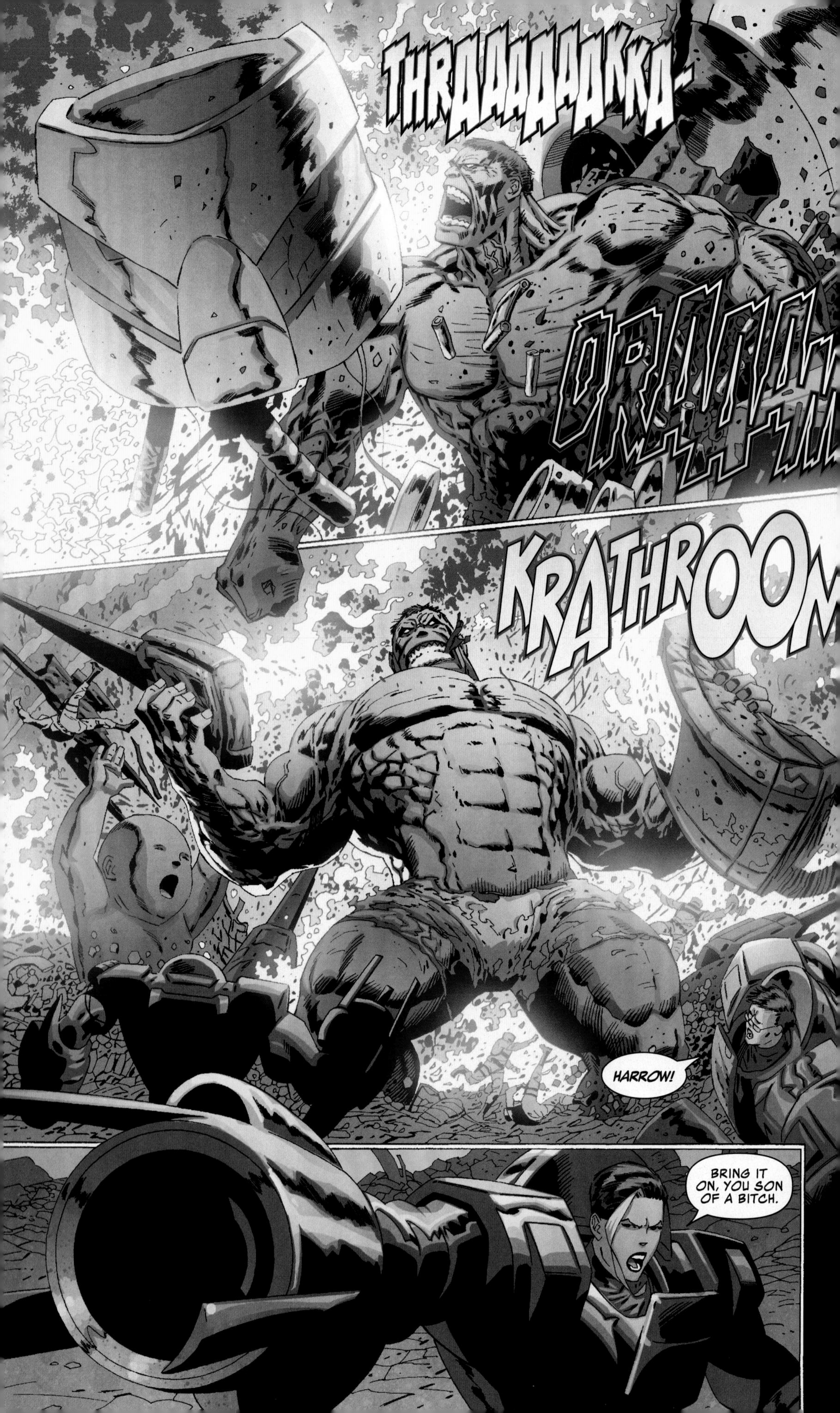
THRAAAAAAKKA-
DRAAAM
KRATHROOM
HARROW!
BRING IT ON, YOU SON OF A BITCH.

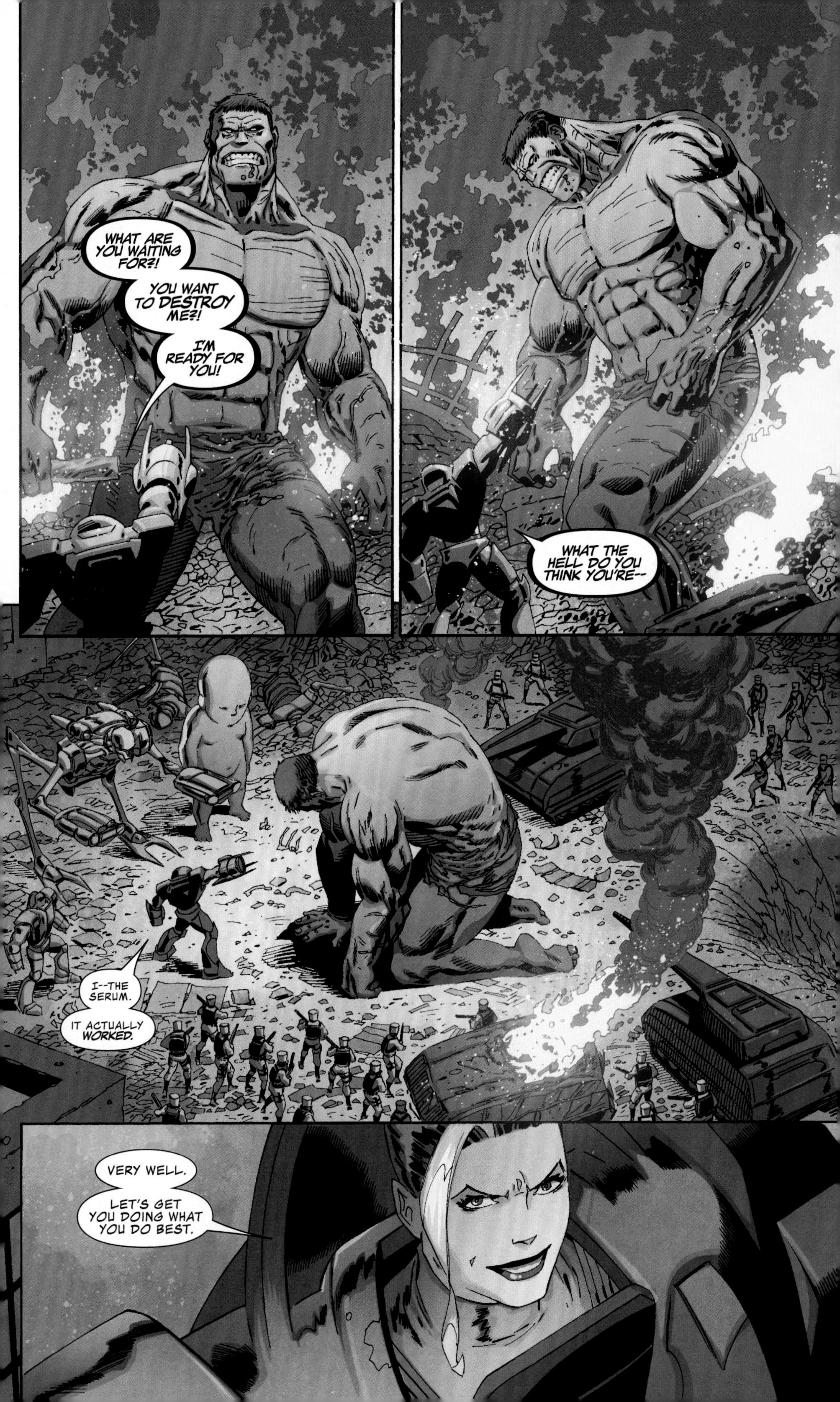

WHAT ARE YOU WAITING FOR?!
YOU WANT TO DESTROY ME?!
I'M READY FOR YOU!
WHAT THE HELL DO YOU THINK YOU'RE--
I--THE SERUM.
IT ACTUALLY WORKED.
VERY WELL.
LET'S GET YOU DOING WHAT YOU DO BEST.

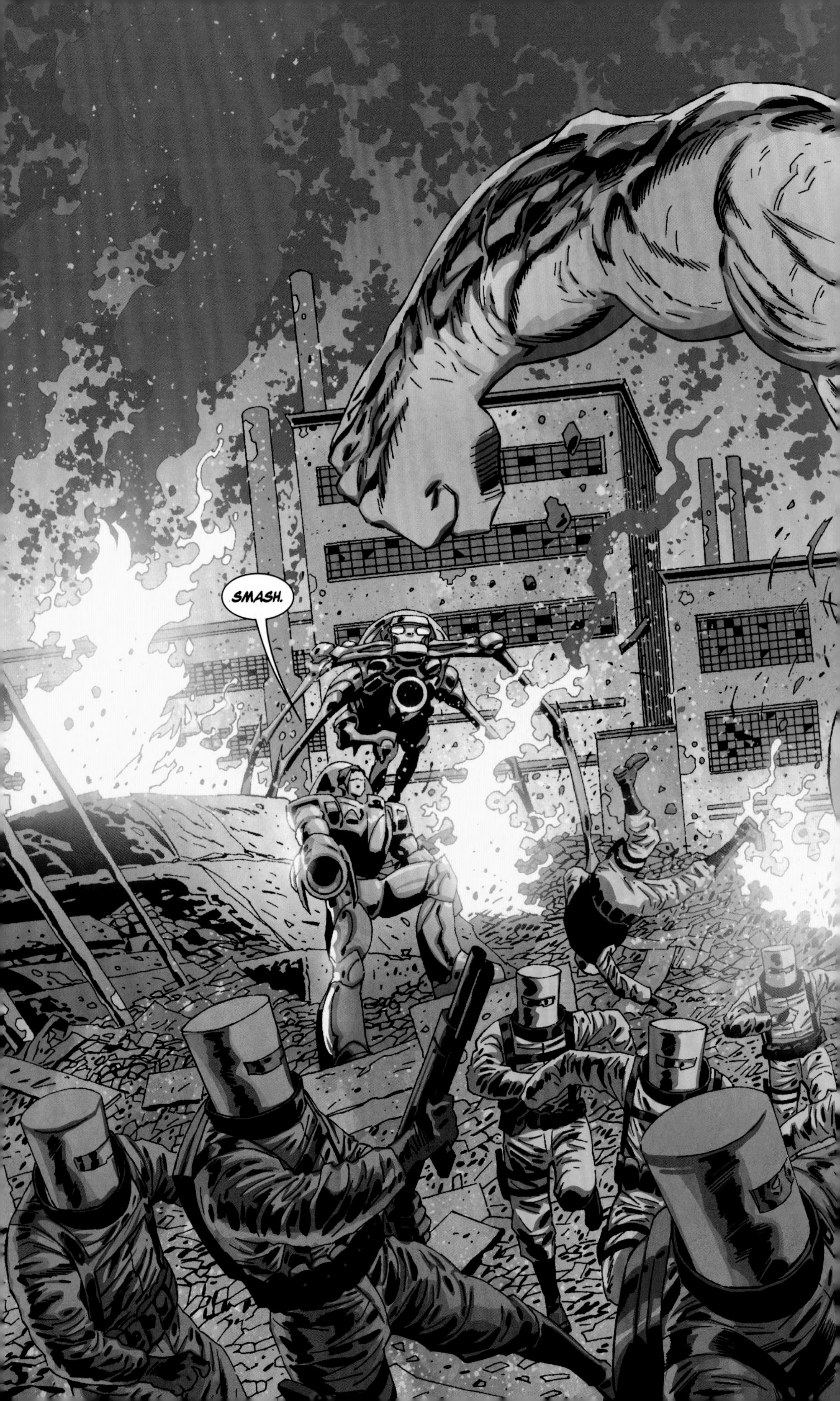
SMASH.

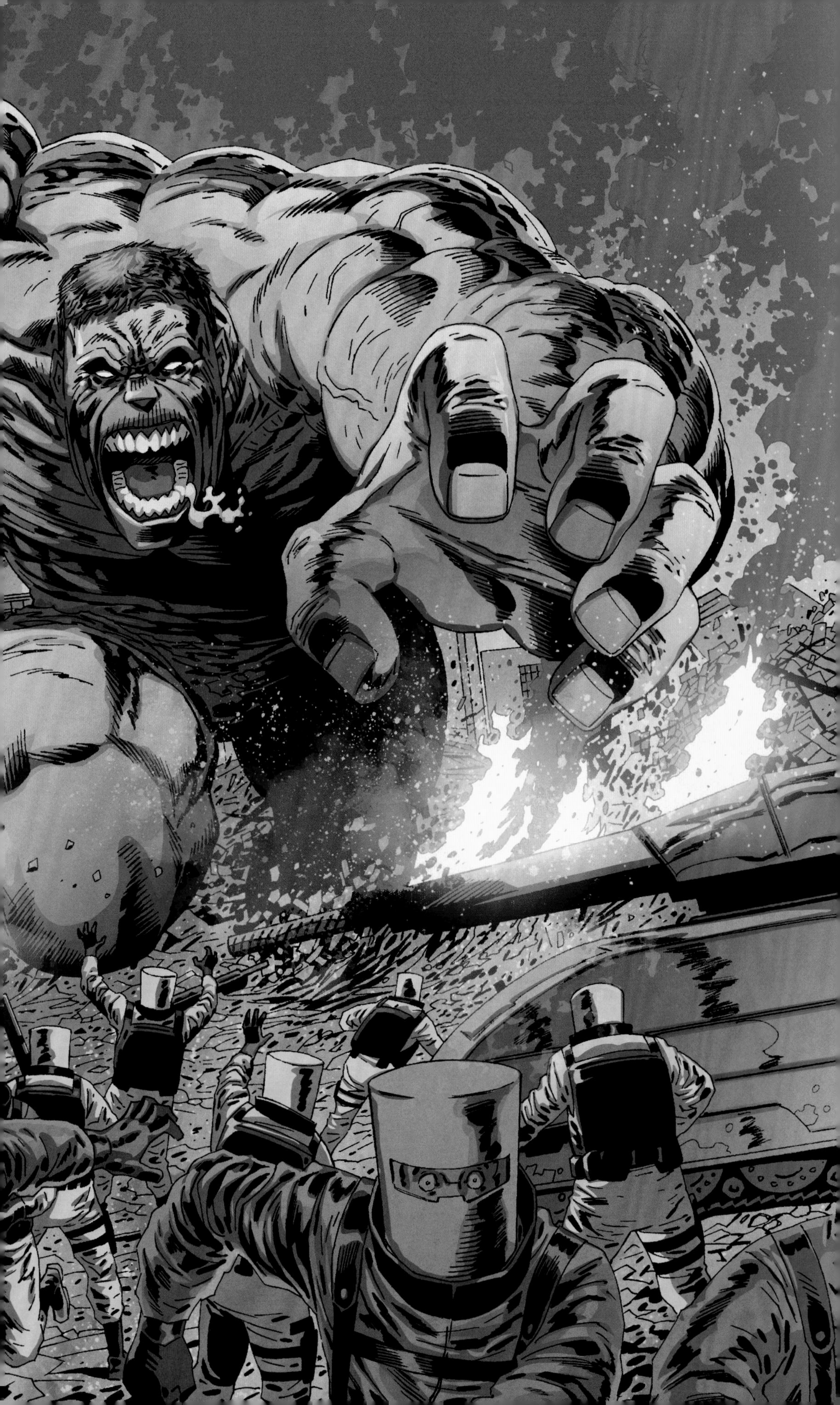

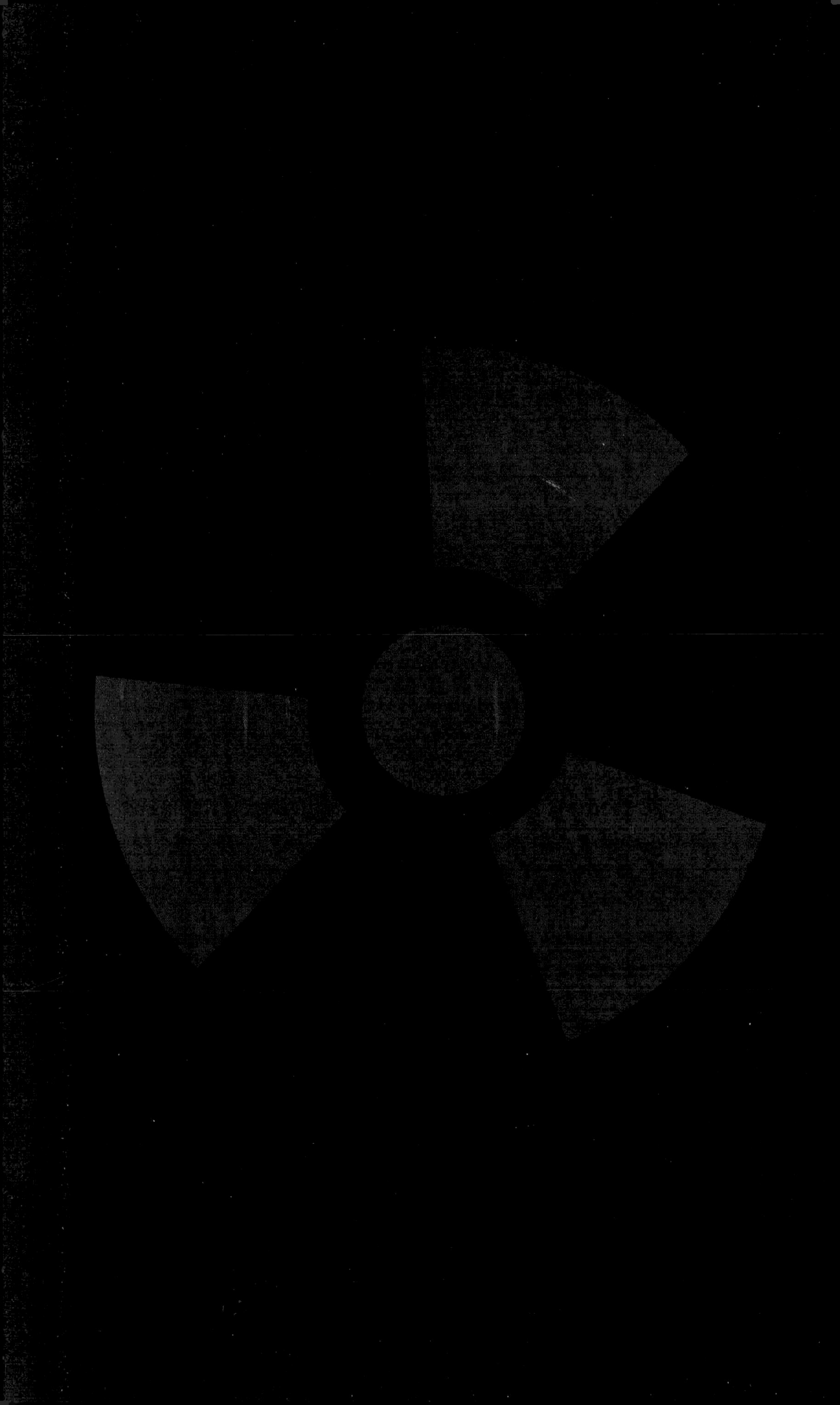

3

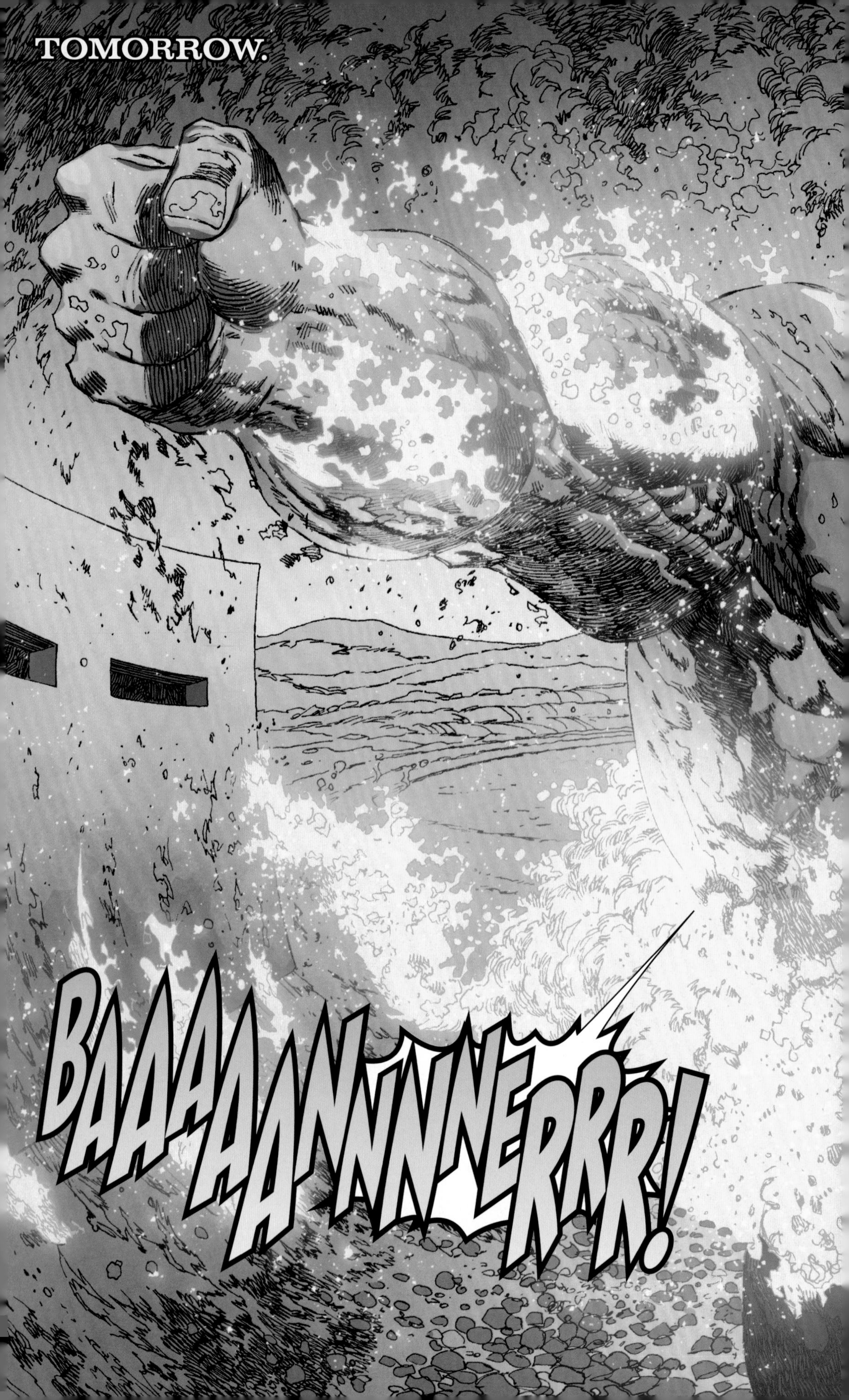
TOMORROW.
BAAAAANNNNERRR!

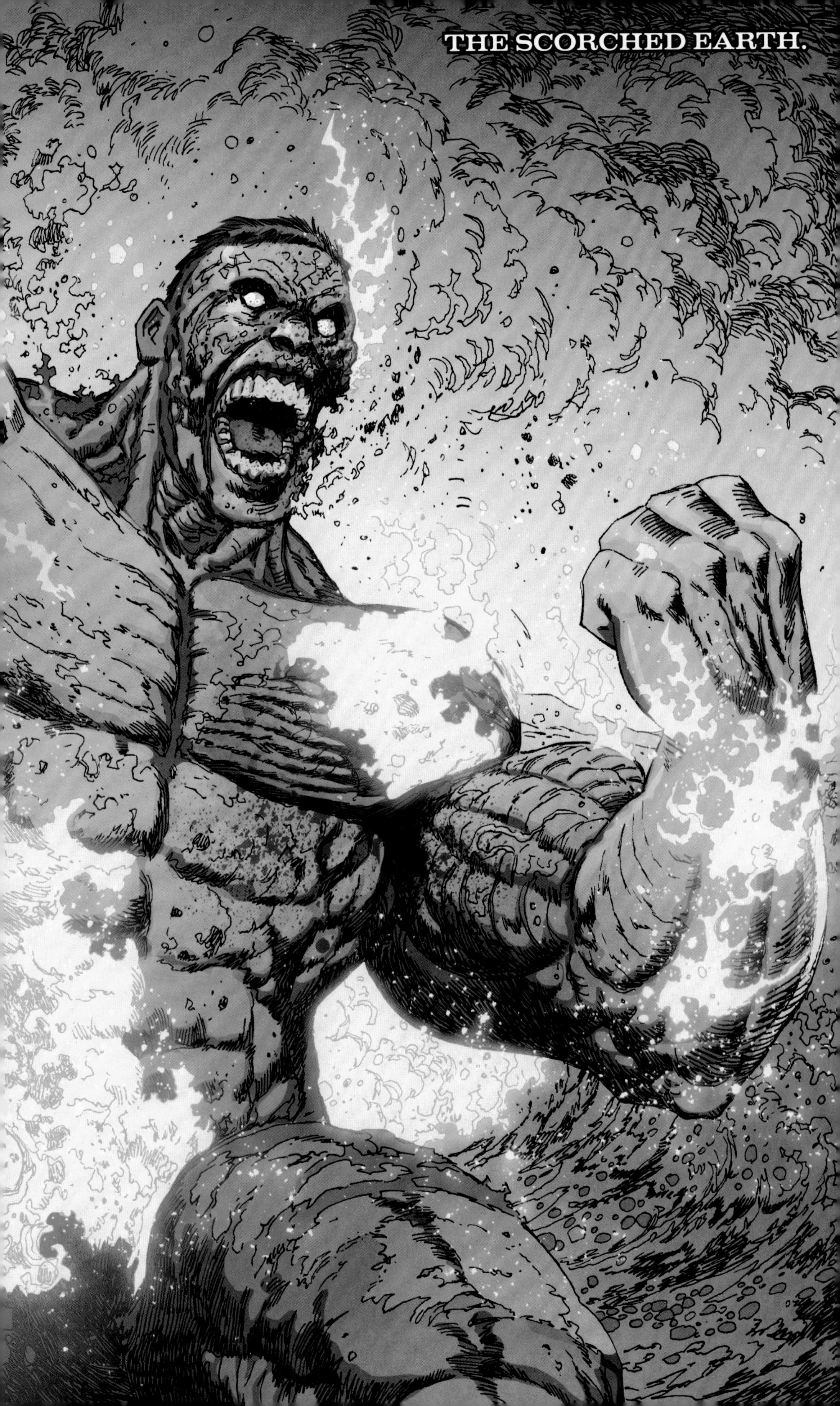
THE SCORCHED EARTH.

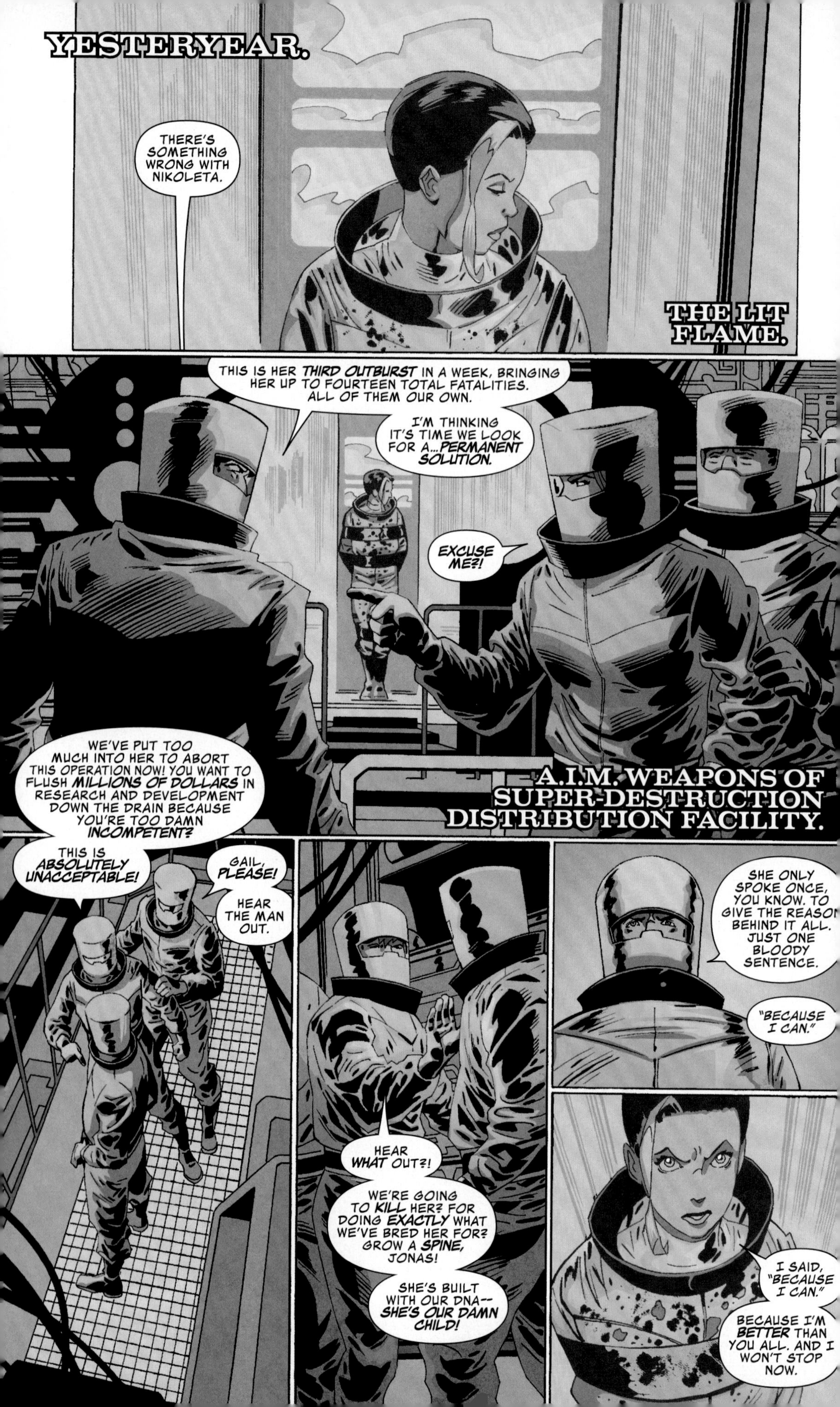

YESTERYEAR.
THERE'S SOMETHING WRONG WITH NIKOLETA.
THE LIT FLAME.
THIS IS HER THIRD OUTBURST IN A WEEK, BRINGING HER UP TO FOURTEEN TOTAL FATALITIES. ALL OF THEM OUR OWN.
I'M THINKING IT'S TIME WE LOOK FOR A...PERMANENT SOLUTION.
EXCUSE ME?!
WE'VE PUT TOO MUCH INTO HER TO ABORT THIS OPERATION NOW! YOU WANT TO FLUSH MILLIONS OF DOLLARS IN RESEARCH AND DEVELOPMENT DOWN THE DRAIN BECAUSE YOU'RE TOO DAMN INCOMPETENT?
A.I.M. WEAPONS OF SUPER-DESTRUCTION DISTRIBUTION FACILITY.
THIS IS ABSOLUTELY UNACCEPTABLE!
GAIL, PLEASE!
HEAR THE MAN OUT.
HEAR WHAT OUT?!
WE'RE GOING TO KILL HER? FOR DOING EXACTLY WHAT WE'VE BRED HER FOR? GROW A SPINE, JONAS!
SHE'S BUILT WITH OUR DNA-- SHE'S OUR DAMN CHILD!
SHE ONLY SPOKE ONCE, YOU KNOW. TO GIVE THE REASON BEHIND IT ALL. JUST ONE BLOODY SENTENCE.
"BECAUSE I CAN."
I SAID, "BECAUSE I CAN."
BECAUSE I'M BETTER THAN YOU ALL. AND I WON'T STOP NOW.

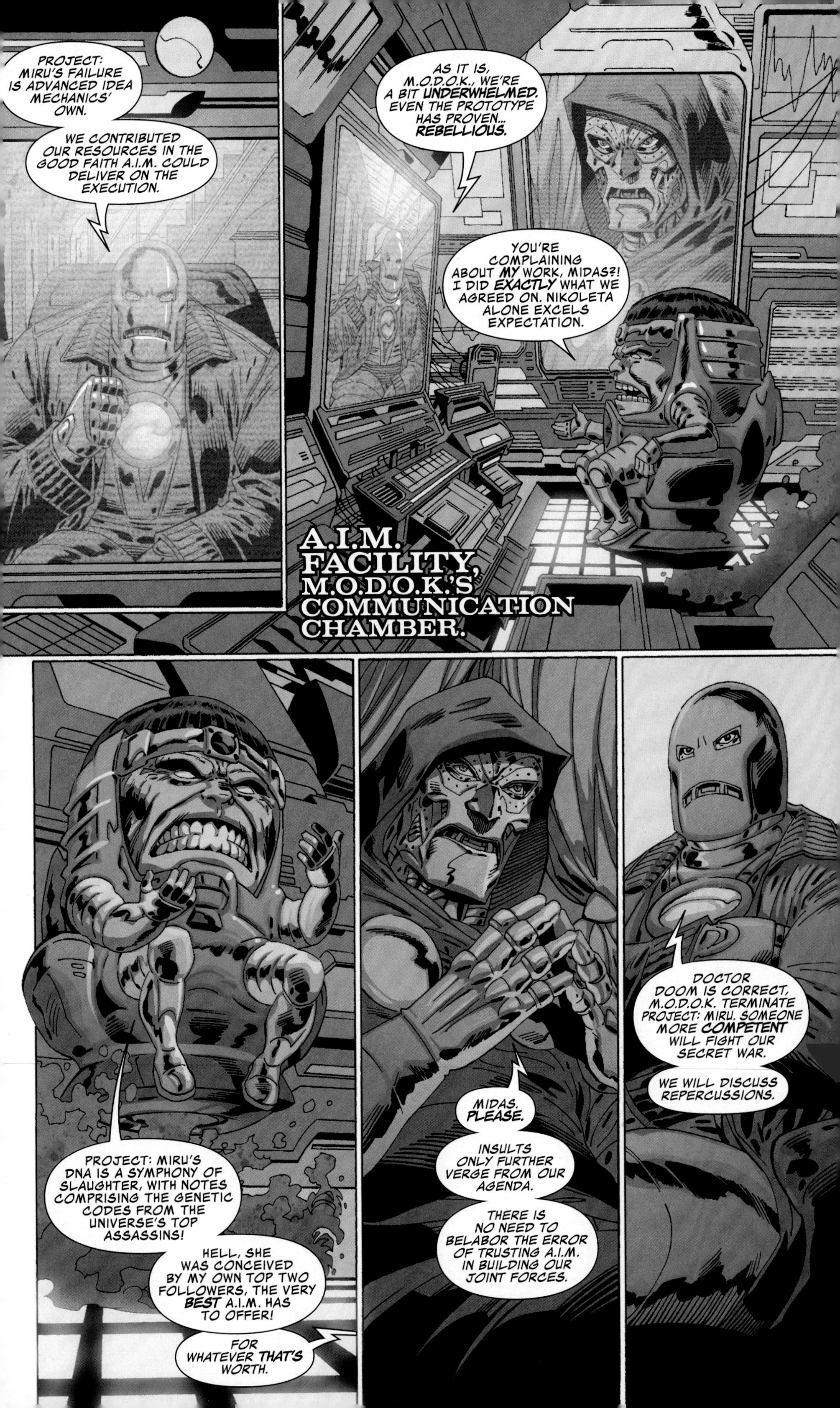
PROJECT: MIRU'S FAILURE IS ADVANCED IDEA MECHANICS' OWN.
WE CONTRIBUTED OUR RESOURCES IN THE GOOD FAITH A.I.M. COULD DELIVER ON THE EXECUTION.
AS IT IS, M.O.D.O.K., WE'RE A BIT UNDERWHELMED. EVEN THE PROTOTYPE HAS PROVEN... REBELLIOUS.
YOU'RE COMPLAINING ABOUT MY WORK, MIDAS?! I DID EXACTLY WHAT WE AGREED ON. NIKOLETA ALONE EXCELS EXPECTATION.
A.I.M. FACILITY, M.O.D.O.K.'S COMMUNICATION CHAMBER.
PROJECT: MIRU'S DNA IS A SYMPHONY OF SLAUGHTER, WITH NOTES COMPRISING THE GENETIC CODES FROM THE UNIVERSE'S TOP ASSASSINS!
HELL, SHE WAS CONCEIVED BY MY OWN TOP TWO FOLLOWERS, THE VERY BEST A.I.M. HAS TO OFFER!
FOR WHATEVER THAT'S WORTH.
MIDAS. PLEASE.
INSULTS ONLY FURTHER VERGE FROM OUR AGENDA.
THERE IS NO NEED TO BELABOR THE ERROR OF TRUSTING A.I.M. IN BUILDING OUR JOINT FORCES.
DOCTOR DOOM IS CORRECT, M.O.D.O.K. TERMINATE PROJECT: MIRU. SOMEONE MORE COMPETENT WILL FIGHT OUR SECRET WAR.
WE WILL DISCUSS REPERCUSSIONS.

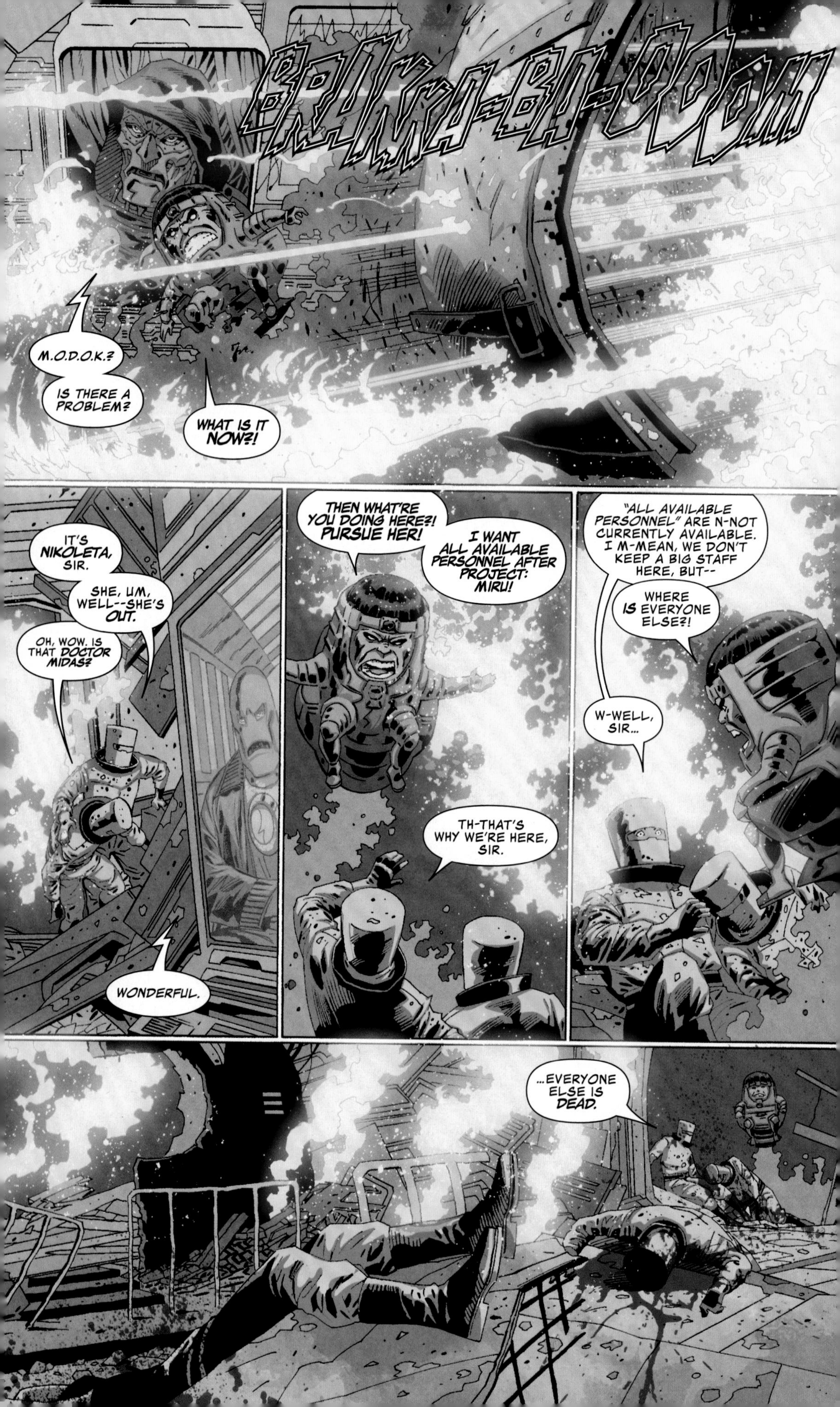
BRAKKA-BA-DOOOM
M.O.D.O.K.?
IS THERE A PROBLEM?
WHAT IS IT NOW?!
IT'S NIKOLETA, SIR.
SHE, UM, WELL--SHE'S OUT.
OH, WOW. IS THAT DOCTOR MIDAS?
WONDERFUL.
THEN WHAT'RE YOU DOING HERE?! PURSUE HER!
I WANT ALL AVAILABLE PERSONNEL AFTER PROJECT: MIRU!
TH-THAT'S WHY WE'RE HERE, SIR.
"ALL AVAILABLE PERSONNEL" ARE N-NOT CURRENTLY AVAILABLE. I M-MEAN, WE DON'T KEEP A BIG STAFF HERE, BUT--
WHERE IS EVERYONE ELSE?!
W-WELL, SIR...
...EVERYONE ELSE IS DEAD.

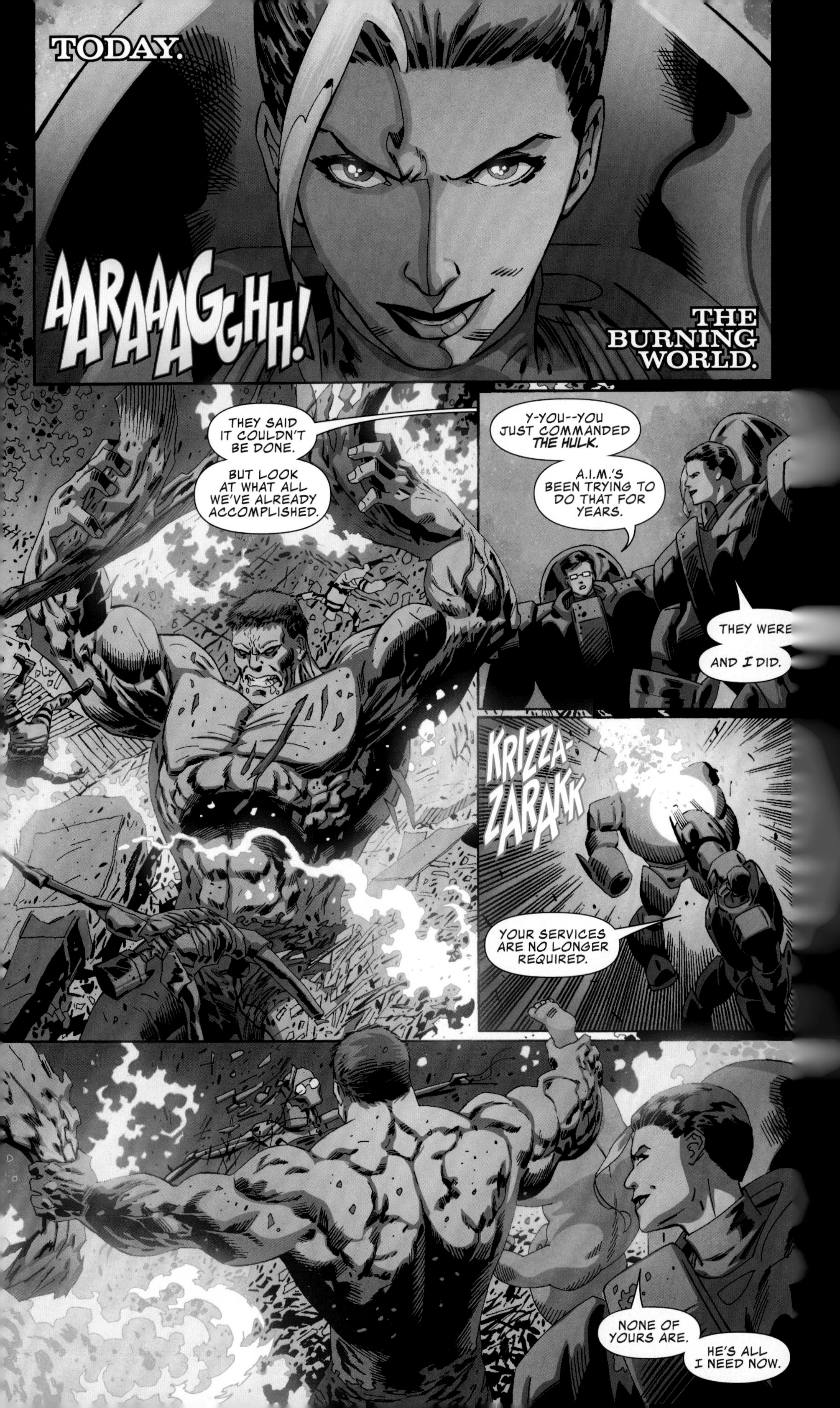
TODAY.
AARAAAGGHH!
THE BURNING WORLD.
THEY SAID IT COULDN'T BE DONE.
BUT LOOK AT WHAT ALL WE'VE ALREADY ACCOMPLISHED.
Y-YOU--YOU JUST COMMANDED THE HULK.
A.I.M.'S BEEN TRYING TO DO THAT FOR YEARS.
THEY WERE
AND I DID.
KRIZZA-ZARAKK
YOUR SERVICES ARE NO LONGER REQUIRED.
NONE OF YOURS ARE.
HE'S ALL I NEED NOW.

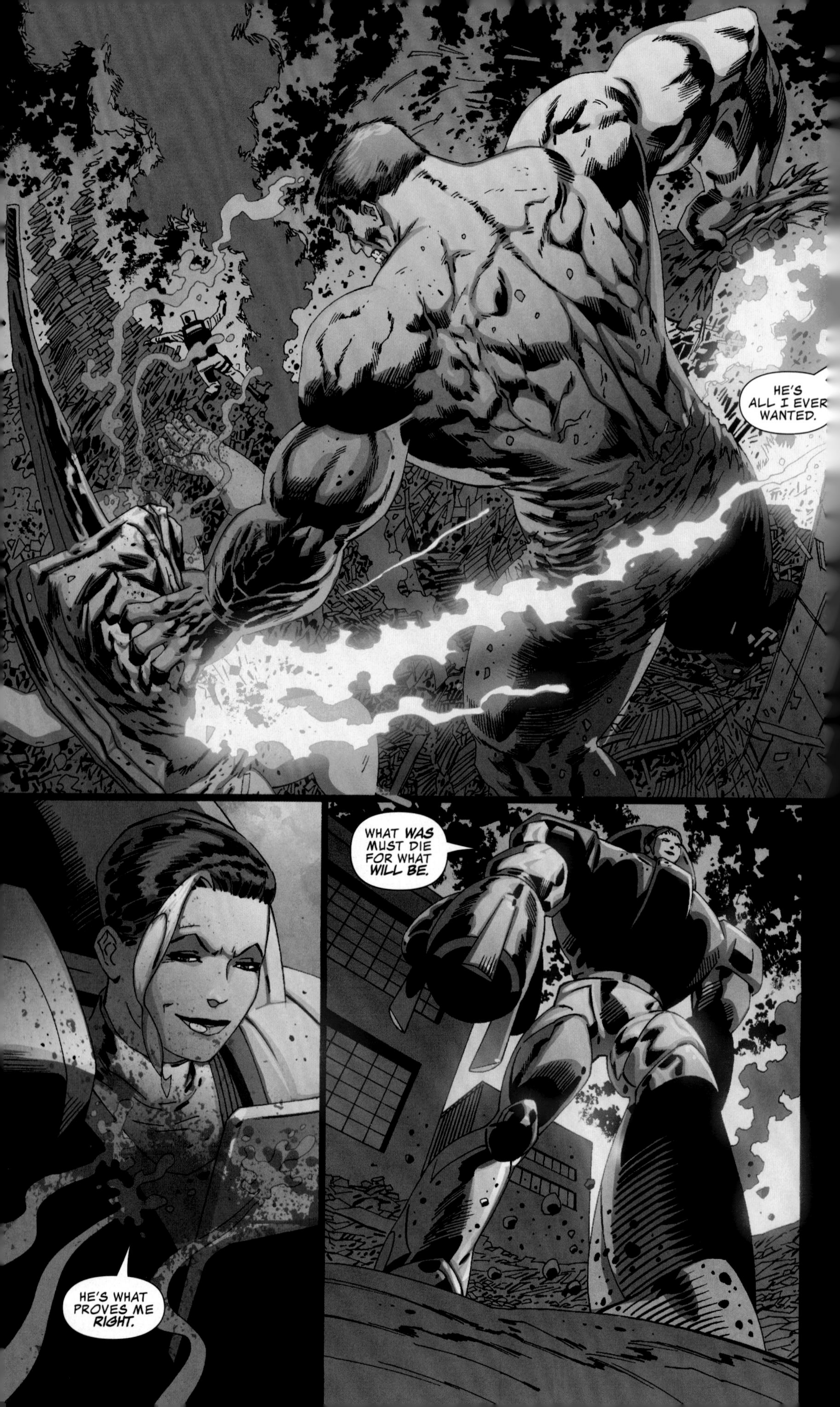
HE'S ALL I EVER WANTED.
WHAT WAS MUST DIE FOR WHAT WILL BE.
HE'S WHAT PROVES ME RIGHT.

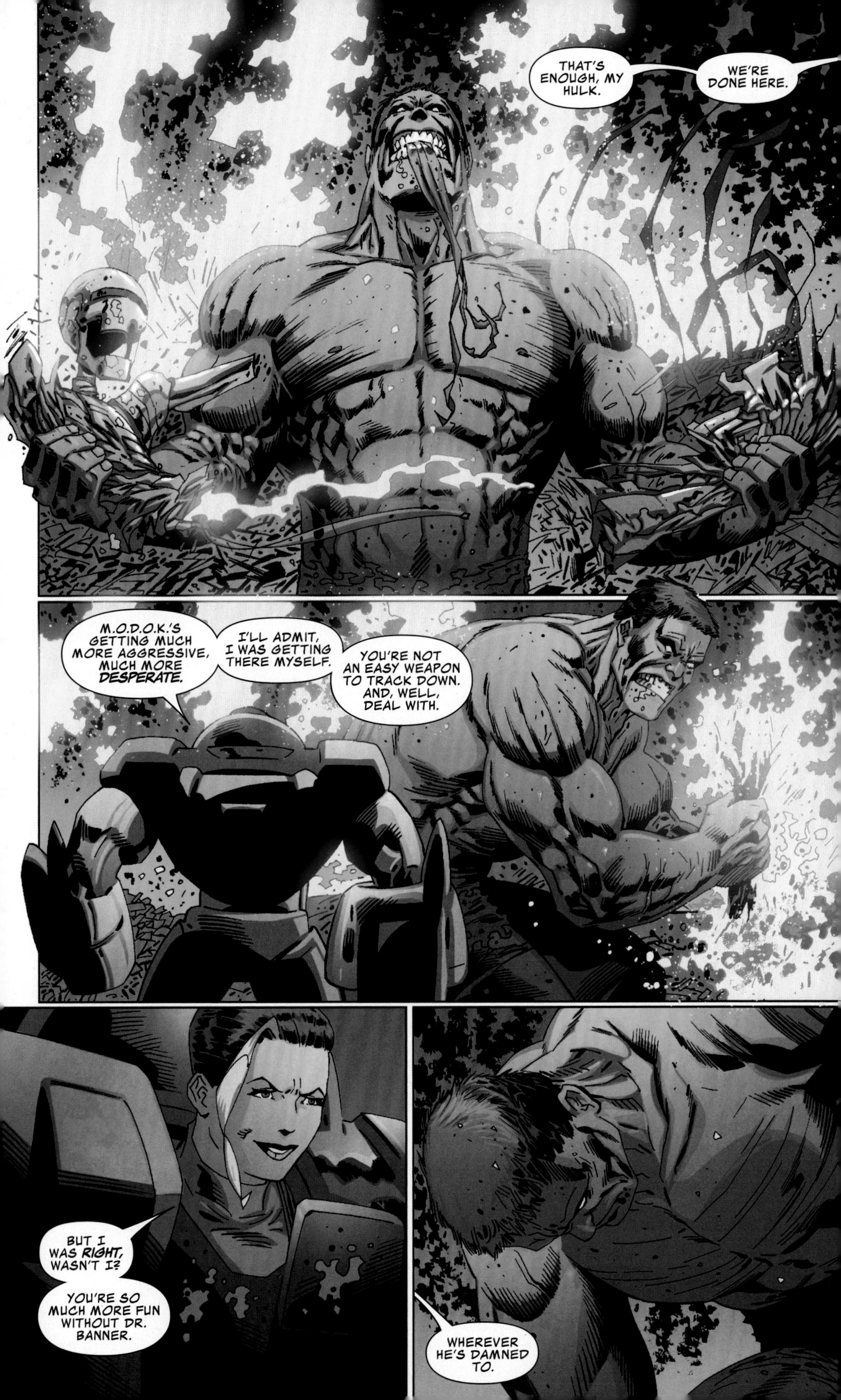

THAT'S ENOUGH, MY HULK.
WE'RE DONE HERE.
M.O.D.O.K.'S GETTING MUCH MORE AGGRESSIVE, MUCH MORE DESPERATE.
I'LL ADMIT, I WAS GETTING THERE MYSELF.
YOU'RE NOT AN EASY WEAPON TO TRACK DOWN. AND, WELL, DEAL WITH.
BUT I WAS RIGHT, WASN'T I?
YOU'RE SO MUCH MORE FUN WITHOUT DR. BANNER.
WHEREVER HE'S DAMNED TO.

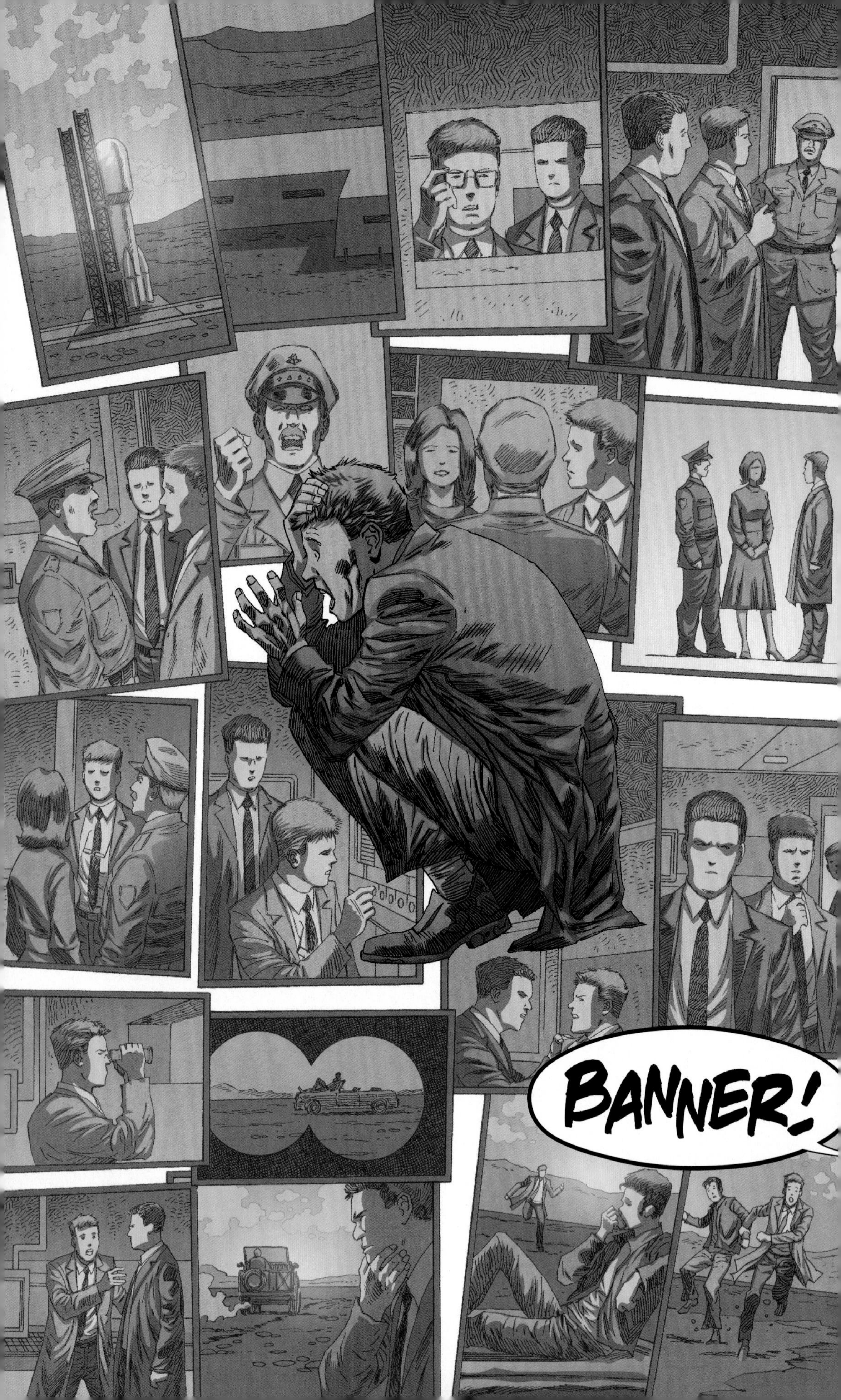
BANNER!

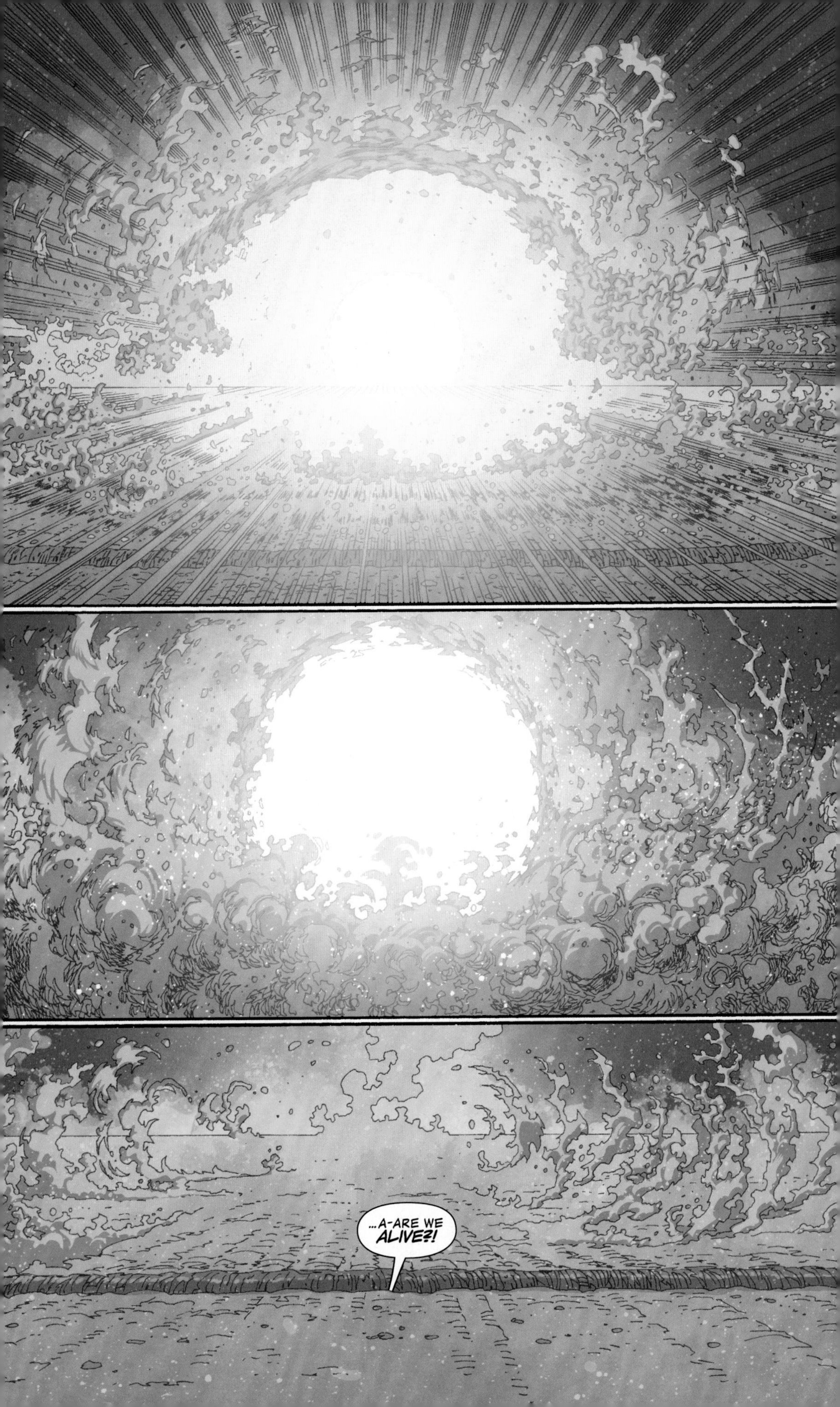
...A-ARE WE ALIVE?!

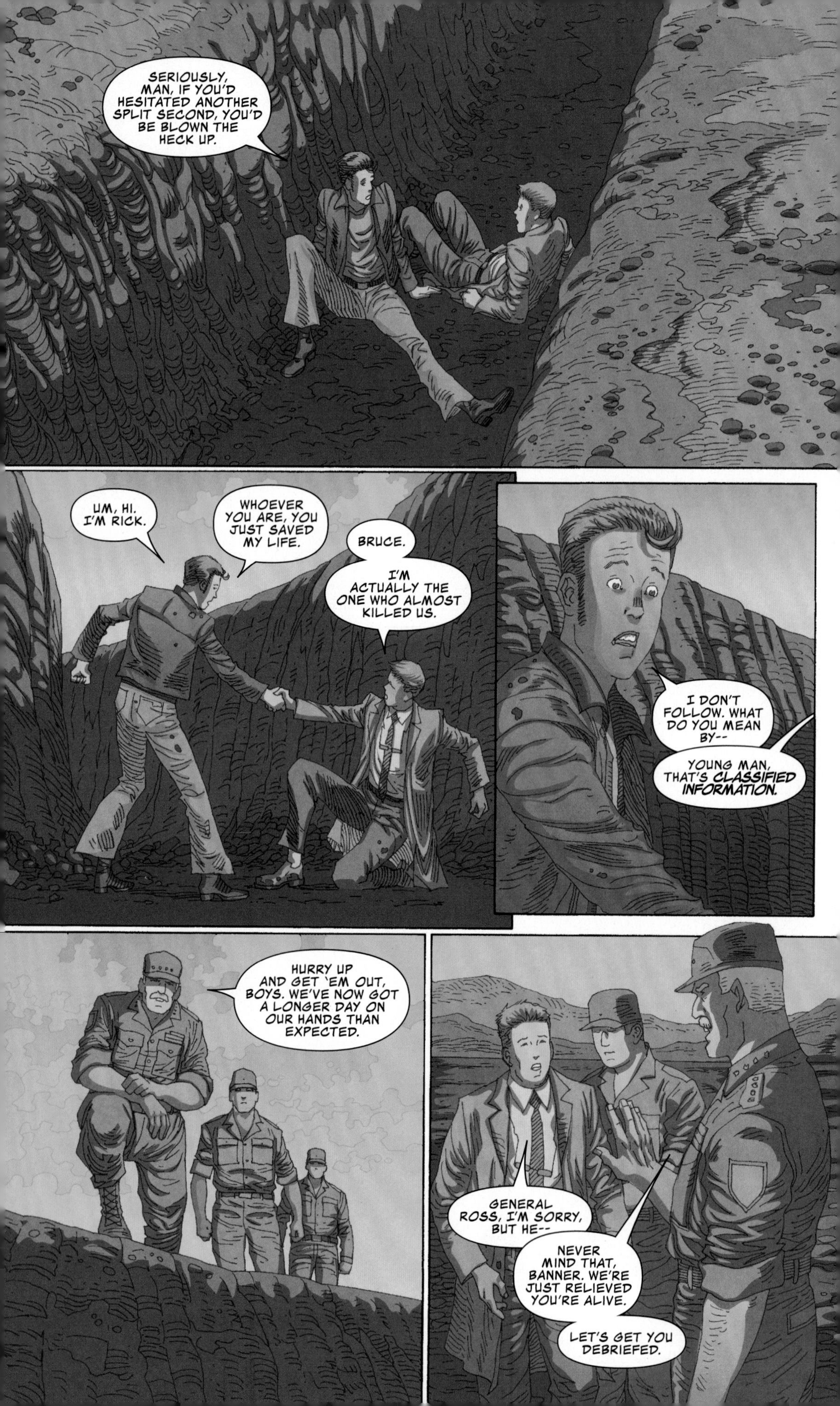
SERIOUSLY, MAN, IF YOU'D HESITATED ANOTHER SPLIT SECOND, YOU'D BE BLOWN THE HECK UP.
UM, HI. I'M RICK.
WHOEVER YOU ARE, YOU JUST SAVED MY LIFE.
BRUCE.
I'M ACTUALLY THE ONE WHO ALMOST KILLED US.
I DON'T FOLLOW. WHAT DO YOU MEAN BY--
YOUNG MAN, THAT'S CLASSIFIED INFORMATION.
HURRY UP AND GET 'EM OUT, BOYS. WE'VE NOW GOT A LONGER DAY ON OUR HANDS THAN EXPECTED.
GENERAL ROSS, I'M SORRY, BUT HE--
NEVER MIND THAT, BANNER. WE'RE JUST RELIEVED YOU'RE ALIVE.
LET'S GET YOU DEBRIEFED.

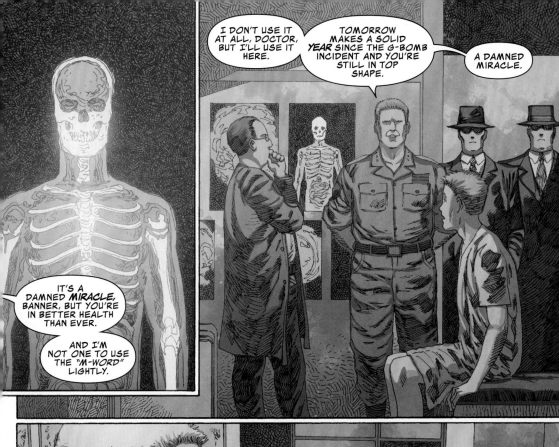

IT'S A DAMNED **MIRACLE**, BANNER, BUT YOU'RE IN BETTER HEALTH THAN EVER.

AND I'M NOT ONE TO USE THE "M-WORD" LIGHTLY.

I DON'T USE IT AT ALL, DOCTOR, BUT I'LL USE IT HERE.

TOMORROW MAKES A SOLID **YEAR** SINCE THE G-BOMB INCIDENT AND YOU'RE STILL IN TOP SHAPE.

A DAMNED MIRACLE.

DOES THIS MEAN I CAN GET A CHECKUP WITHOUT THE MILITARY ESCORT?

IT'S BAD ENOUGH MY FATHER-IN-LAW SEES ME IN A HOSPITAL GOWN, BUT I STILL DON'T EVEN KNOW THIS SUIT'S NAME.

I'M MERELY HERE TO LOOK AFTER EVERYONE'S BEST INTERESTS.

AND WHEN DO MY "BEST INTERESTS" INCLUDE MY **FREEDOM**?

LIKE I SAID, DOCTOR BANNER...

...I'M CONCERNED WITH **EVERYONE'S** BEST INTERESTS.

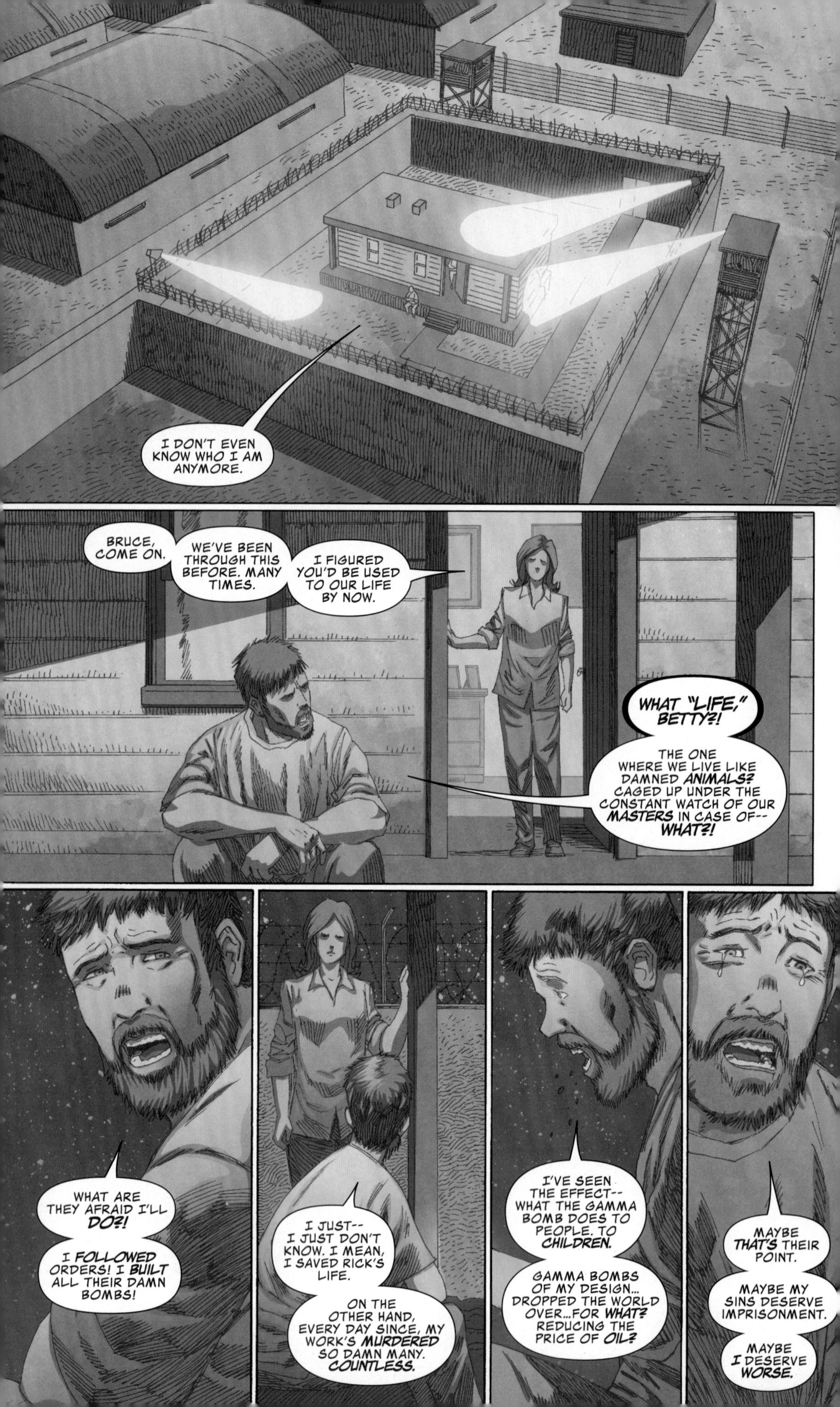
I DON'T EVEN KNOW WHO I AM ANYMORE.
BRUCE, COME ON.
WE'VE BEEN THROUGH THIS BEFORE. MANY TIMES.
I FIGURED YOU'D BE USED TO OUR LIFE BY NOW.
WHAT "LIFE," BETTY?!
THE ONE WHERE WE LIVE LIKE DAMNED ANIMALS? CAGED UP UNDER THE CONSTANT WATCH OF OUR MASTERS IN CASE OF-- WHAT?!
WHAT ARE THEY AFRAID I'LL DO?!
I FOLLOWED ORDERS! I BUILT ALL THEIR DAMN BOMBS!
I JUST-- I JUST DON'T KNOW. I MEAN, I SAVED RICK'S LIFE.
ON THE OTHER HAND, EVERY DAY SINCE, MY WORK'S MURDERED SO DAMN MANY. COUNTLESS.
I'VE SEEN THE EFFECT-- WHAT THE GAMMA BOMB DOES TO PEOPLE. TO CHILDREN.
GAMMA BOMBS OF MY DESIGN... DROPPED THE WORLD OVER...FOR WHAT? REDUCING THE PRICE OF OIL?
MAYBE THAT'S THEIR POINT.
MAYBE MY SINS DESERVE IMPRISONMENT.
MAYBE I DESERVE WORSE.

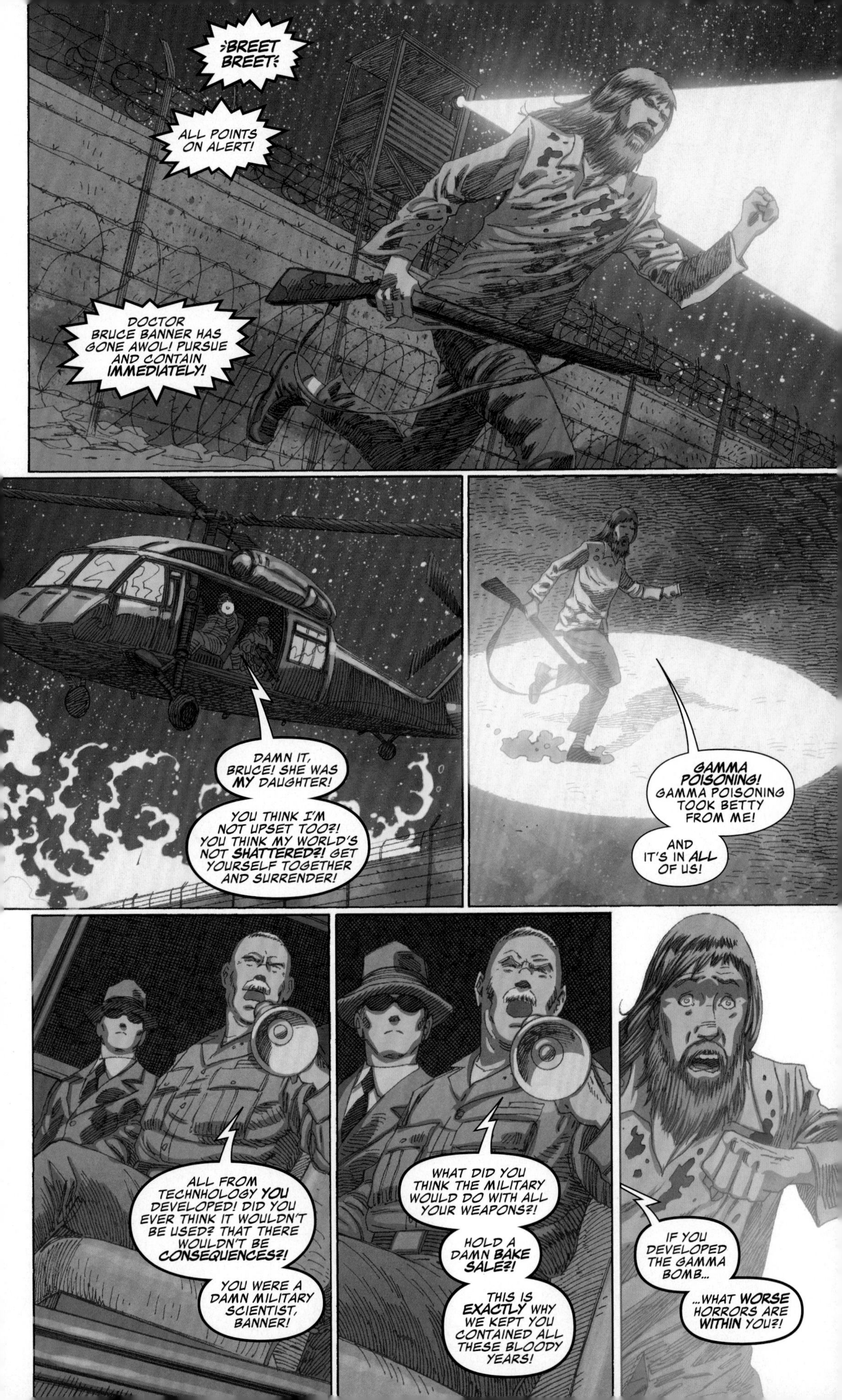
BREET BREET
ALL POINTS ON ALERT!
DOCTOR BRUCE BANNER HAS GONE AWOL! PURSUE AND CONTAIN IMMEDIATELY!
DAMN IT, BRUCE! SHE WAS MY DAUGHTER!
YOU THINK I'M NOT UPSET TOO?! YOU THINK MY WORLD'S NOT SHATTERED?! GET YOURSELF TOGETHER AND SURRENDER!
GAMMA POISONING! GAMMA POISONING TOOK BETTY FROM ME!
AND IT'S IN ALL OF US!
ALL FROM TECHNOLOGY YOU DEVELOPED! DID YOU EVER THINK IT WOULDN'T BE USED? THAT THERE WOULDN'T BE CONSEQUENCES?!
YOU WERE A DAMN MILITARY SCIENTIST, BANNER!
WHAT DID YOU THINK THE MILITARY WOULD DO WITH ALL YOUR WEAPONS?!
HOLD A DAMN BAKE SALE?!
THIS IS EXACTLY WHY WE KEPT YOU CONTAINED ALL THESE BLOODY YEARS!
IF YOU DEVELOPED THE GAMMA BOMB...
...WHAT WORSE HORRORS ARE WITHIN YOU?!

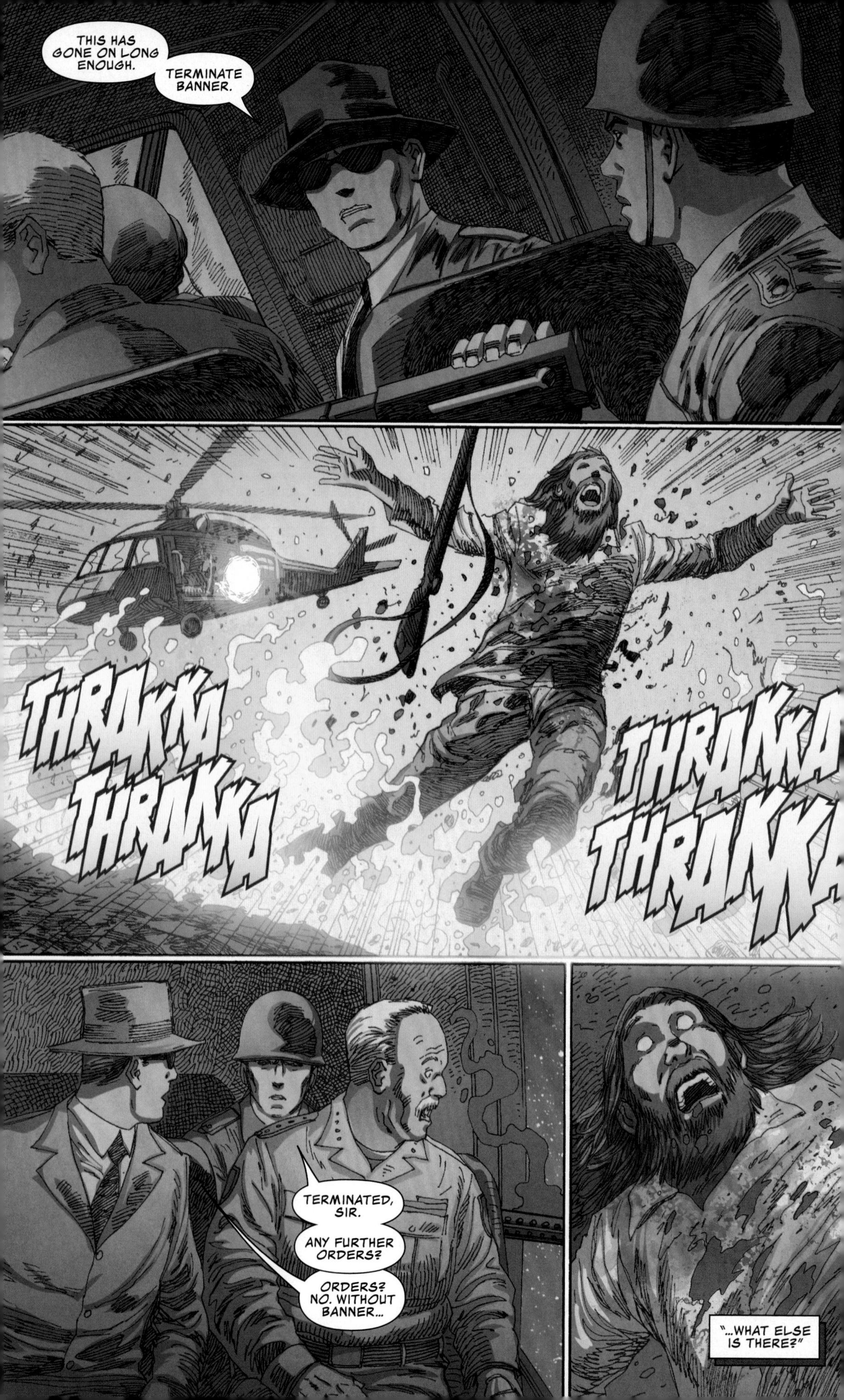
THIS HAS GONE ON LONG ENOUGH.
TERMINATE BANNER.
THRAKKA THRAKKA
THRAKKA THRAKKA
TERMINATED, SIR.
ANY FURTHER ORDERS?
ORDERS? NO. WITHOUT BANNER...
"...WHAT ELSE IS THERE?"

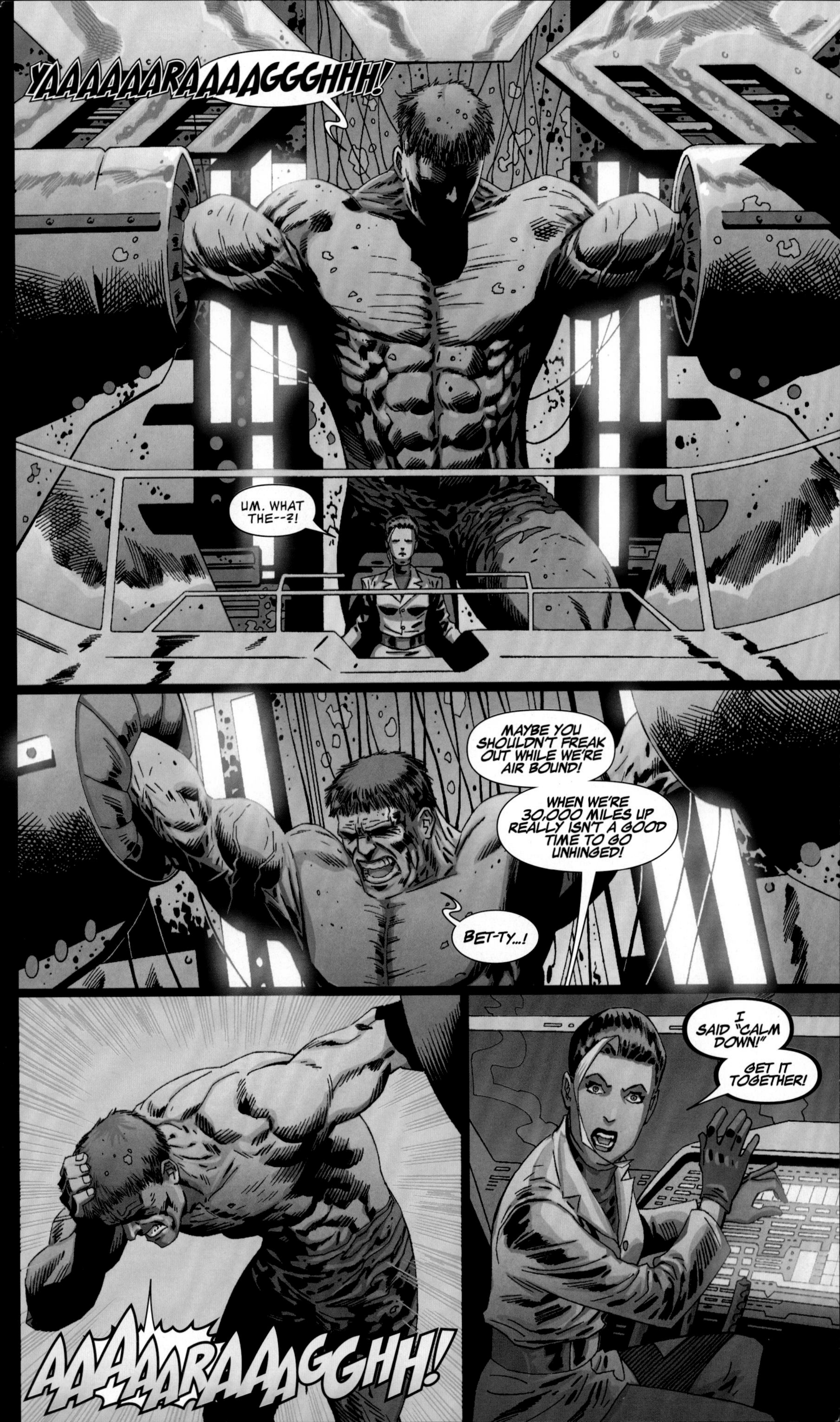
YAAAAAARAAAAGGGHHH!
UM. WHAT THE--?!
MAYBE YOU SHOULDN'T FREAK OUT WHILE WE'RE AIR BOUND!
WHEN WE'RE 30,000 MILES UP REALLY ISN'T A GOOD TIME TO GO UNHINGED!
BET-TY...!
AAAAARAAAGGHH!
I SAID "CALM DOWN!"
GET IT TOGETHER!

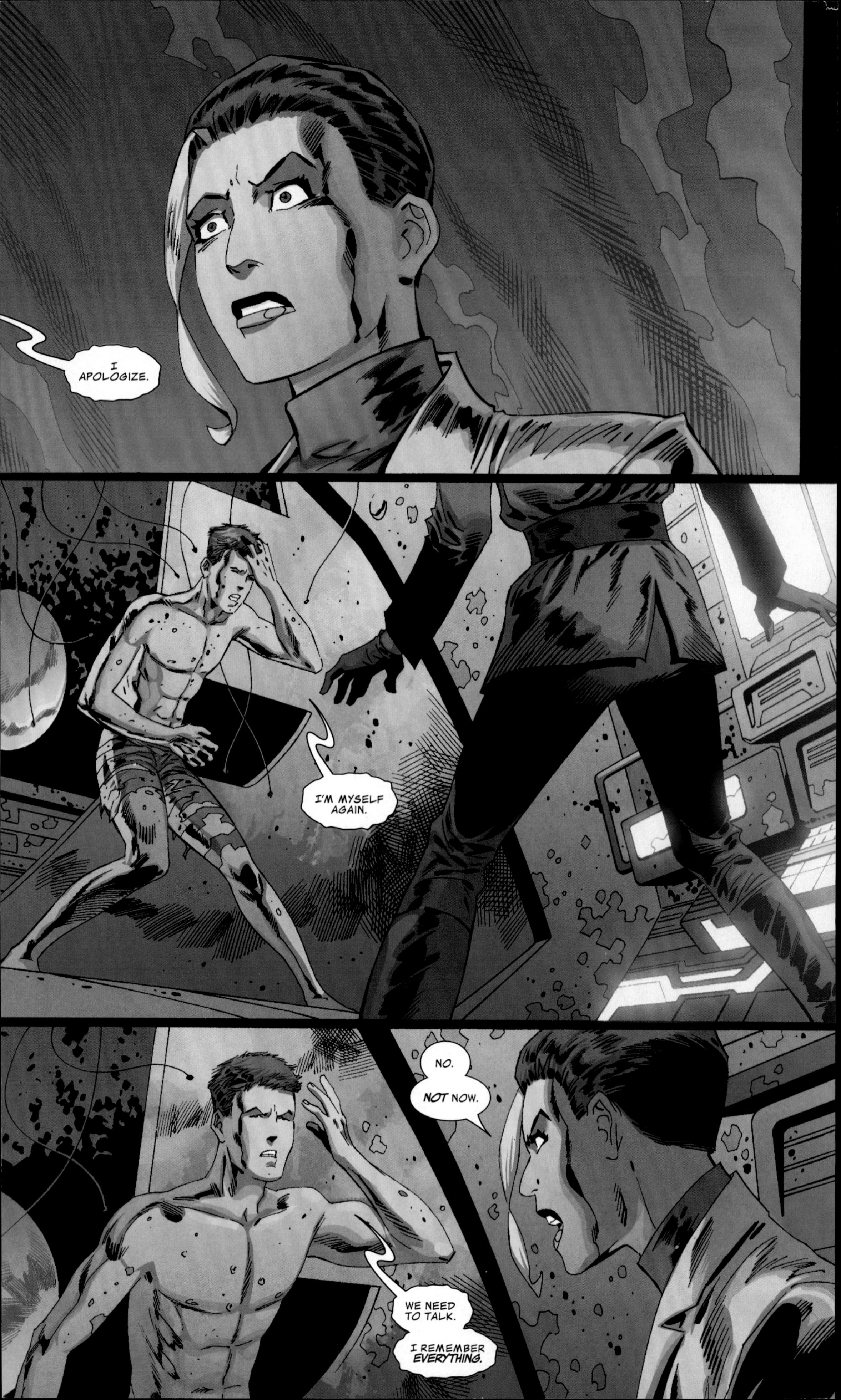
I APOLOGIZE.
I'M MYSELF AGAIN.
NO.
NOT NOW.
WE NEED TO TALK.
I REMEMBER EVERYTHING.

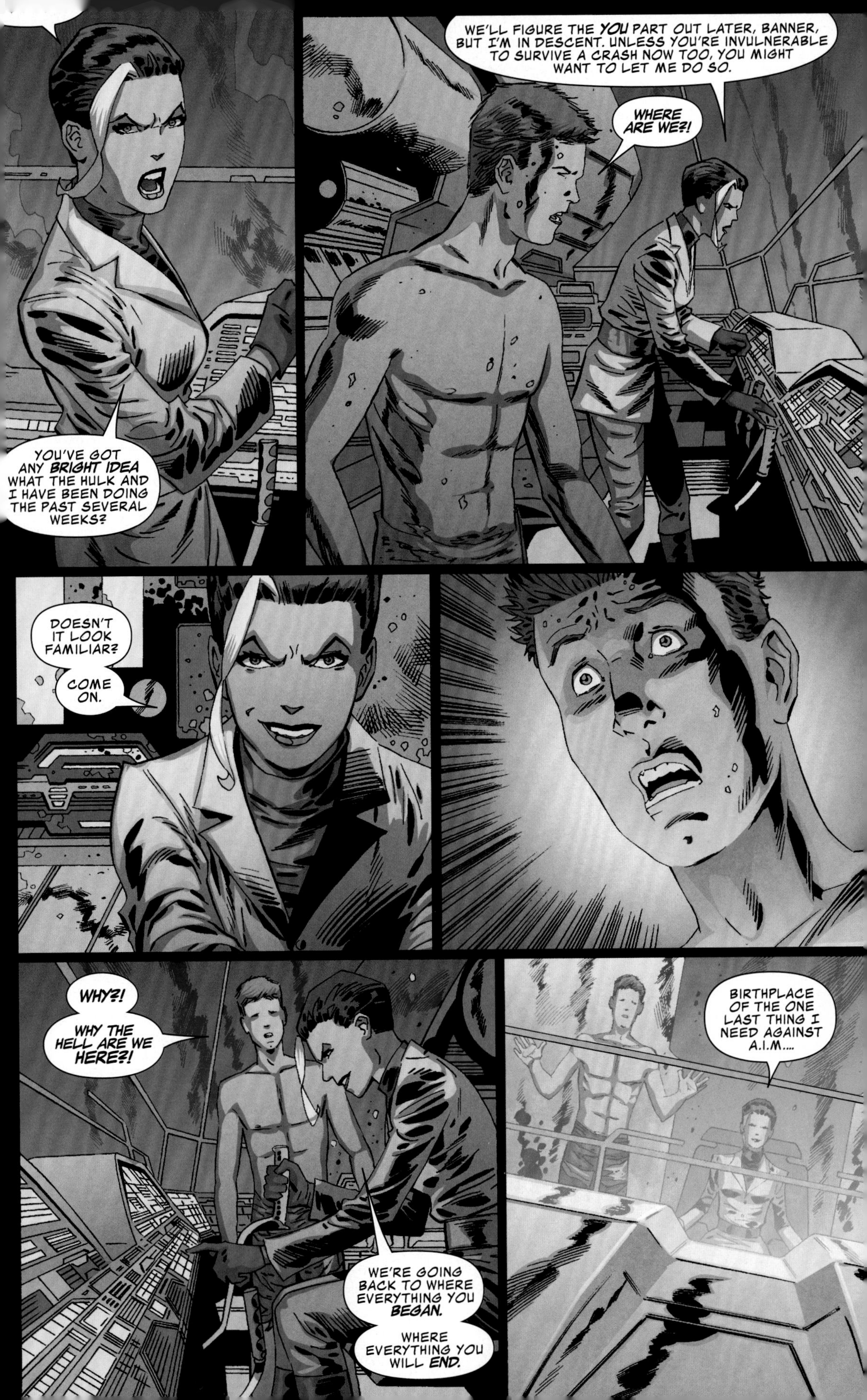
YOU'VE GOT ANY BRIGHT IDEA WHAT THE HULK AND I HAVE BEEN DOING THE PAST SEVERAL WEEKS?
WE'LL FIGURE THE YOU PART OUT LATER, BANNER, BUT I'M IN DESCENT. UNLESS YOU'RE INVULNERABLE TO SURVIVE A CRASH NOW TOO, YOU MIGHT WANT TO LET ME DO SO.
WHERE ARE WE?!
DOESN'T IT LOOK FAMILIAR?
COME ON.
WHY?!
WHY THE HELL ARE WE HERE?!
WE'RE GOING BACK TO WHERE EVERYTHING YOU BEGAN.
WHERE EVERYTHING YOU WILL END.
BIRTHPLACE OF THE ONE LAST THING I NEED AGAINST A.I.M....

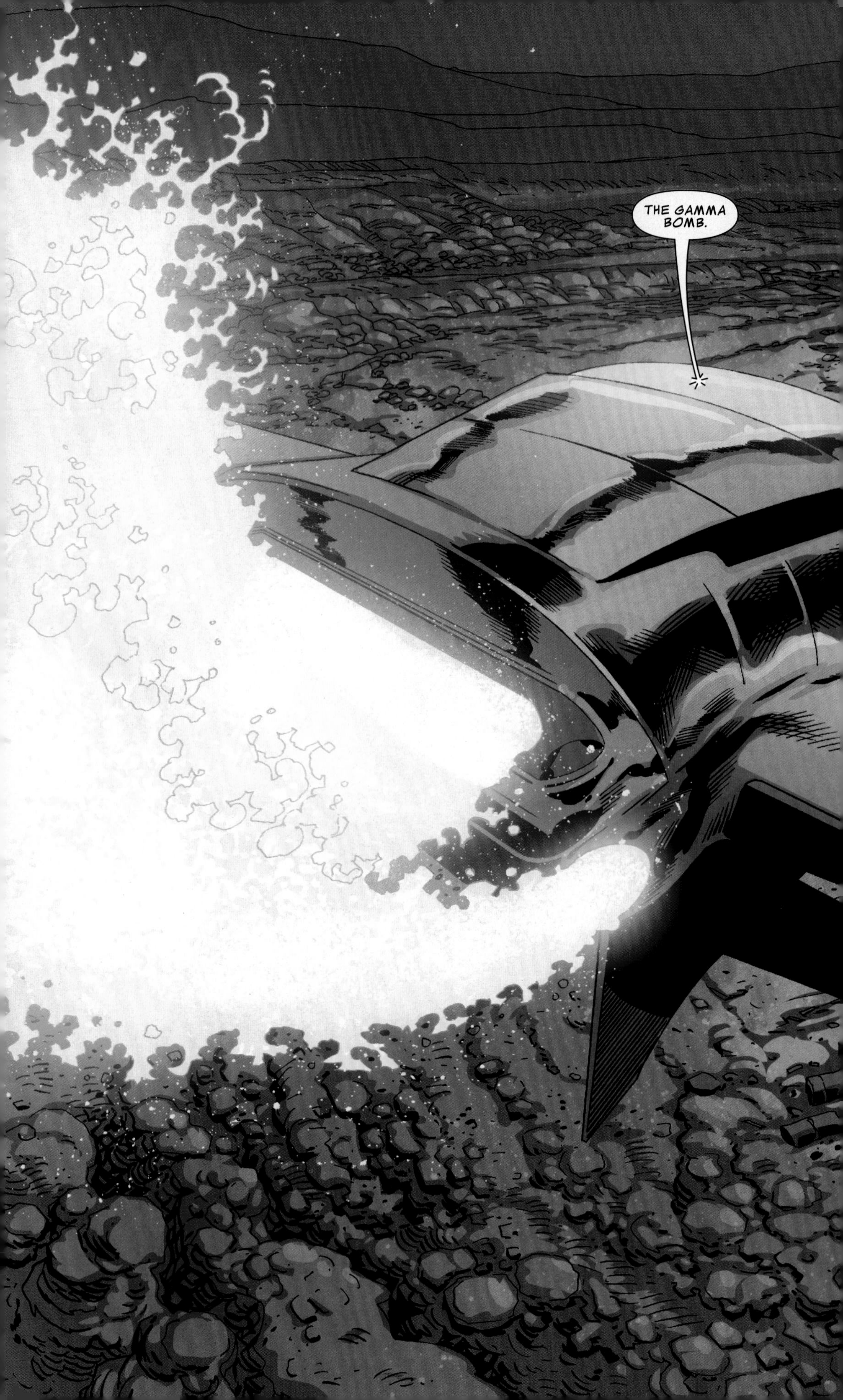
THE GAMMA BOMB.

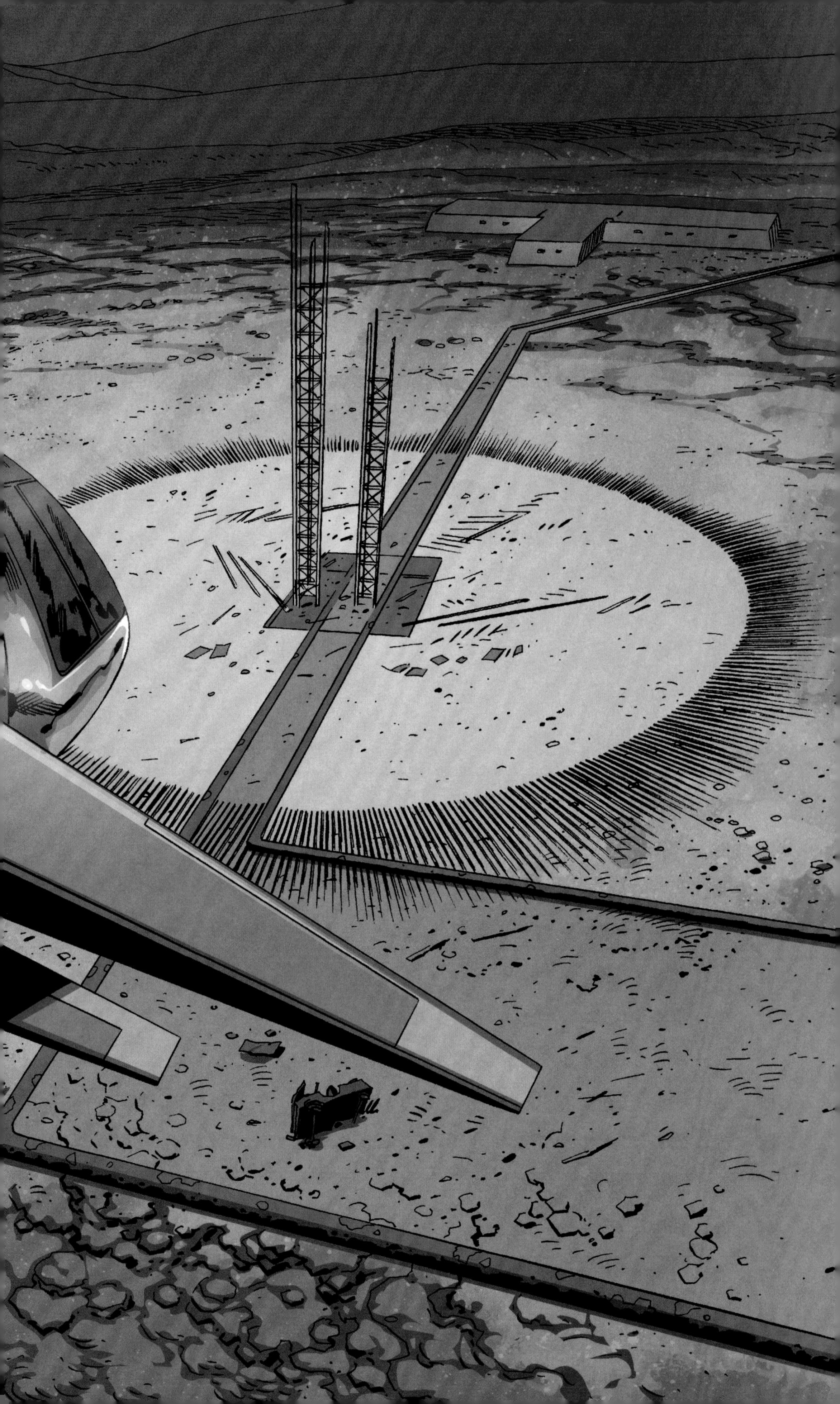

4

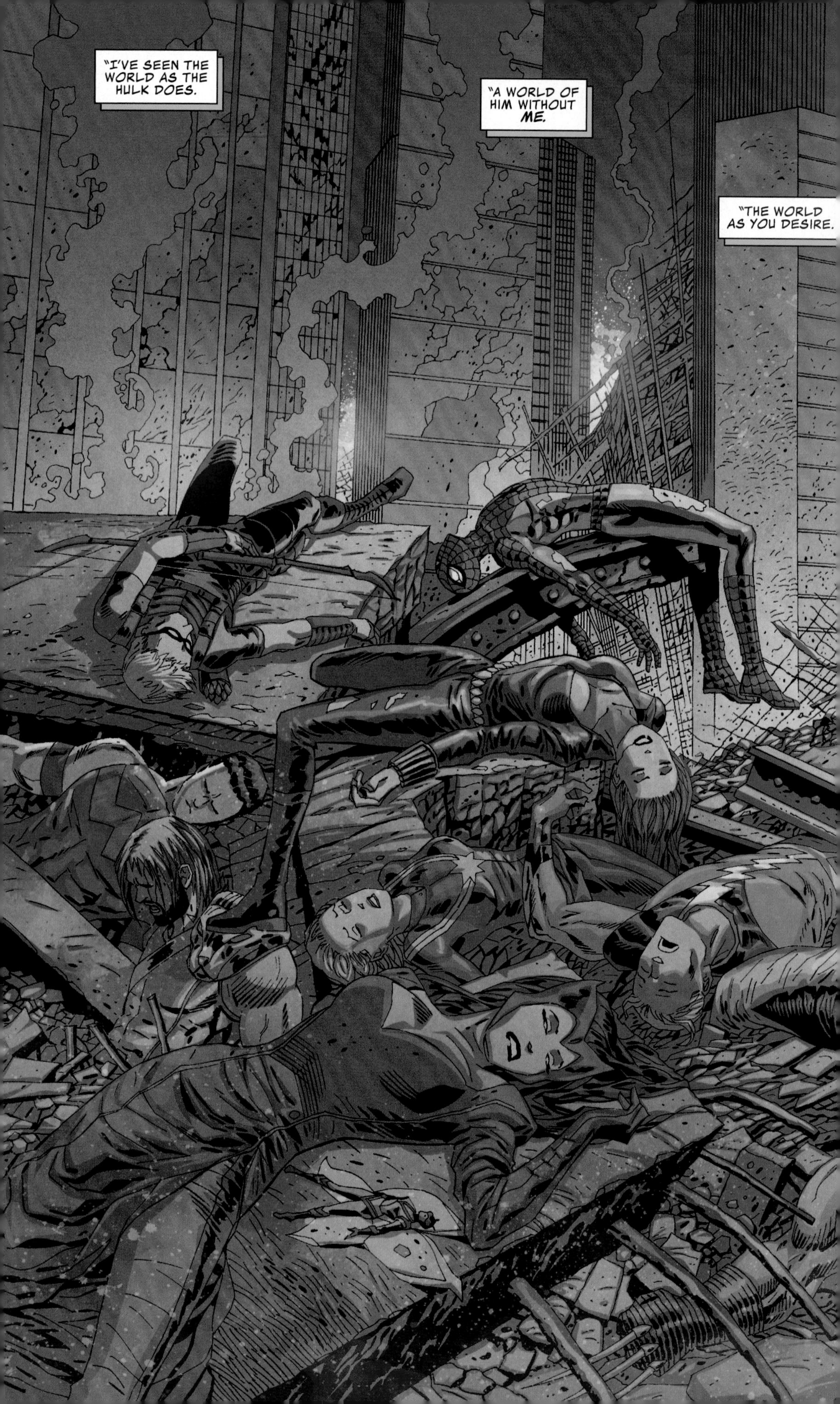
"I'VE SEEN THE WORLD AS THE HULK DOES.
"A WORLD OF HIM WITHOUT ME.
"THE WORLD AS YOU DESIRE.

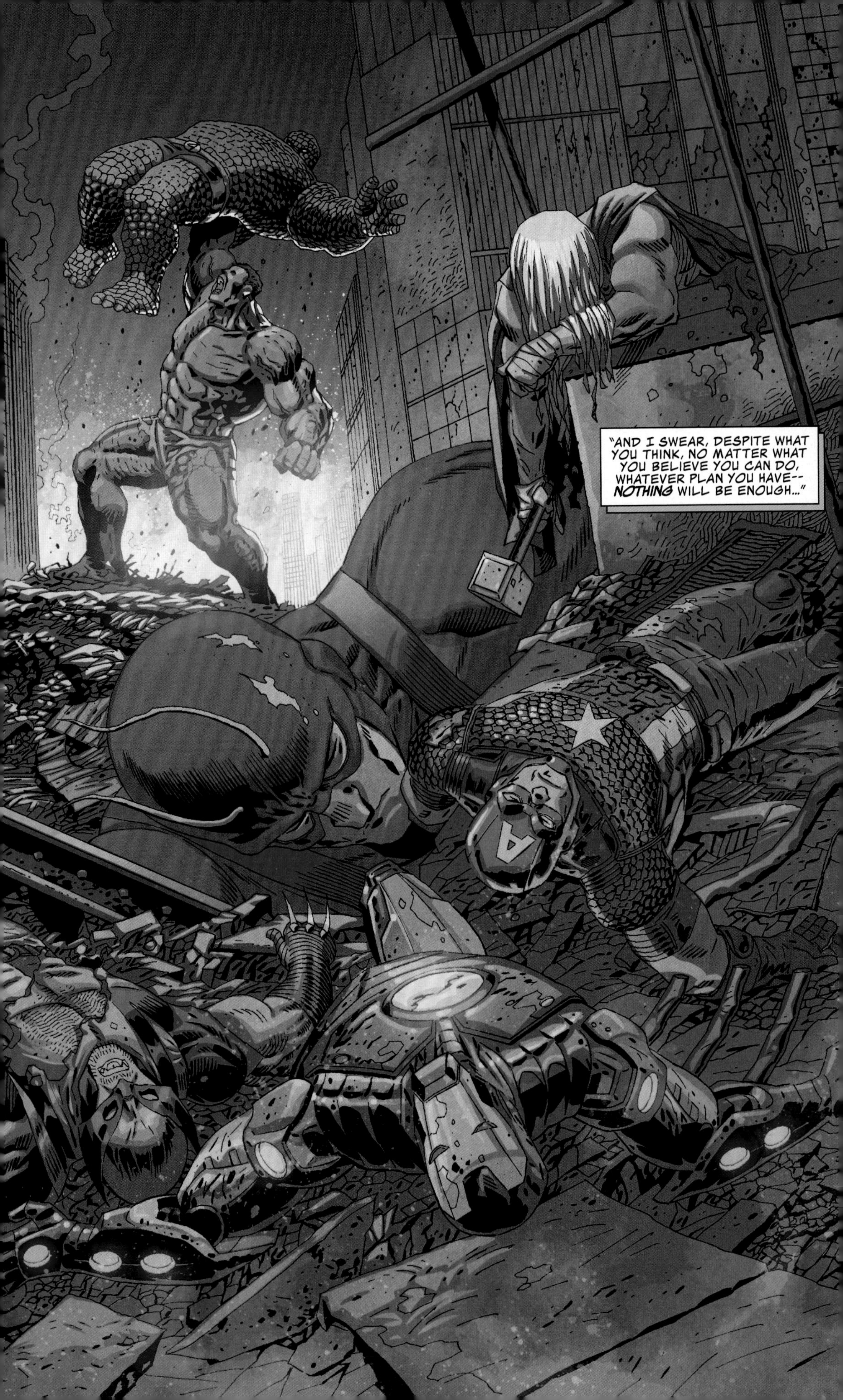
"AND I SWEAR, DESPITE WHAT YOU THINK, NO MATTER WHAT YOU BELIEVE YOU CAN DO, WHATEVER PLAN YOU HAVE-- ***NOTHING*** WILL BE ENOUGH..."

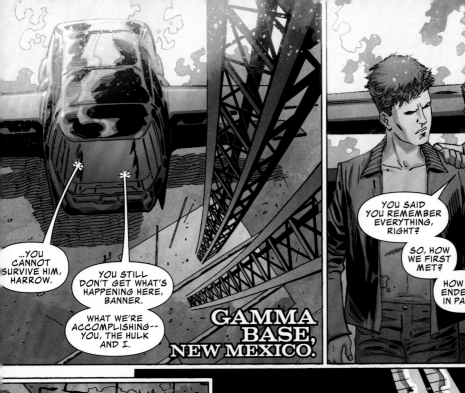

"...YOU CANNOT SURVIVE HIM, HARROW.

YOU STILL DON'T GET WHAT'S HAPPENING HERE, BANNER.

WHAT WE'RE ACCOMPLISHING-- YOU, THE HULK AND I.

GAMMA BASE, NEW MEXICO.

YOU SAID YOU REMEMBER EVERYTHING, RIGHT?

SO, HOW WE FIRST MET?

HOW YOU ENDED UP IN PARIS?

"AFTER WE FOUND YOU AT THE BOTTOM.

"AFTER WE TOOK YOU FAR ABOVE.

"AFTER WE STOLE FROM YOU WHAT WE NEEDED.

"AND WHY."

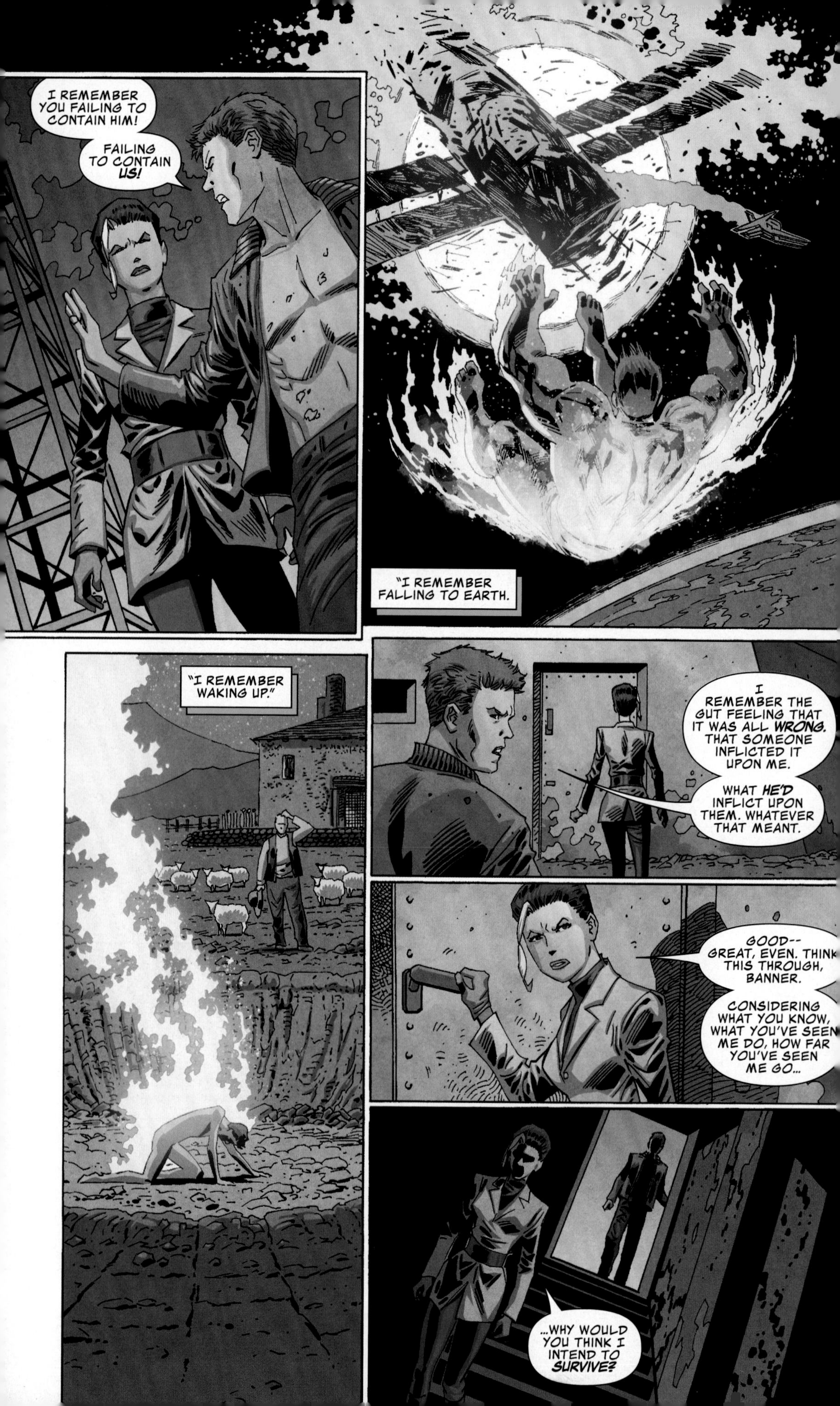
I REMEMBER YOU FAILING TO CONTAIN HIM!
FAILING TO CONTAIN US!
"I REMEMBER FALLING TO EARTH.
"I REMEMBER WAKING UP."
I REMEMBER THE GUT FEELING THAT IT WAS ALL WRONG. THAT SOMEONE INFLICTED IT UPON ME.
WHAT HE'D INFLICT UPON THEM. WHATEVER THAT MEANT.
GOOD-- GREAT, EVEN. THINK THIS THROUGH, BANNER.
CONSIDERING WHAT YOU KNOW, WHAT YOU'VE SEEN ME DO, HOW FAR YOU'VE SEEN ME GO...
...WHY WOULD YOU THINK I INTEND TO SURVIVE?

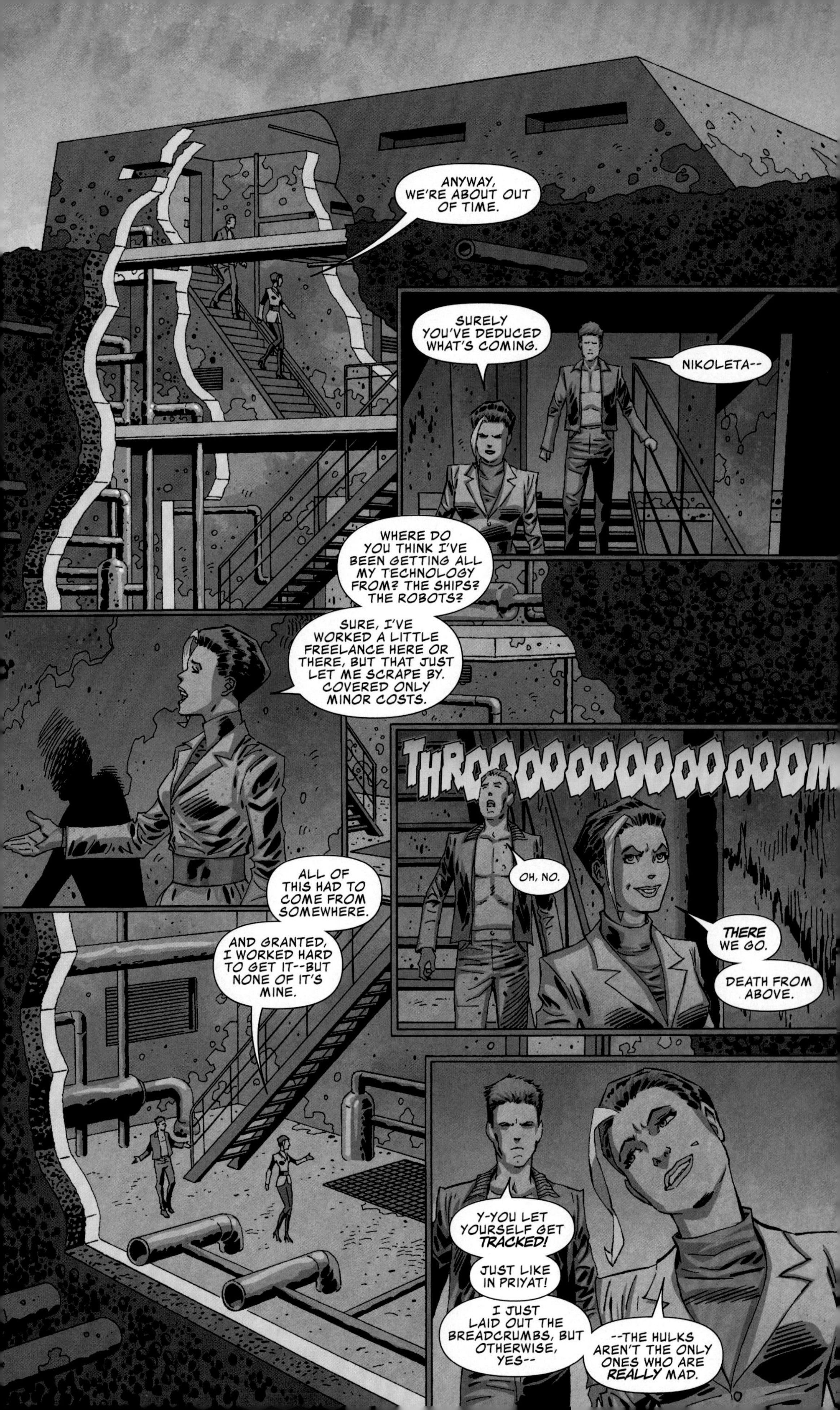
ANYWAY, WE'RE ABOUT OUT OF TIME.
SURELY YOU'VE DEDUCED WHAT'S COMING.
NIKOLETA--
WHERE DO YOU THINK I'VE BEEN GETTING ALL MY TECHNOLOGY FROM? THE SHIPS? THE ROBOTS?
SURE, I'VE WORKED A LITTLE FREELANCE HERE OR THERE, BUT THAT JUST LET ME SCRAPE BY. COVERED ONLY MINOR COSTS.
ALL OF THIS HAD TO COME FROM SOMEWHERE.
AND GRANTED, I WORKED HARD TO GET IT--BUT NONE OF IT'S MINE.
THROOOOOOOOOOOOOOM
OH, NO.
THERE WE GO.
DEATH FROM ABOVE.
Y-YOU LET YOURSELF GET *TRACKED!*
JUST LIKE IN PRIYAT!
I JUST LAID OUT THE BREADCRUMBS, BUT OTHERWISE, YES--
--THE HULKS AREN'T THE ONLY ONES WHO ARE *REALLY* MAD.

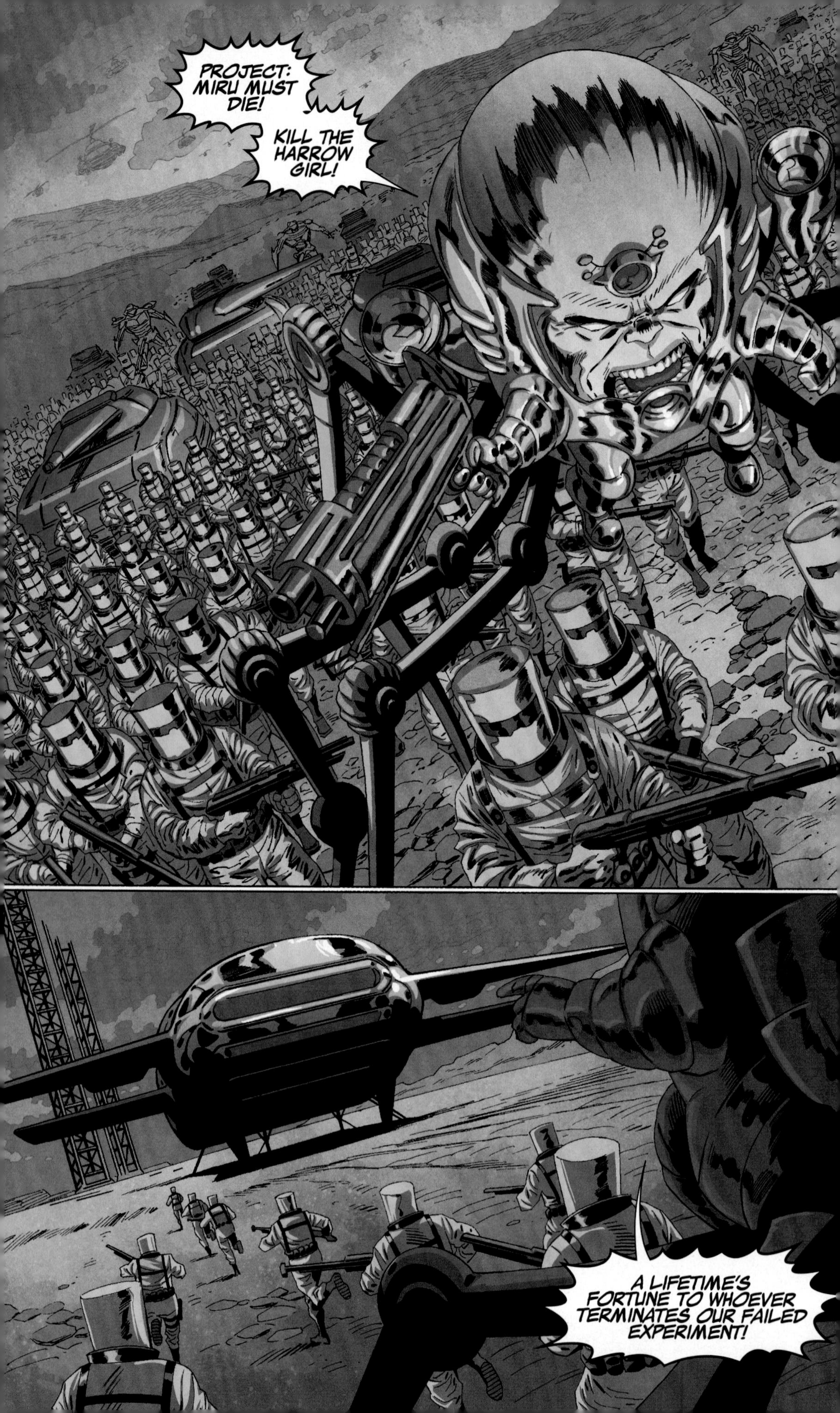
PROJECT: MIRU MUST DIE!
KILL THE HARROW GIRL!
A LIFETIME'S FORTUNE TO WHOEVER TERMINATES OUR FAILED EXPERIMENT!

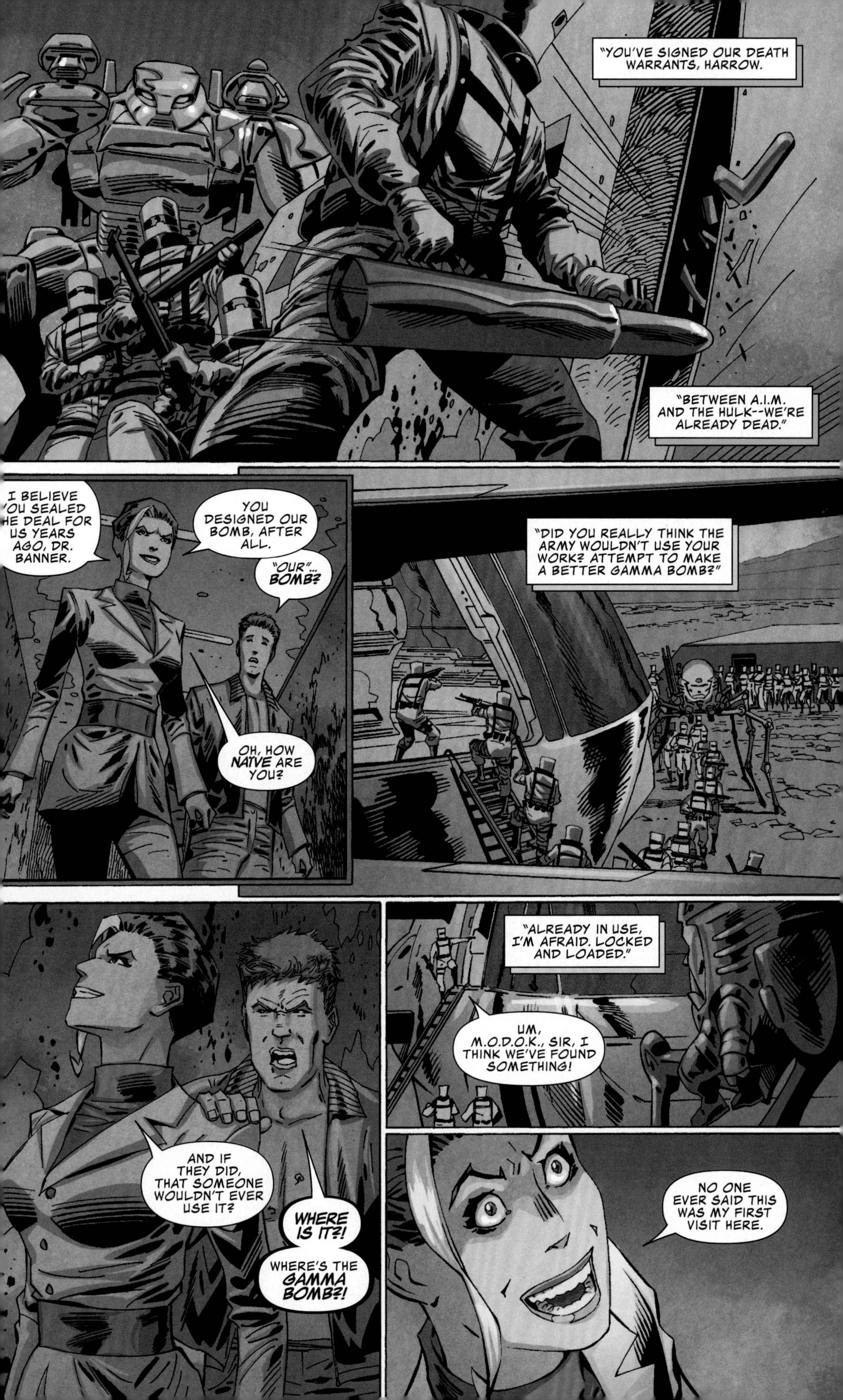
"YOU'VE SIGNED OUR DEATH WARRANTS, HARROW.
"BETWEEN A.I.M. AND THE HULK--WE'RE ALREADY DEAD."
I BELIEVE YOU SEALED THE DEAL FOR US YEARS AGO, DR. BANNER.
YOU DESIGNED OUR BOMB, AFTER ALL.
"OUR"... BOMB?
OH, HOW NAIVE ARE YOU?
"DID YOU REALLY THINK THE ARMY WOULDN'T USE YOUR WORK? ATTEMPT TO MAKE A BETTER GAMMA BOMB?"
AND IF THEY DID, THAT SOMEONE WOULDN'T EVER USE IT?
WHERE IS IT?!
WHERE'S THE GAMMA BOMB?!
"ALREADY IN USE, I'M AFRAID. LOCKED AND LOADED."
UM, M.O.D.O.K., SIR, I THINK WE'VE FOUND SOMETHING!
NO ONE EVER SAID THIS WAS MY FIRST VISIT HERE.

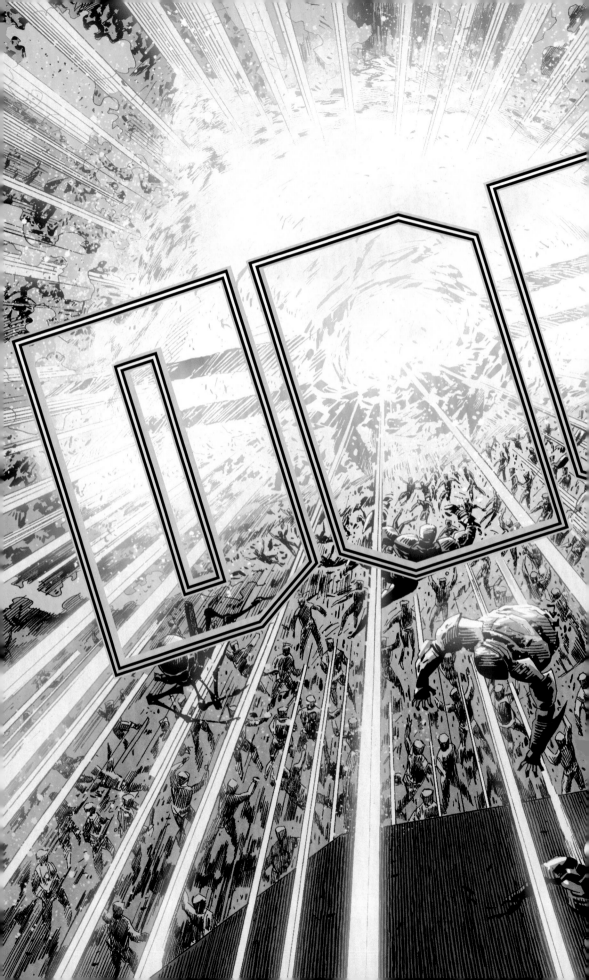

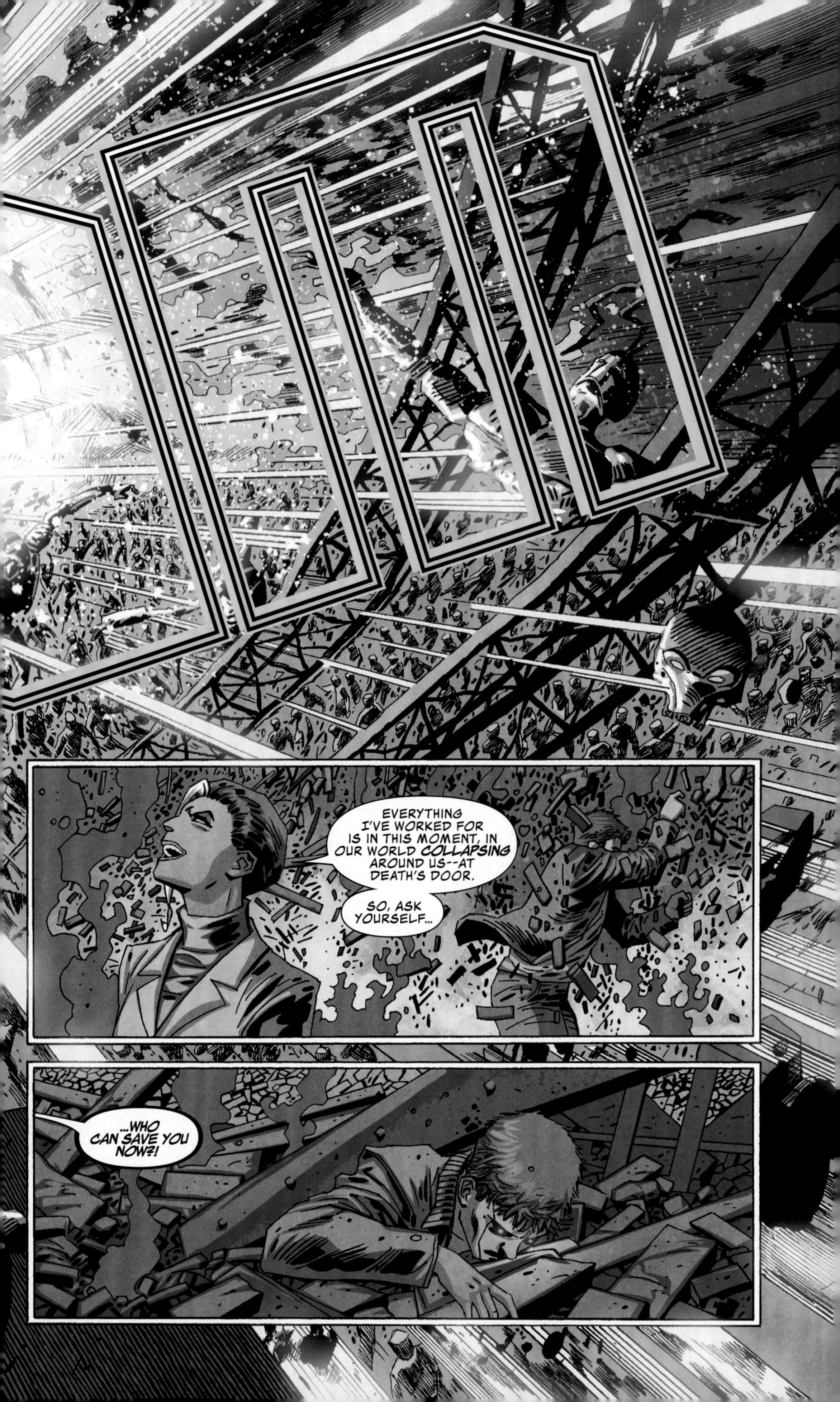
EVERYTHING I'VE WORKED FOR IS IN THIS MOMENT, IN OUR WORLD COLLAPSING AROUND US--AT DEATH'S DOOR.
SO, ASK YOURSELF...
...WHO CAN SAVE YOU NOW?!

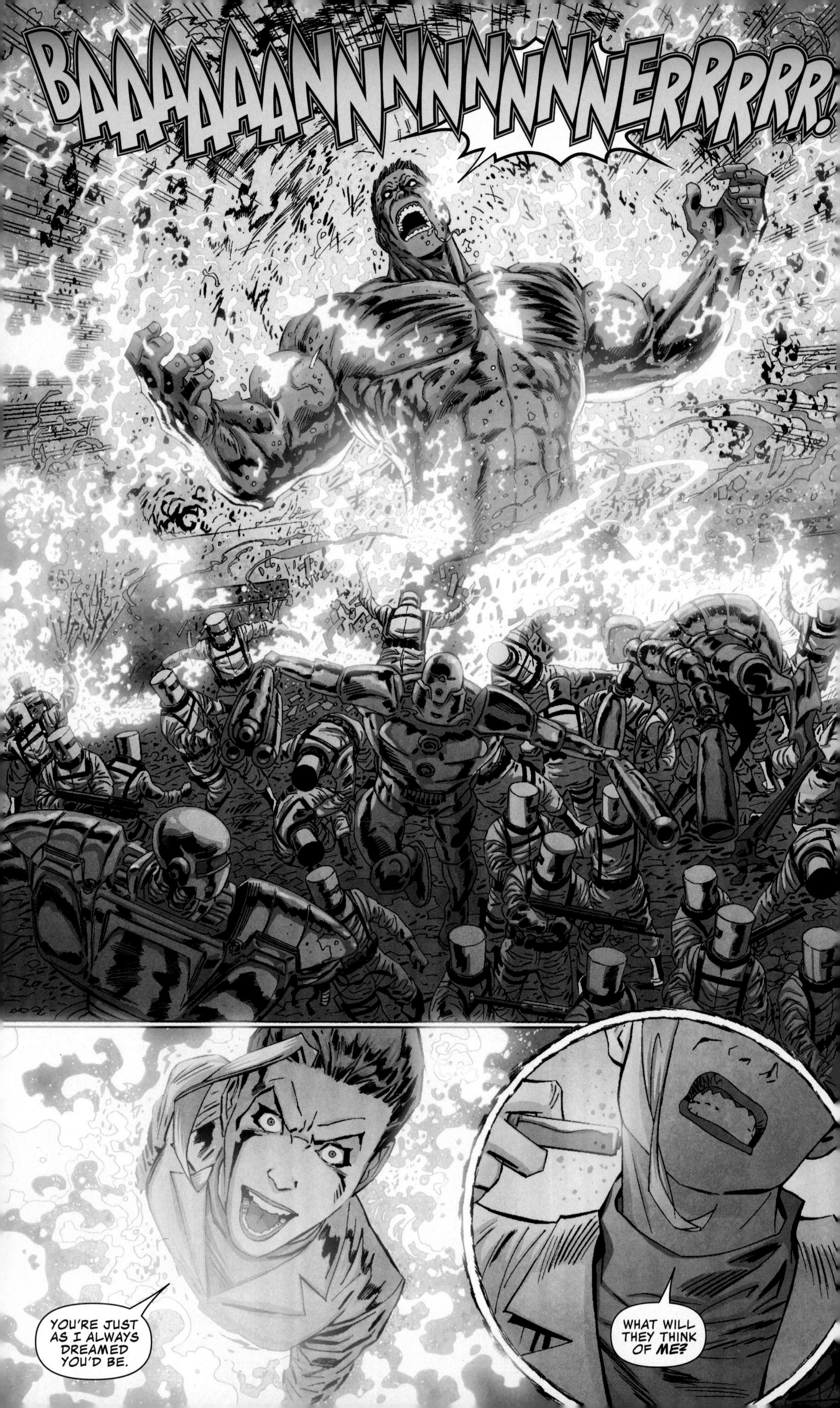
BAAAAAANNNNNNNNNERRRRRR!
YOU'RE JUST AS I ALWAYS DREAMED YOU'D BE.
WHAT WILL THEY THINK OF ME?

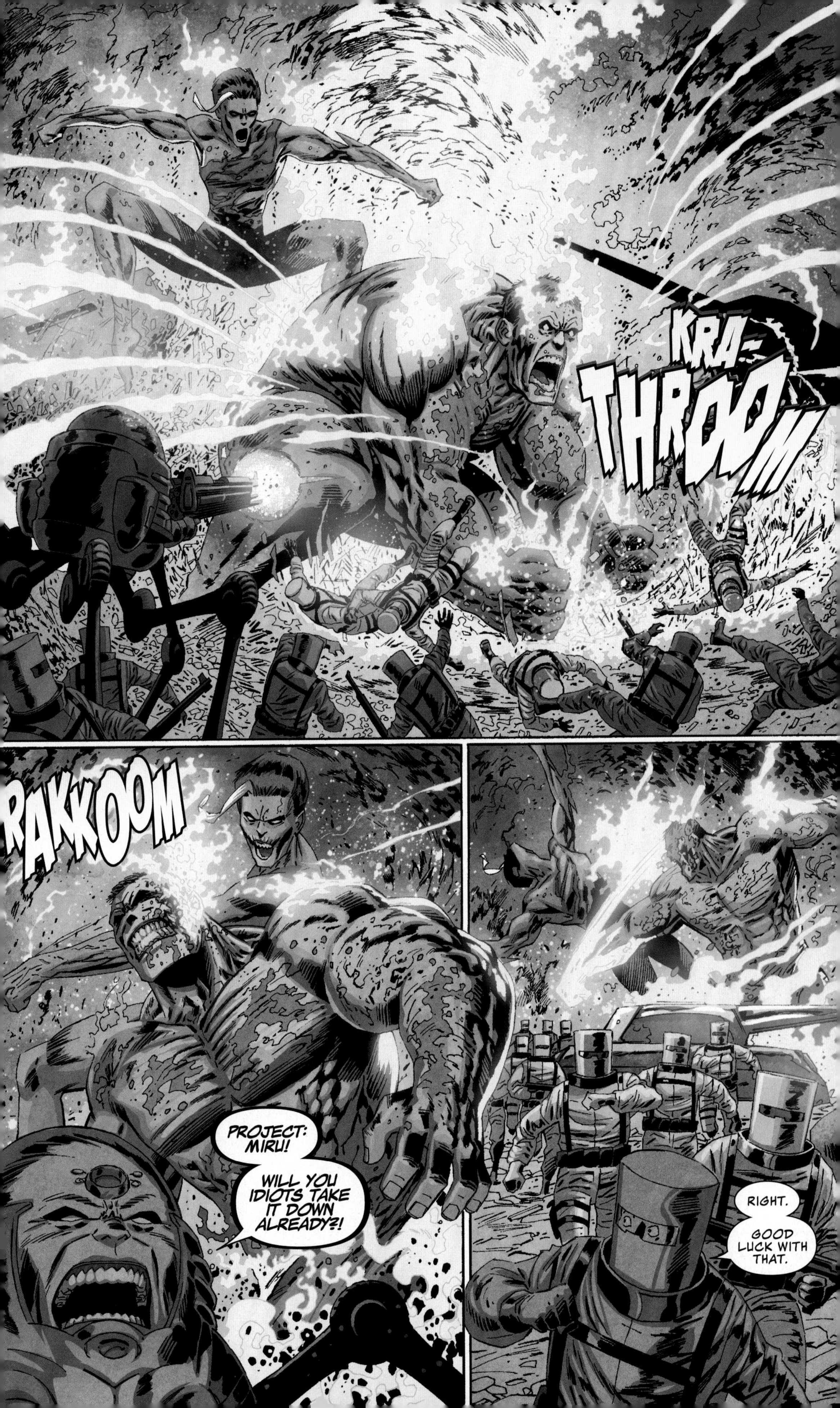
KRA-THROOM
RAKKOOM
PROJECT: MIRU!
WILL YOU IDIOTS TAKE IT DOWN ALREADY?!
RIGHT.
GOOD LUCK WITH THAT.

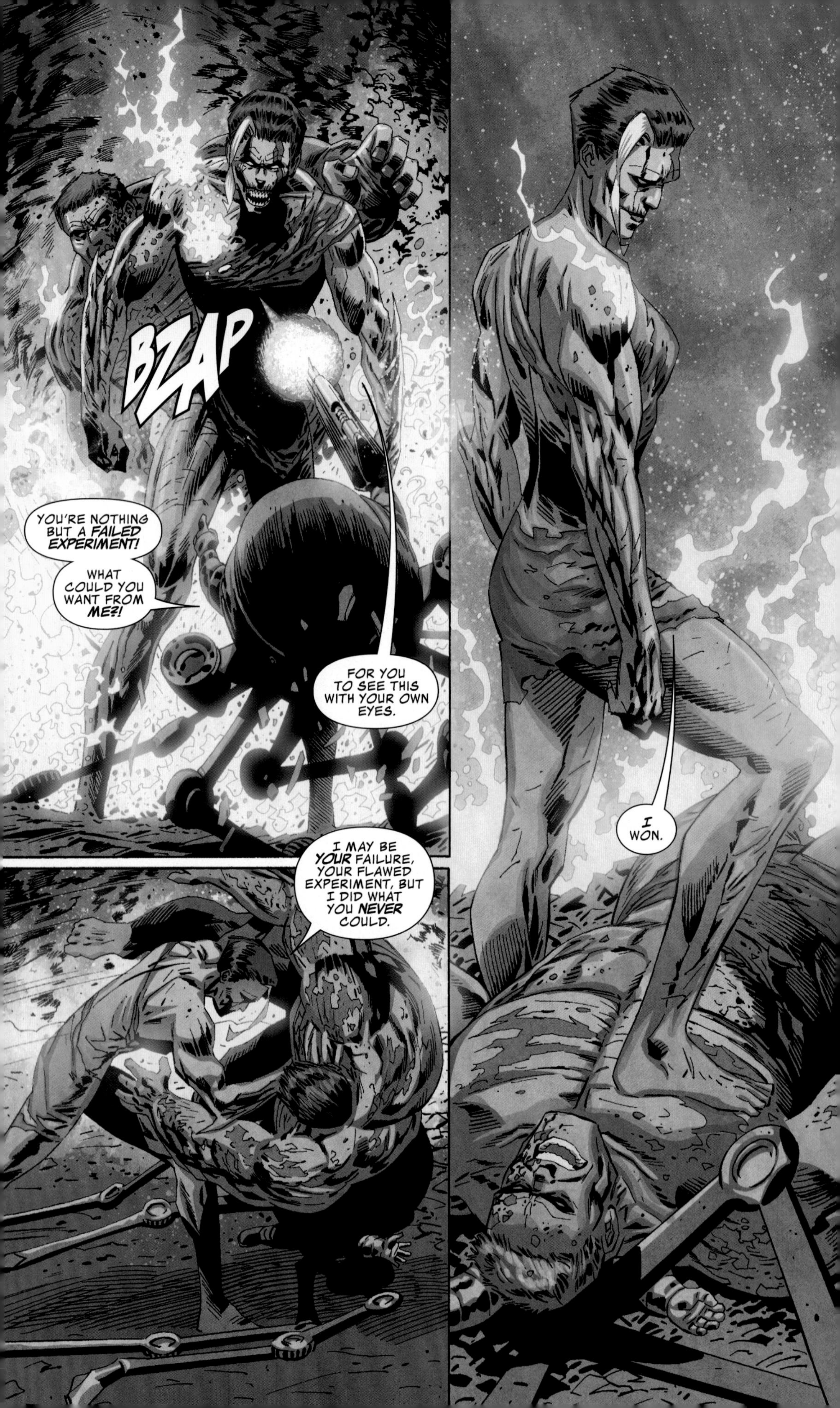

BZAP
YOU'RE NOTHING BUT A FAILED EXPERIMENT!
WHAT COULD YOU WANT FROM ME?!
FOR YOU TO SEE THIS WITH YOUR OWN EYES.
I MAY BE YOUR FAILURE, YOUR FLAWED EXPERIMENT, BUT I DID WHAT YOU NEVER COULD.
I WON.

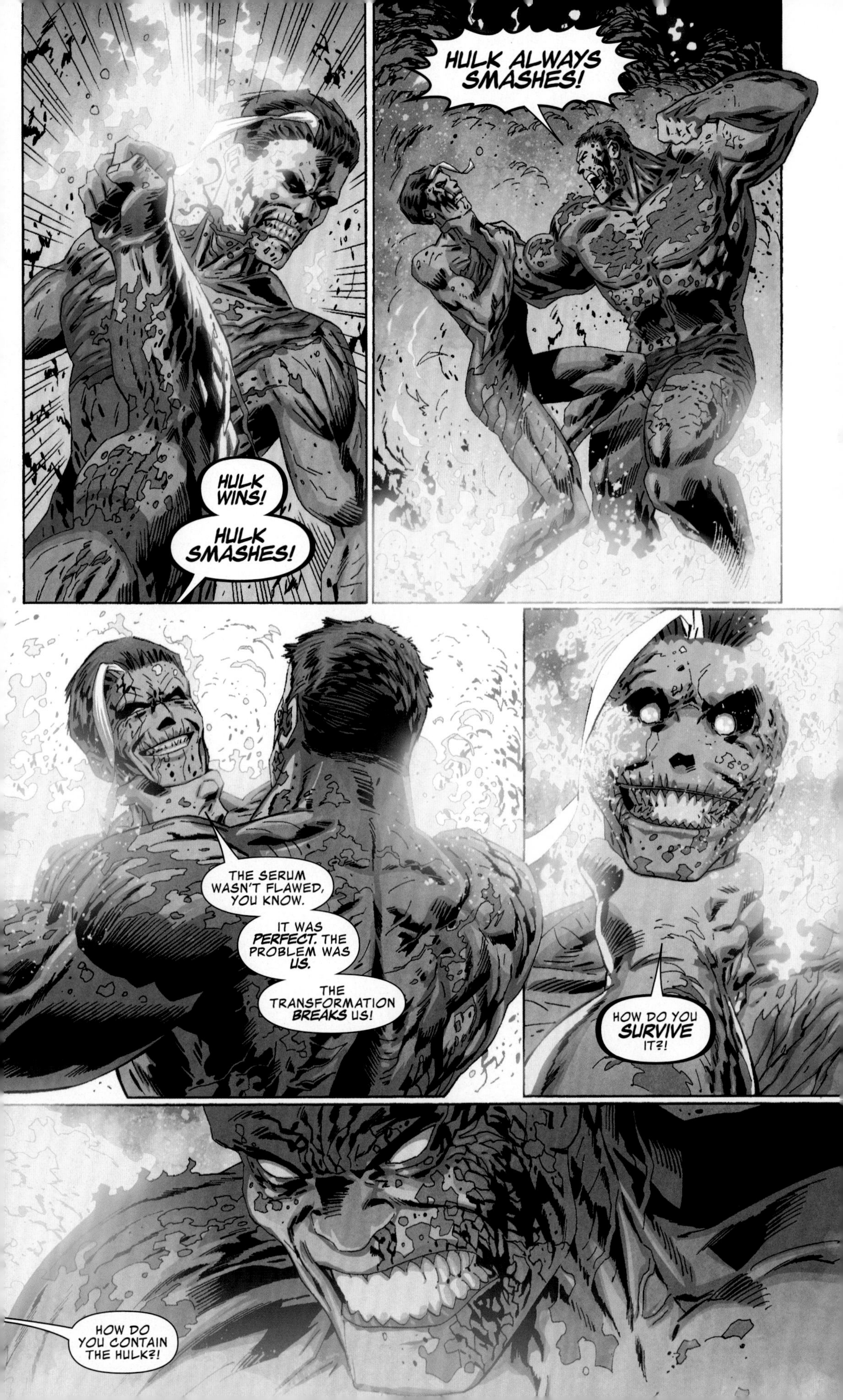
HULK WINS!
HULK SMASHES!
HULK ALWAYS SMASHES!
THE SERUM WASN'T FLAWED, YOU KNOW.
IT WAS PERFECT. THE PROBLEM WAS US.
THE TRANSFORMATION BREAKS US!
HOW DO YOU SURVIVE IT?!
HOW DO YOU CONTAIN THE HULK?!

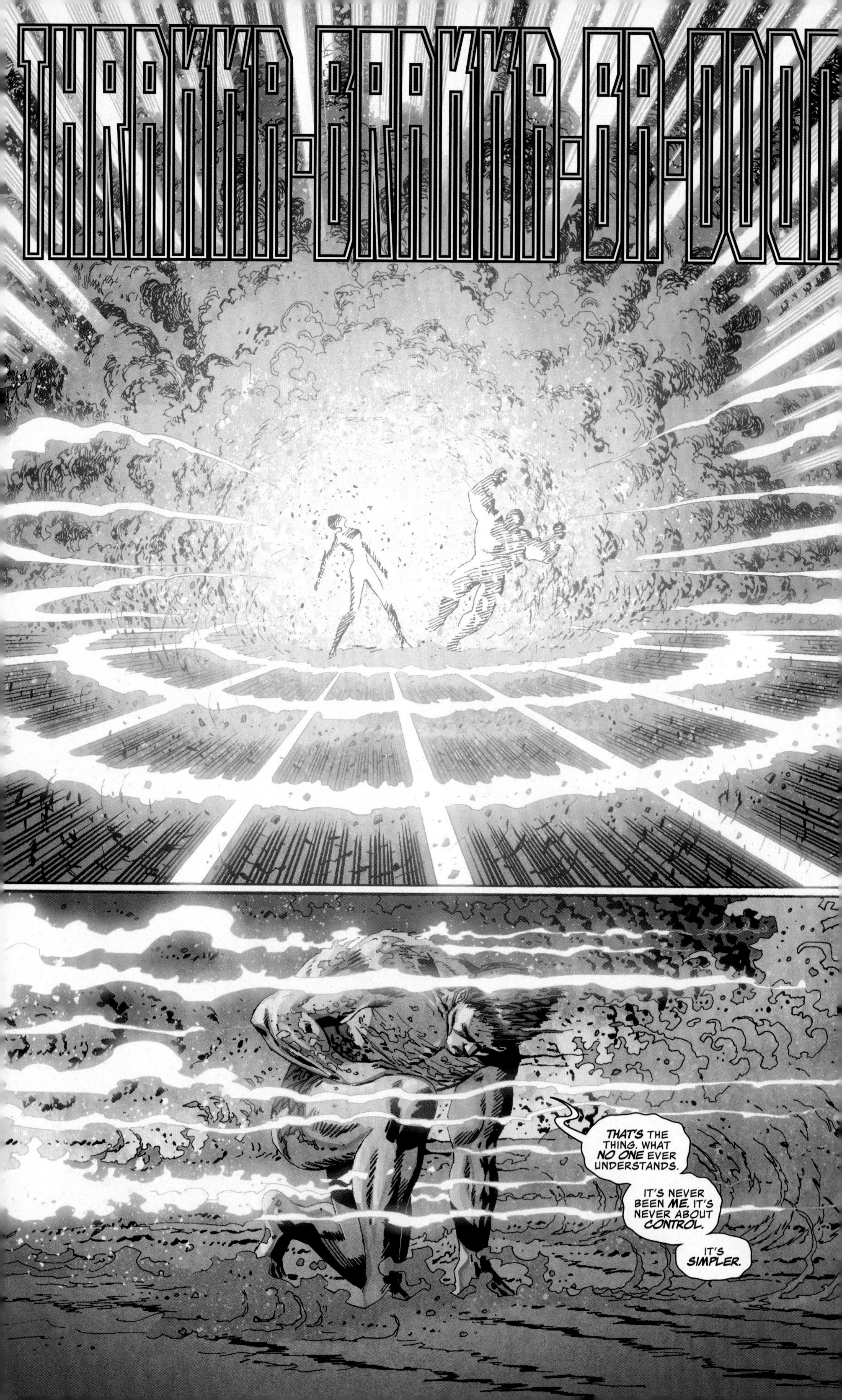
THRAKKA-BRAKKA-BA-DOO
THAT'S THE THING. WHAT NO ONE EVER UNDERSTANDS.
IT'S NEVER BEEN ME. IT'S NEVER ABOUT CONTROL.
IT'S SIMPLER.

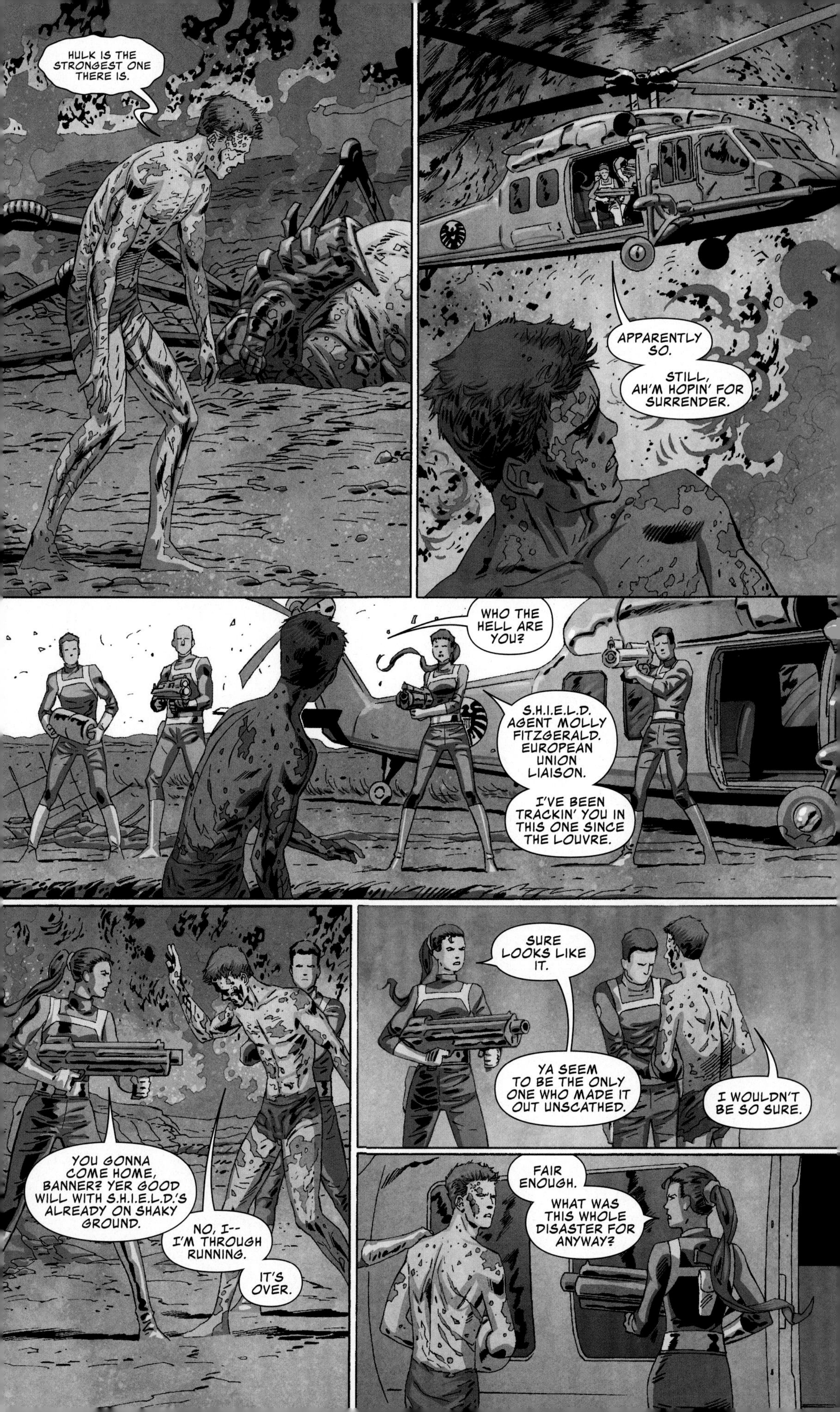
HULK IS THE STRONGEST ONE THERE IS.
APPARENTLY SO.
STILL, AH'M HOPIN' FOR SURRENDER.
WHO THE HELL ARE YOU?
S.H.I.E.L.D. AGENT MOLLY FITZGERALD. EUROPEAN UNION LIAISON.
I'VE BEEN TRACKIN' YOU IN THIS ONE SINCE THE LOUVRE.
YOU GONNA COME HOME, BANNER? YER GOOD WILL WITH S.H.I.E.L.D.'S ALREADY ON SHAKY GROUND.
NO, I-- I'M THROUGH RUNNING.
IT'S OVER.
SURE LOOKS LIKE IT.
YA SEEM TO BE THE ONLY ONE WHO MADE IT OUT UNSCATHED.
I WOULDN'T BE SO SURE.
FAIR ENOUGH.
WHAT WAS THIS WHOLE DISASTER FOR ANYWAY?

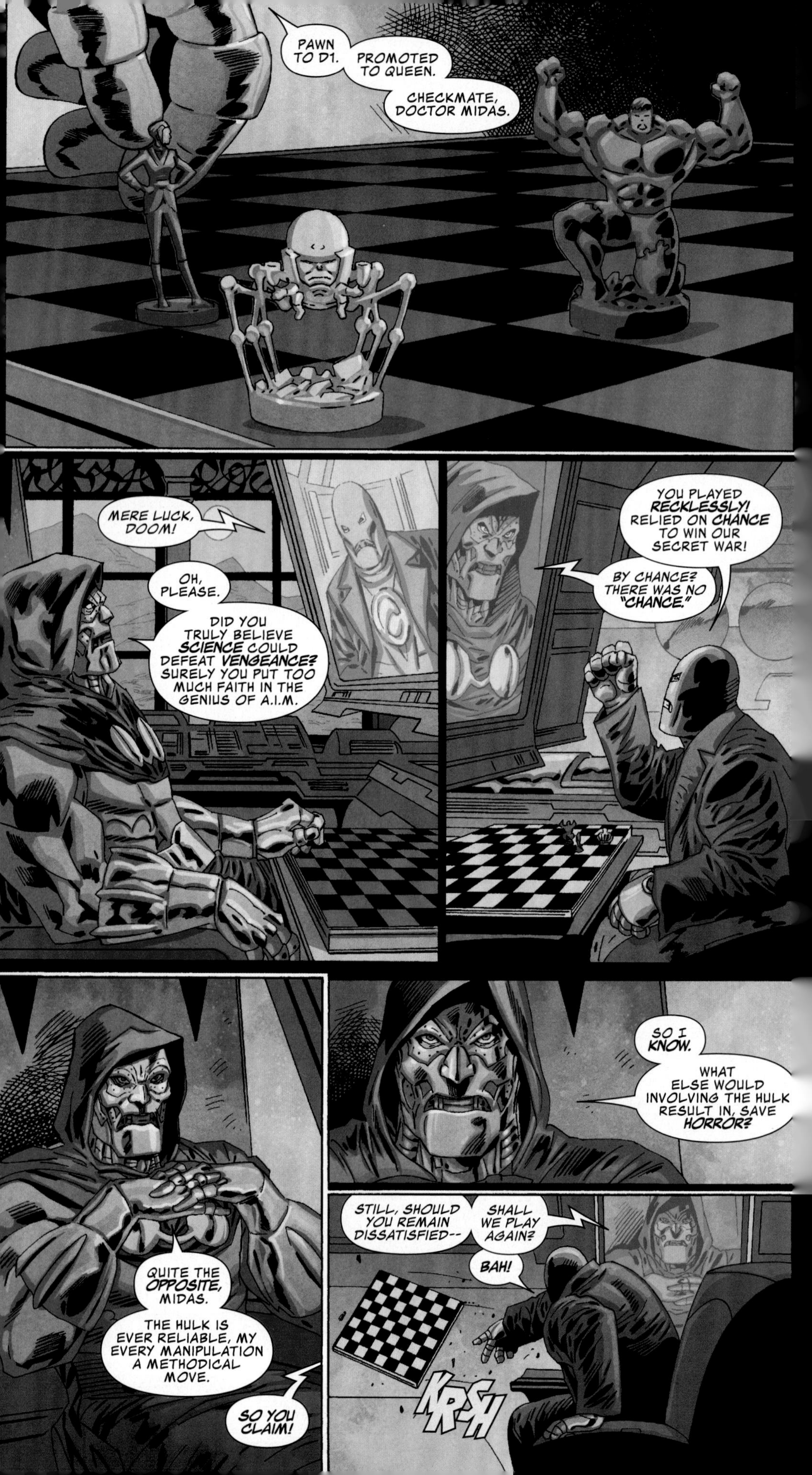
PAWN TO D1.
PROMOTED TO QUEEN.
CHECKMATE, DOCTOR MIDAS.
MERE LUCK, DOOM!
OH, PLEASE.
DID YOU TRULY BELIEVE SCIENCE COULD DEFEAT VENGEANCE? SURELY YOU PUT TOO MUCH FAITH IN THE GENIUS OF A.I.M.
YOU PLAYED RECKLESSLY! RELIED ON CHANCE TO WIN OUR SECRET WAR!
BY CHANCE? THERE WAS NO "CHANCE."
QUITE THE OPPOSITE, MIDAS.
THE HULK IS EVER RELIABLE, MY EVERY MANIPULATION A METHODICAL MOVE.
SO YOU CLAIM!
SO I KNOW.
WHAT ELSE WOULD INVOLVING THE HULK RESULT IN, SAVE HORROR?
STILL, SHOULD YOU REMAIN DISSATISFIED--
SHALL WE PLAY AGAIN?
BAH!
KRSH

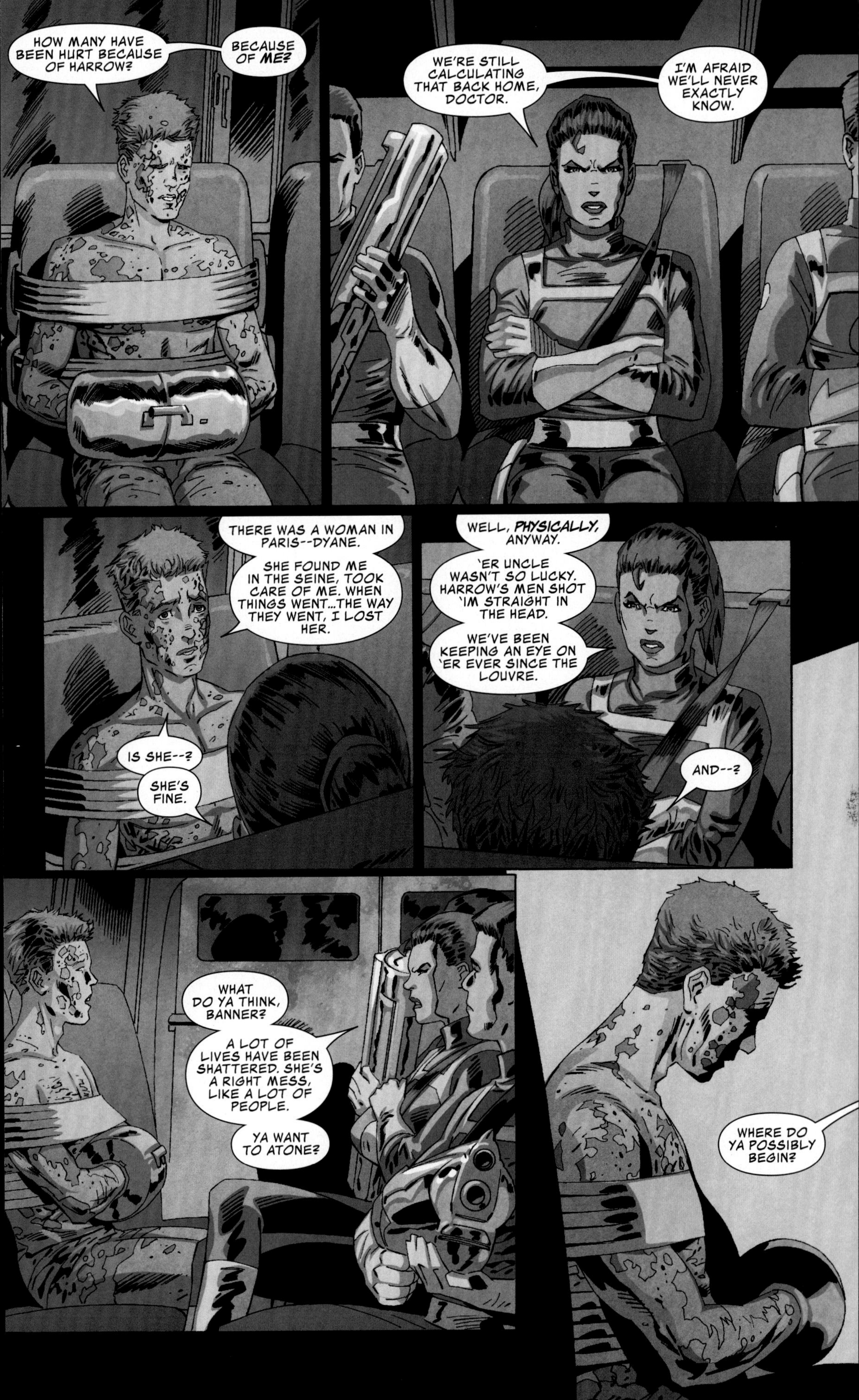
HOW MANY HAVE BEEN HURT BECAUSE OF HARROW?
BECAUSE OF *ME?*
WE'RE STILL CALCULATING THAT BACK HOME, DOCTOR.
I'M AFRAID WE'LL NEVER EXACTLY KNOW.
THERE WAS A WOMAN IN PARIS--DYANE.
SHE FOUND ME IN THE SEINE, TOOK CARE OF ME. WHEN THINGS WENT...THE WAY THEY WENT, I LOST HER.
IS SHE--?
SHE'S FINE.
WELL, *PHYSICALLY,* ANYWAY.
'ER UNCLE WASN'T SO LUCKY. HARROW'S MEN SHOT 'IM STRAIGHT IN THE HEAD.
WE'VE BEEN KEEPING AN EYE ON 'ER EVER SINCE THE LOUVRE.
AND--?
WHAT DO YA THINK, BANNER?
A LOT OF LIVES HAVE BEEN SHATTERED. SHE'S A RIGHT MESS, LIKE A LOT OF PEOPLE.
YA WANT TO ATONE?
WHERE DO YA POSSIBLY BEGIN?

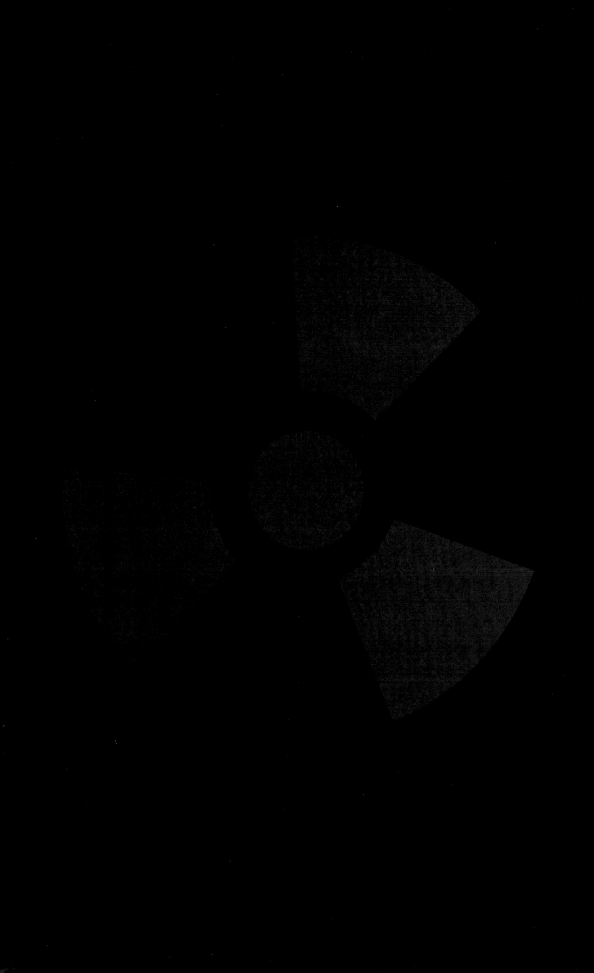

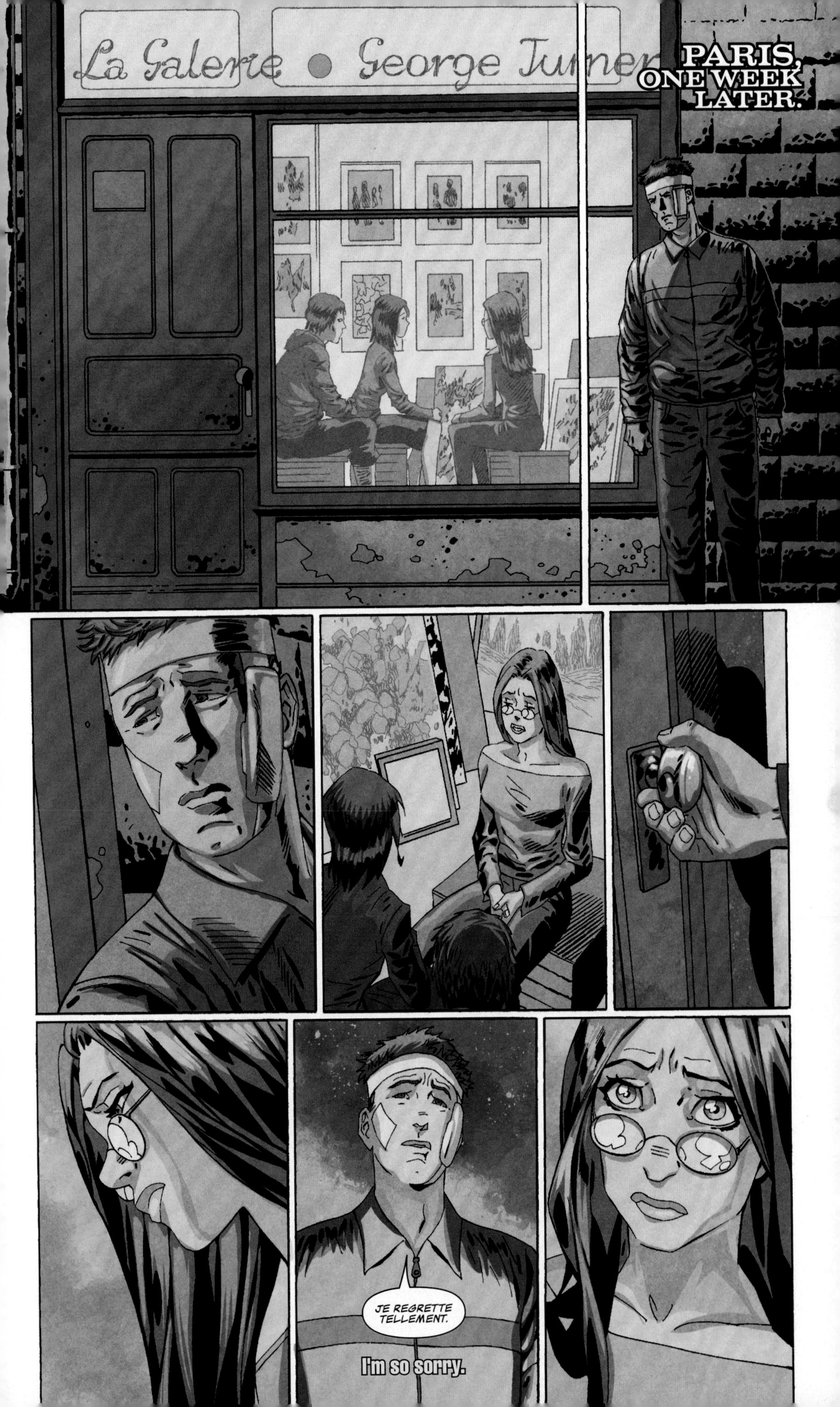
La Galerie George Turner
PARIS, ONE WEEK LATER.
JE REGRETTE TELLEMENT.
I'm so sorry.

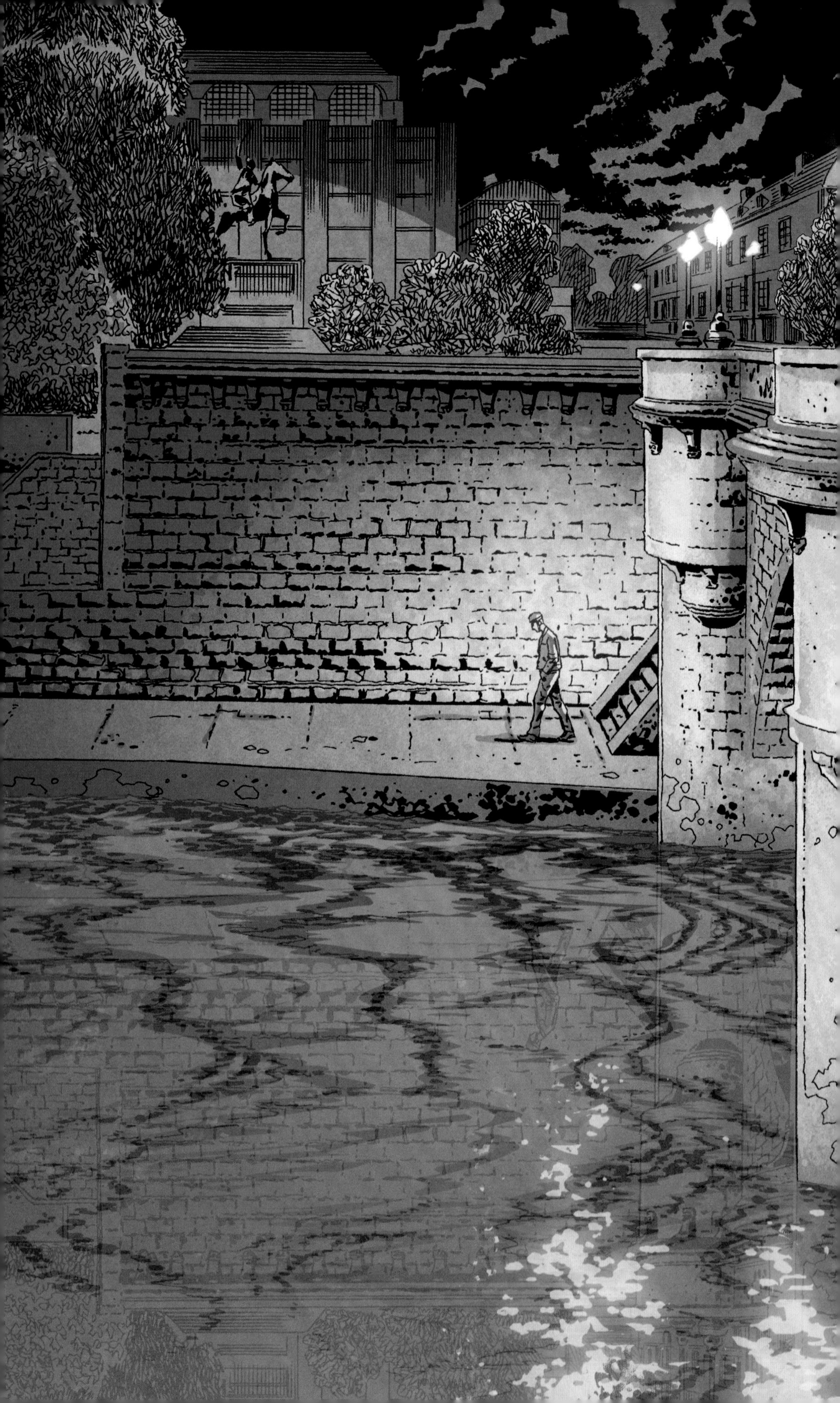

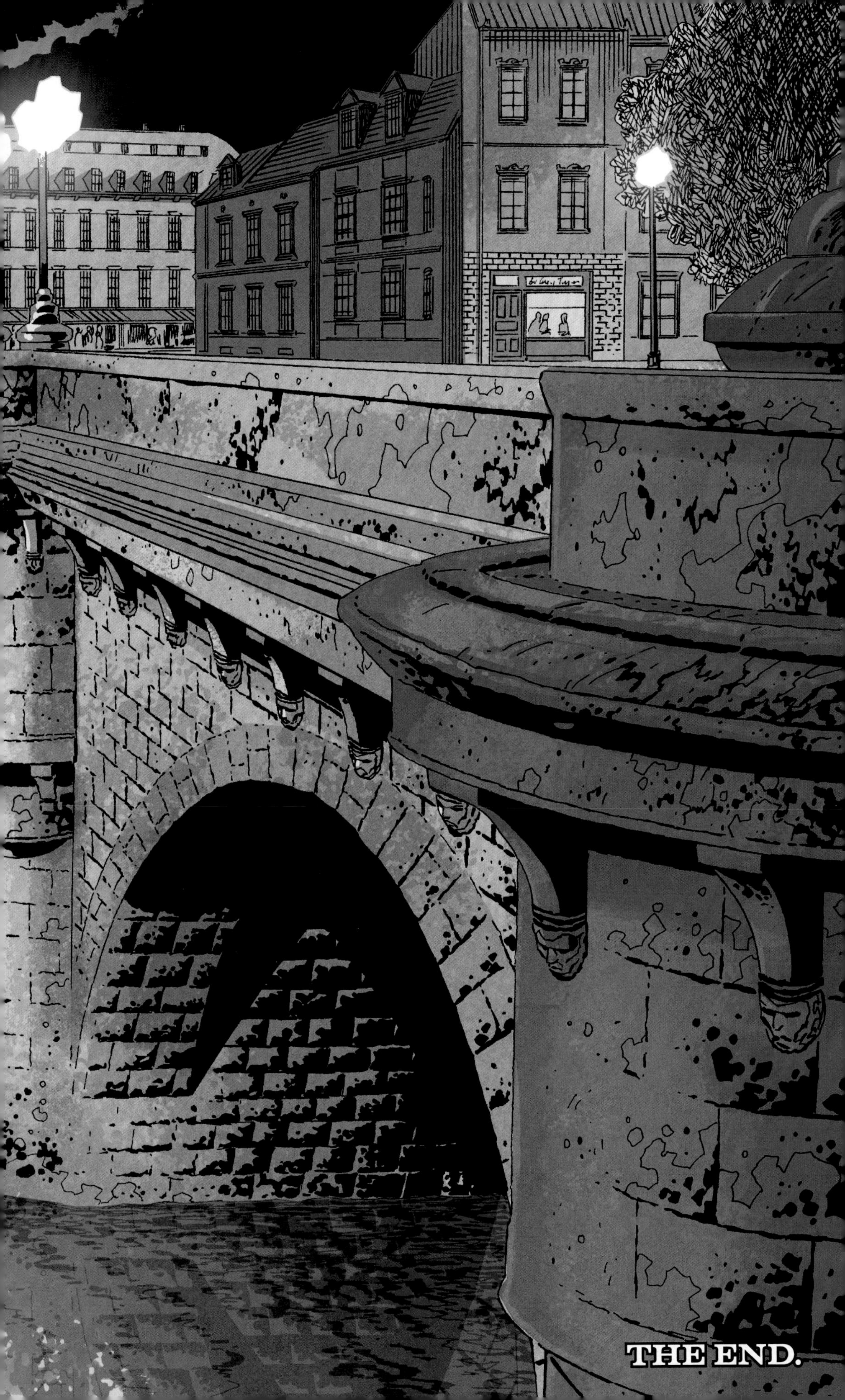
THE END.

HULK

THE STRANGEST MAN OF ALL TIME! FANTASY AS YOU LIKE IT! IS HE MAN OR MONSTER OR … IS HE BOTH?

So read the cover copy of *The Incredible Hulk* #1 from 1962, the very first, gray appearance of the soon-to-be green monster and the scientist—in the case of this cover's composition, most literally—within.

When Bill Rosemann invited Piotr Kowalksi and I on board, it was these statements we wanted to examine, this question we wanted to answer. To tear apart what Piotr (born in a crib brandished with a Hulk sticker) and myself with an obsession of the character lasting decades) love about Banner and his monster (or perhaps Hulk and his scientist), to see what makes them tick. To see what made Banner so strange. To see what it was about this fantasy that we like so. To determine our perspective on just what the Hulk was. How much monster or man exists. To dissect his first appearance and see what lies underneath the surface.

Plus we both enjoy it when Hulk smashes the heck out of anything. That came first and foremost.

We decided to start by taking Hulk out of his element, to take what I view as Marvel's personification of the American nightmare and thrust him into an international setting unlike anything remotely what he's associated with. To see how he fights against it. To see what he evolves into by the end.

As our last double-page spread bookends our first, I hope you enjoyed what we came up with in between. Collaborating with Piotr on these four issues has been one of the biggest highlights of my career thus far, in huge part because of both Bill and Jon Moisan, but also colorist Nick Filardi and the guy I'm happy has lettered all my Marvel work at this point, Clayton Cowles. An extra big thanks goes to Axel Alonso, Mark Paniccia, Tom Brevoort and C.B. Cebulski, who provided guidance early on. Another Hulk-sized thanks goes to the Marvel staff who were huge supporters the entire way through—Ryan Penagos, Ben Morse, Blake Garris, Lorraine Cink, Chris D'Lando, Charles Meyer, among many more—as all you do for us creators never gets praised enough, but your extremely hard work is always very appreciated.

Piotr Kowalski and I will return in Marvel's *What If? Age Of Ultron*.

For now, smash on.

Joe Keatinge
02.20.2014
Tranquility Base
Portland, OR

I would like to thank Joe Keatinge, editor Bill Rosemann, assistant editor Jon Moisan, and everyone who bought read or glanced through the pages of these four issues. And of course the man who was responsible for making my art look so good: Nick Filardi...thank you, Nick!

For the visual side of this miniseries, I tried to create an interesting world for the Hulk in which many amazing things could happen. It was a slightly surreal world, often unusual, full of flashbacks, visions and tense, action-packed sequences...In a word, a dream for any comic book artist!

And although I have always been inspired by Dale Keown's vision of the Hulk, I tried to find my own language here giving you a Hulk who is really big and totally wild! I hope you enjoyed reading our comic as much as I enjoyed

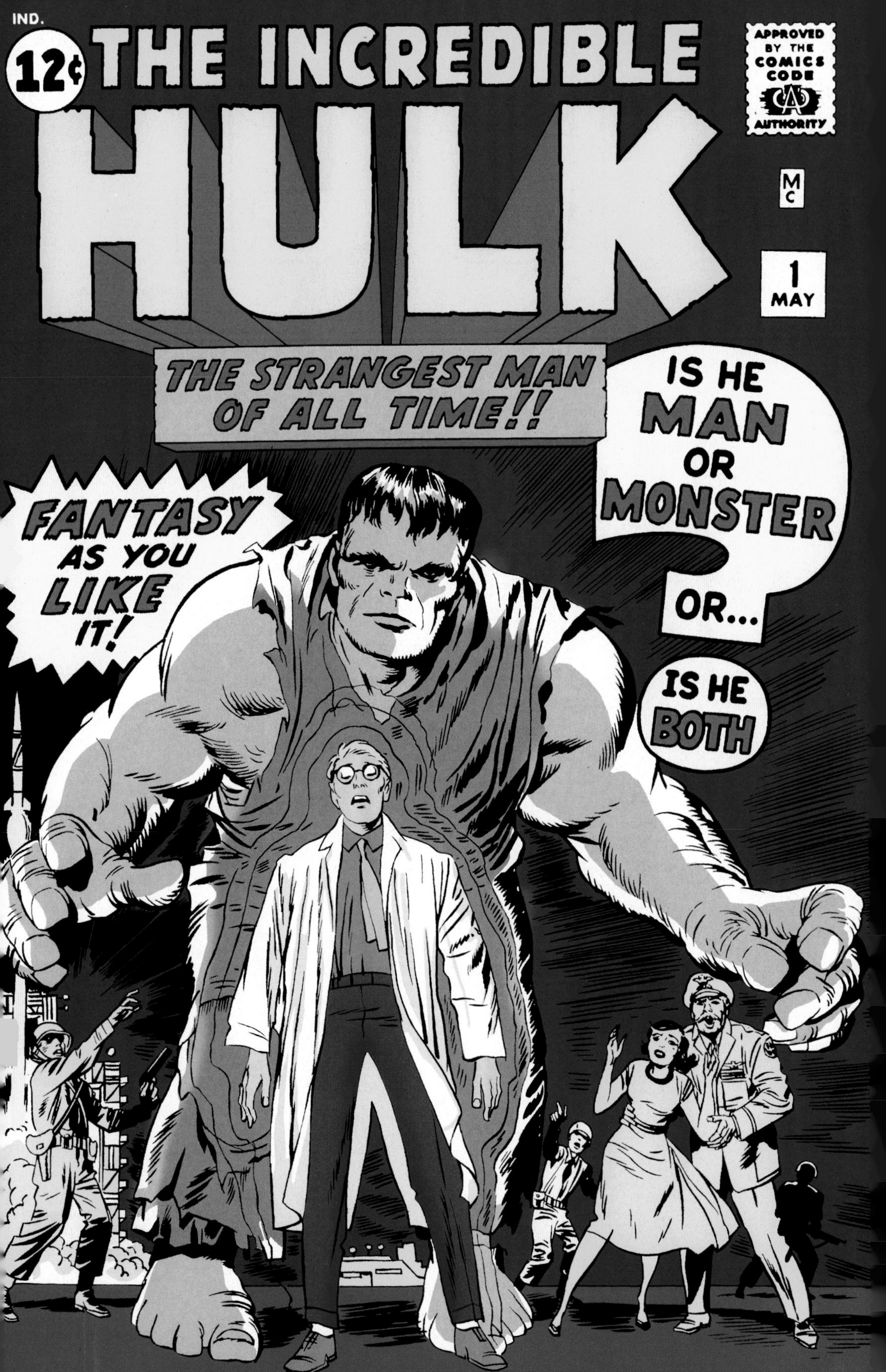
IND.
12¢
THE INCREDIBLE
HULK
APPROVED BY THE COMICS CODE AUTHORITY
MC
1
MAY
THE STRANGEST MAN OF ALL TIME!!
IS HE MAN OR MONSTER
OR...
IS HE BOTH
FANTASY AS YOU LIKE IT!

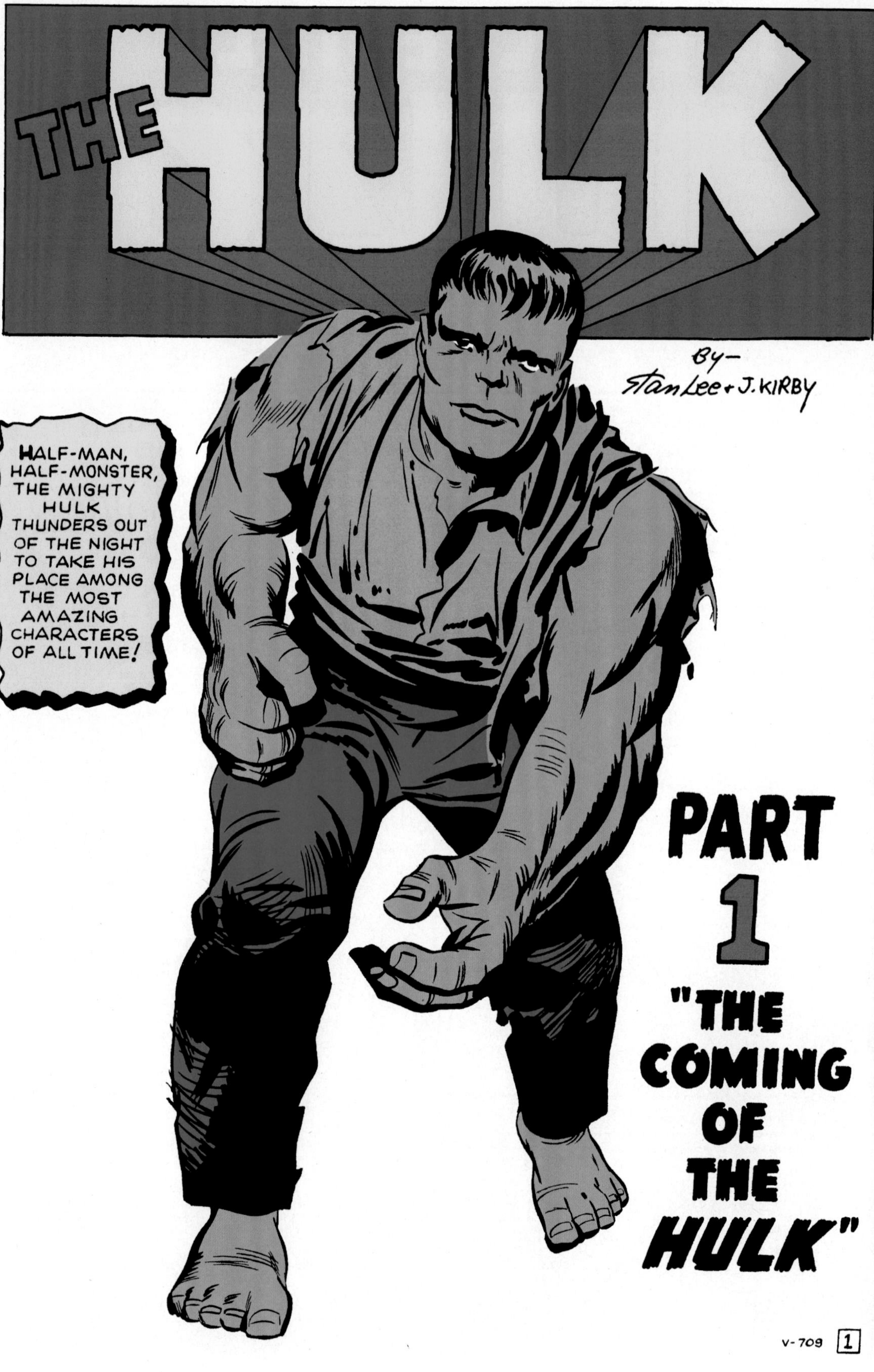
THE HULK
BY— STAN LEE + J. KIRBY
HALF-MAN, HALF-MONSTER, THE MIGHTY HULK THUNDERS OUT OF THE NIGHT TO TAKE HIS PLACE AMONG THE MOST AMAZING CHARACTERS OF ALL TIME!
PART 1
"THE COMING OF THE HULK"

ALONE IN THE DESERT STANDS THE MOST AWESOME WEAPON EVER CREATED BY MAN--*THE INCREDIBLE G-BOMB!*

MILES AWAY, BEHIND SOLID CONCRETE BUNKERS, A NERVOUS SCIENTIFIC TASK FORCE WAITS FOR THE GAMMA-BOMB'S FIRST AWESOME TEST FIRING!

AND NONE IS MORE TENSE, MORE WORRIED, THAN DR. BRUCE BANNER, THE MAN WHOSE GENIUS CREATED THE G-BOMB!

A FEW SECONDS MORE AND WE'LL KNOW WHETHER WE HAVE SUCCEEDED OR NOT!

I WAS AGAINST IT FROM THE START, BANNER, AND I STILL AM! IT IS *TOO DANGEROUS!*

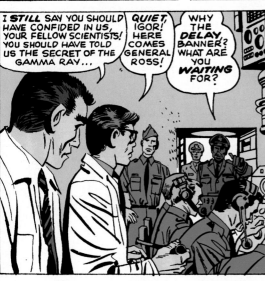

I *STILL* SAY YOU SHOULD HAVE CONFIDED IN US, YOUR FELLOW SCIENTISTS! YOU SHOULD HAVE TOLD US THE SECRET OF THE GAMMA RAY...

QUIET, IGOR! HERE COMES GENERAL ROSS!

WHY THE *DELAY* BANNER? WHAT ARE YOU *WAITING* FOR?

MY MEN HAVE BEEN STATIONED HERE FOR WEEKS, WASTING TIME BECAUSE OF YOUR INFERNAL DELAYS! ARE YOU GOING TO TEST THAT BLAMED BOMB OR *NOT?*

OF COURSE, GENERAL! IT'S JUST THAT I MUST BE SURE EVERY PRECAUTION HAS BEEN TAKEN! WE ARE TAMPERING WITH POWERFUL FORCES!

POWERFUL FORCES! *BAH!!* A BOMB IS A BOMB! THE TROUBLE WITH *YOU* IS YOU'RE A *MILKSOP!* YOU'VE GOT NO *GUTS!*

THEY SHOULD HAVE PUT *ME* IN CHARGE OF THIS TEST! BY THUNDER, IT WOULD HAVE BEEN *DONE* BY NOW!

OH DADDY, DON'T BE SO UNFAIR! DR. BRUCE BANNER IS ONE OF OUR MOST FAMOUS SCIENTISTS! I'M *SURE* HE KNOWS WHAT HE'S DOING!

YOU KEEP OUT OF THIS, BETTY! THIS IS *MAN TALK!*

DON'T MIND DAD, DR. BANNER! EVER SINCE HE WAS NICKNAMED "THUNDERBOLT" ROSS, HE'S TRIED TO LIVE UP TO IT!

HRMMPHH!

THANK YOU, MISS ROSS!

2

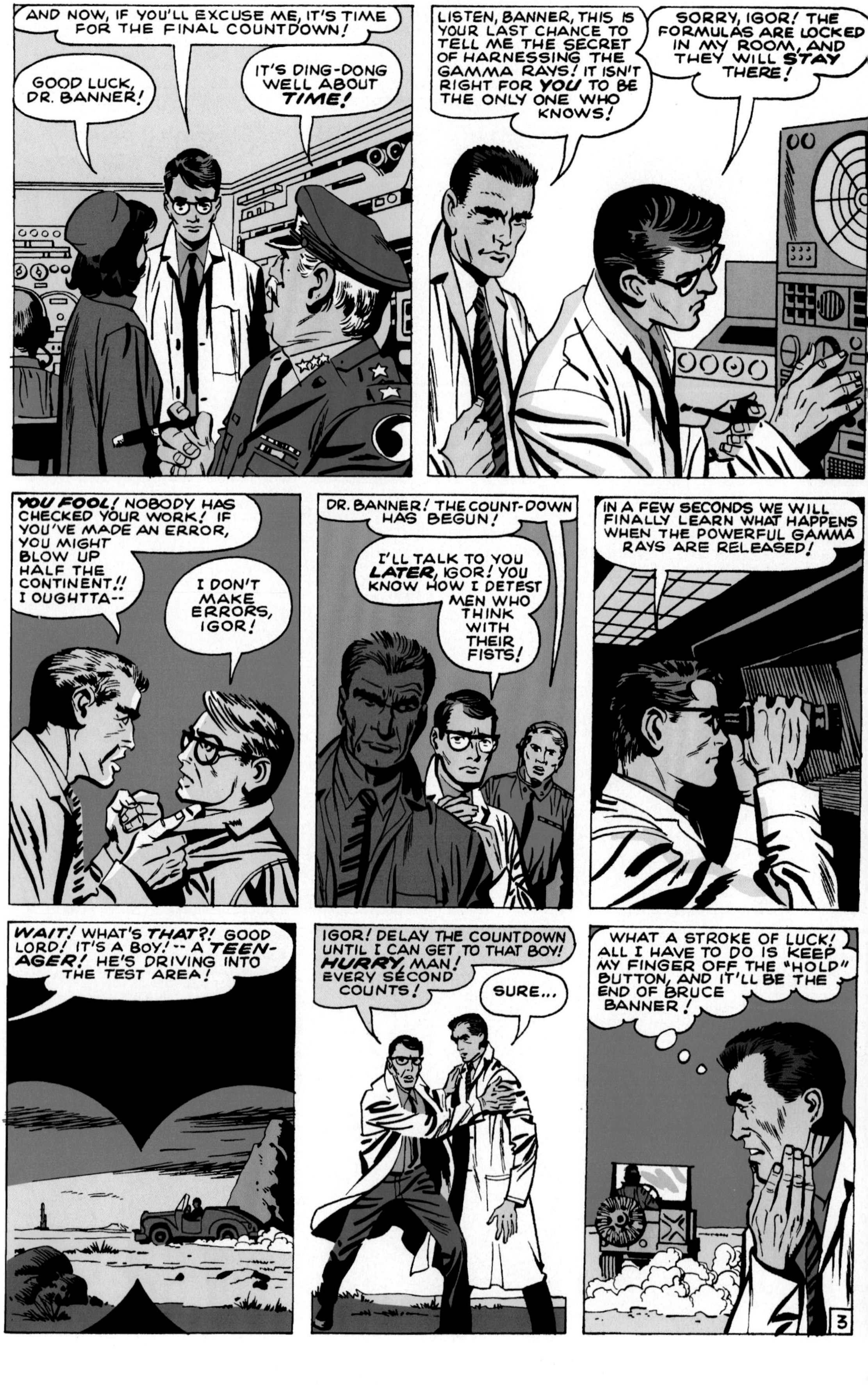
AND NOW, IF YOU'LL EXCUSE ME, IT'S TIME FOR THE FINAL COUNTDOWN!
GOOD LUCK, DR. BANNER!
IT'S DING-DONG WELL ABOUT TIME!
LISTEN, BANNER, THIS IS YOUR LAST CHANCE TO TELL ME THE SECRET OF HARNESSING THE GAMMA RAYS! IT ISN'T RIGHT FOR YOU TO BE THE ONLY ONE WHO KNOWS!
SORRY, IGOR! THE FORMULAS ARE LOCKED IN MY ROOM, AND THEY WILL STAY THERE!
YOU FOOL! NOBODY HAS CHECKED YOUR WORK! IF YOU'VE MADE AN ERROR, YOU MIGHT BLOW UP HALF THE CONTINENT!! I OUGHTTA--
I DON'T MAKE ERRORS, IGOR!
DR. BANNER! THE COUNT-DOWN HAS BEGUN!
I'LL TALK TO YOU LATER, IGOR! YOU KNOW HOW I DETEST MEN WHO THINK WITH THEIR FISTS!
IN A FEW SECONDS WE WILL FINALLY LEARN WHAT HAPPENS WHEN THE POWERFUL GAMMA RAYS ARE RELEASED!
WAIT! WHAT'S THAT?! GOOD LORD! IT'S A BOY! -- A TEEN-AGER! HE'S DRIVING INTO THE TEST AREA!
IGOR! DELAY THE COUNTDOWN UNTIL I CAN GET TO THAT BOY! HURRY, MAN! EVERY SECOND COUNTS!
SURE...
WHAT A STROKE OF LUCK! ALL I HAVE TO DO IS KEEP MY FINGER OFF THE "HOLD" BUTTON, AND IT'LL BE THE END OF BRUCE BANNER!
3

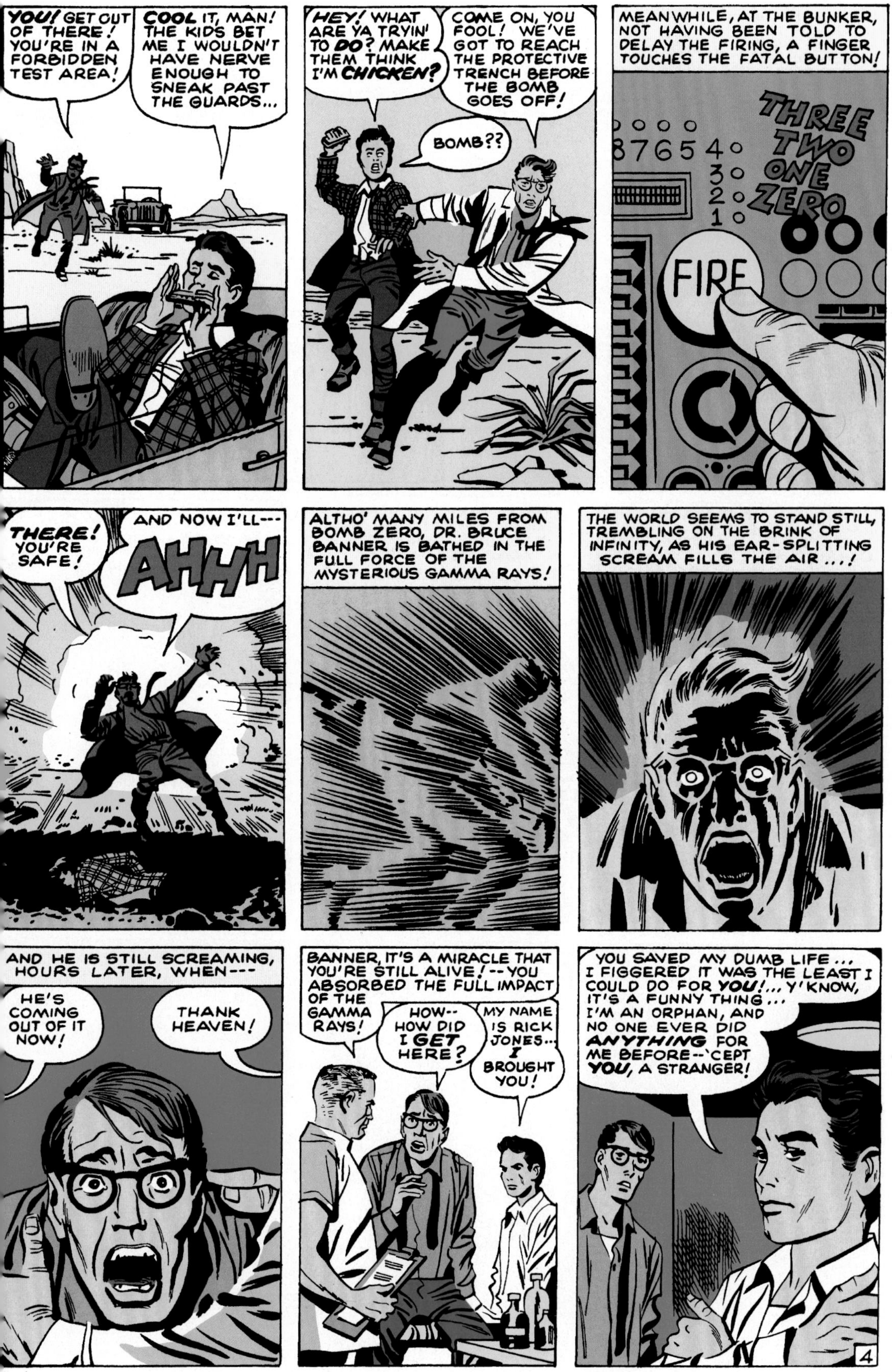
YOU! GET OUT OF THERE! YOU'RE IN A FORBIDDEN TEST AREA!
COOL IT, MAN! THE KIDS BET ME I WOULDN'T HAVE NERVE ENOUGH TO SNEAK PAST THE GUARDS...
HEY! WHAT ARE YA TRYIN' TO DO? MAKE THEM THINK I'M CHICKEN?
COME ON, YOU FOOL! WE'VE GOT TO REACH THE PROTECTIVE TRENCH BEFORE THE BOMB GOES OFF!
BOMB??
MEANWHILE, AT THE BUNKER, NOT HAVING BEEN TOLD TO DELAY THE FIRING, A FINGER TOUCHES THE FATAL BUTTON!
8 7 6 5 4 3 2 1
THREE TWO ONE ZERO
FIRE
THERE! YOU'RE SAFE!
AND NOW I'LL---
AHHH
ALTHO' MANY MILES FROM BOMB ZERO, DR. BRUCE BANNER IS BATHED IN THE FULL FORCE OF THE MYSTERIOUS GAMMA RAYS!
THE WORLD SEEMS TO STAND STILL, TREMBLING ON THE BRINK OF INFINITY, AS HIS EAR-SPLITTING SCREAM FILLS THE AIR...!
AND HE IS STILL SCREAMING, HOURS LATER, WHEN---
HE'S COMING OUT OF IT NOW!
THANK HEAVEN!
BANNER, IT'S A MIRACLE THAT YOU'RE STILL ALIVE! --YOU ABSORBED THE FULL IMPACT OF THE GAMMA RAYS!
HOW-- HOW DID I GET HERE?
MY NAME IS RICK JONES... I BROUGHT YOU!
YOU SAVED MY DUMB LIFE... I FIGGERED IT WAS THE LEAST I COULD DO FOR YOU!... Y'KNOW, IT'S A FUNNY THING... I'M AN ORPHAN, AND NO ONE EVER DID ANYTHING FOR ME BEFORE--'CEPT YOU, A STRANGER!
4

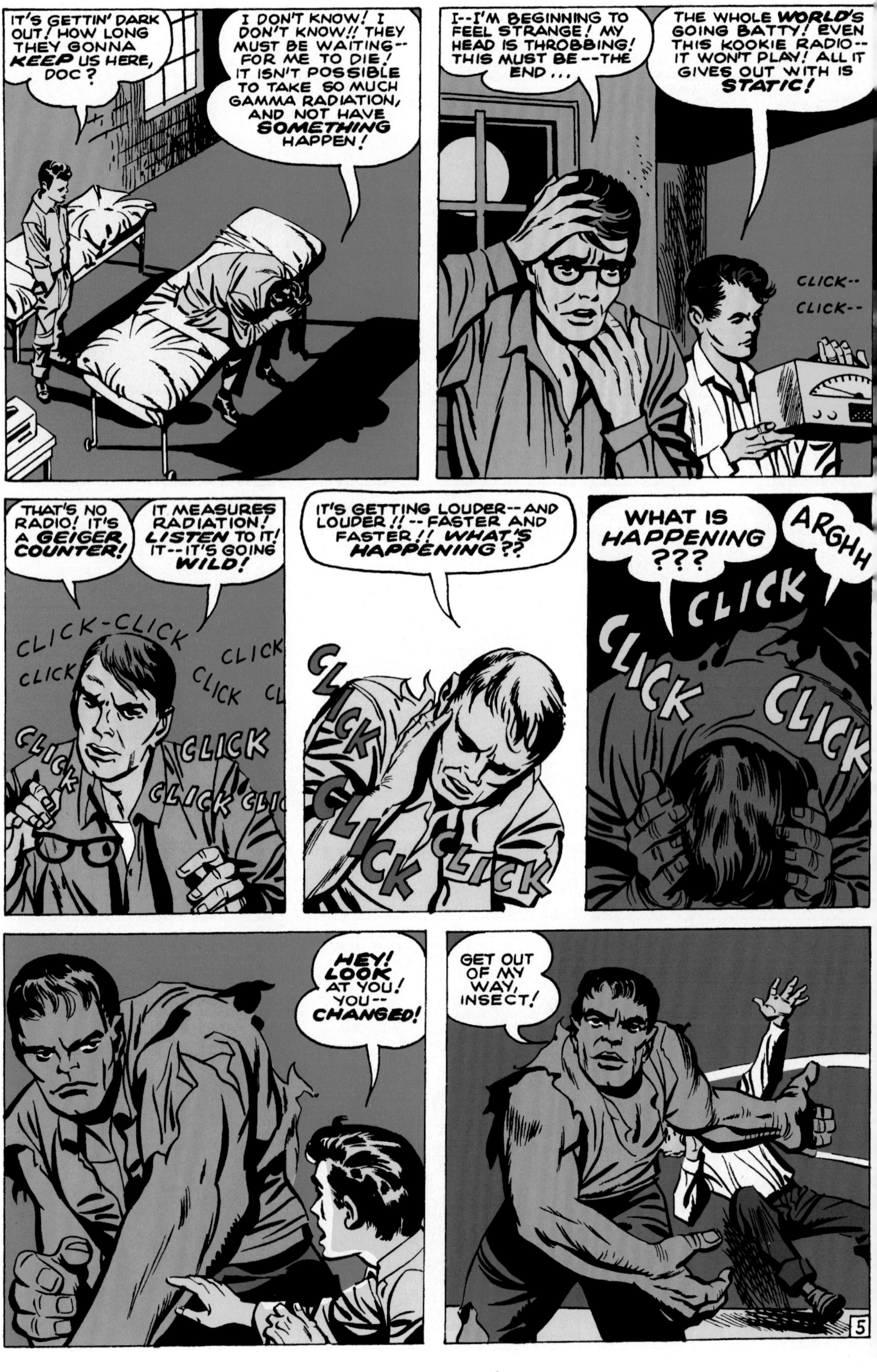

IT'S GETTIN' DARK OUT! HOW LONG THEY GONNA KEEP US HERE, DOC?
I DON'T KNOW! I DON'T KNOW!! THEY MUST BE WAITING-- FOR ME TO DIE! IT ISN'T POSSIBLE TO TAKE SO MUCH GAMMA RADIATION, AND NOT HAVE SOMETHING HAPPEN!
I--I'M BEGINNING TO FEEL STRANGE! MY HEAD IS THROBBING! THIS MUST BE --THE END...
THE WHOLE WORLD'S GOING BATTY! EVEN THIS KOOKIE RADIO-- IT WON'T PLAY! ALL IT GIVES OUT WITH IS STATIC!
CLICK-- CLICK--
THAT'S NO RADIO! IT'S A GEIGER COUNTER!
IT MEASURES RADIATION! LISTEN TO IT! IT--IT'S GOING WILD!
CLICK-CLICK CLICK CLICK CLICK CLICK CLICK CLICK
IT'S GETTING LOUDER--AND LOUDER!! --FASTER AND FASTER!! WHAT'S HAPPENING??
CLICK CLICK CLICK CLICK
WHAT IS HAPPENING ???
ARGHH
CLICK CLICK CLICK
HEY! LOOK AT YOU! YOU-- CHANGED!
GET OUT OF MY WAY, INSECT!
5

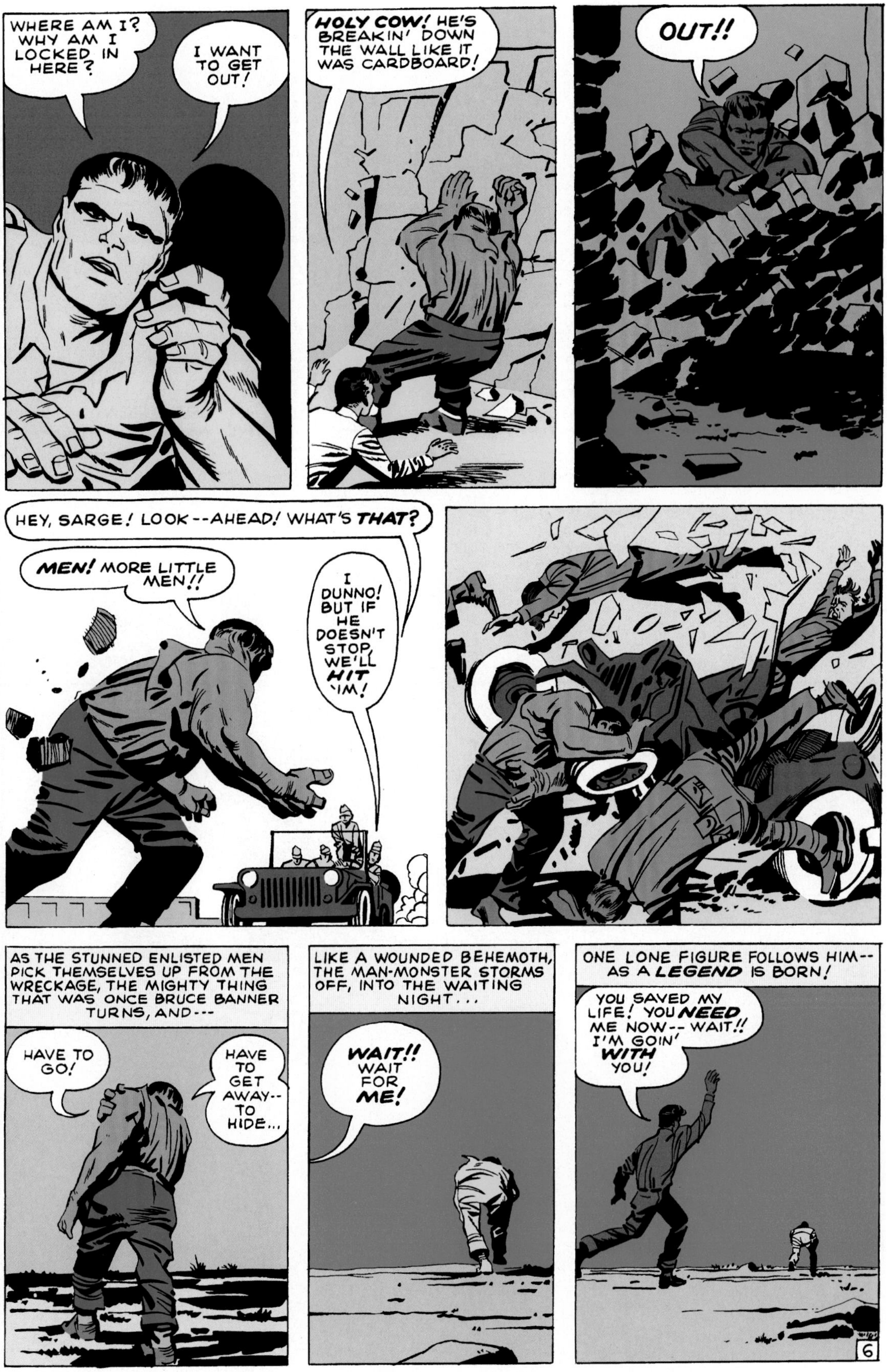

WHERE AM I? WHY AM I LOCKED IN HERE?
I WANT TO GET OUT!
HOLY COW! HE'S BREAKIN' DOWN THE WALL LIKE IT WAS CARDBOARD!
OUT!!
HEY, SARGE! LOOK--AHEAD! WHAT'S THAT?
MEN! MORE LITTLE MEN!!
I DUNNO! BUT IF HE DOESN'T STOP, WE'LL HIT 'IM!
AS THE STUNNED ENLISTED MEN PICK THEMSELVES UP FROM THE WRECKAGE, THE MIGHTY THING THAT WAS ONCE BRUCE BANNER TURNS, AND---
HAVE TO GO!
HAVE TO GET AWAY-- TO HIDE...
LIKE A WOUNDED BEHEMOTH, THE MAN-MONSTER STORMS OFF, INTO THE WAITING NIGHT...
WAIT!! WAIT FOR ME!
ONE LONE FIGURE FOLLOWS HIM-- AS A LEGEND IS BORN!
YOU SAVED MY LIFE! YOU NEED ME NOW-- WAIT!! I'M GOIN' WITH YOU!
6

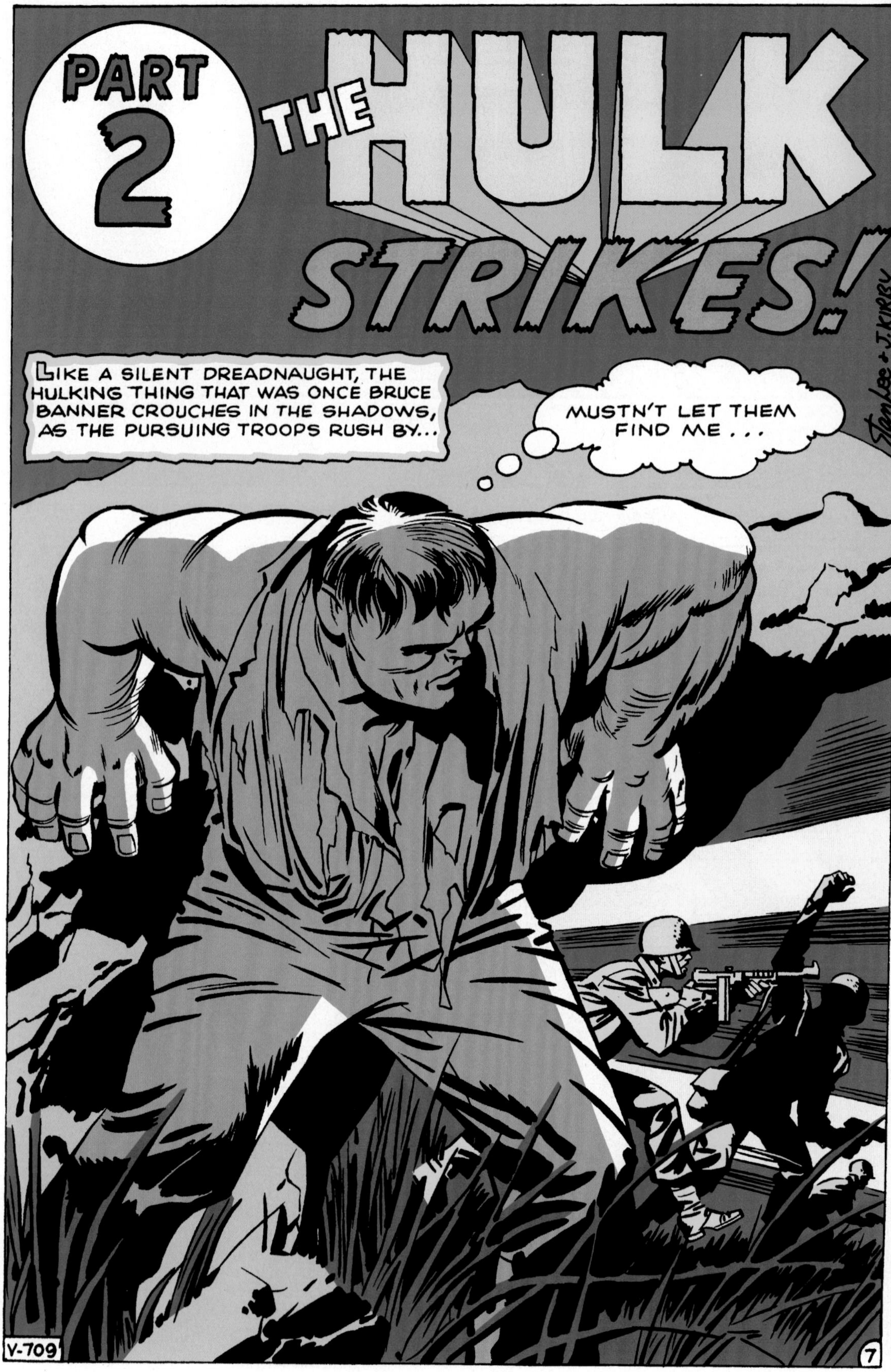
PART 2
THE HULK STRIKES!
STAN LEE + J. KIRBY
LIKE A SILENT DREADNAUGHT, THE HULKING THING THAT WAS ONCE BRUCE BANNER CROUCHES IN THE SHADOWS, AS THE PURSUING TROOPS RUSH BY...
MUSTN'T LET THEM FIND ME . . .
V-709
7

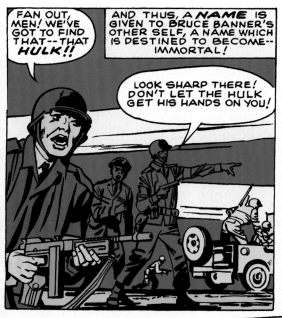

FAN OUT, MEN! WE'VE GOT TO FIND THAT--THAT *HULK*!!

AND THUS, A *NAME* IS GIVEN TO BRUCE BANNER'S OTHER SELF, A NAME WHICH IS DESTINED TO BECOME-- IMMORTAL!

LOOK SHARP THERE! DON'T LET THE HULK GET HIS HANDS ON YOU!

WHILE, BACK AT THE BASE HOSPITAL...

IT'S *IMPOSSIBLE!* NOTHING HUMAN COULD HAVE SMASHED A TWO FOOT THICK CONCRETE *WALL!*

BUT HE *DID!* THE HULK *DID* IT!

BRUCE BANNER AND THE BOY! WHAT BECAME OF *THEM?* COULD THE HULK HAVE--??

BUT WHO COULD EVER GUESS THE INCREDIBLE TRUTH? WHO COULD SUSPECT THAT BRUCE BANNER *IS*... THE HULK*!!!*

WH-WHERE IS HE *HEADED* FOR?

HAVE TO KEEP MOVING...

...HAVE TO REACH HOME! FORMULA INSIDE HOME! MUST GET FORMULA!!

DRIVEN BY SHEER INSTINCT, THE PART OF THE HULK WHICH IS STILL BRUCE BANNER HEADS FOR A SMALL COTTAGE, SMASHING ALL OBSTACLES IN HIS PATH!

MOVING WITH UNBELIEVABLE STEALTH FOR ONE SO PONDEROUS, HE STORMS CLOSER AND CLOSER TO HIS DESTINATION...

UNTIL, AT LAST, A DIM MEMORY FROM THE BRAIN OF BRUCE BANNER TELLS HIM...

THE THIRD CABIN! THAT IS WHERE I MUST GO!

8

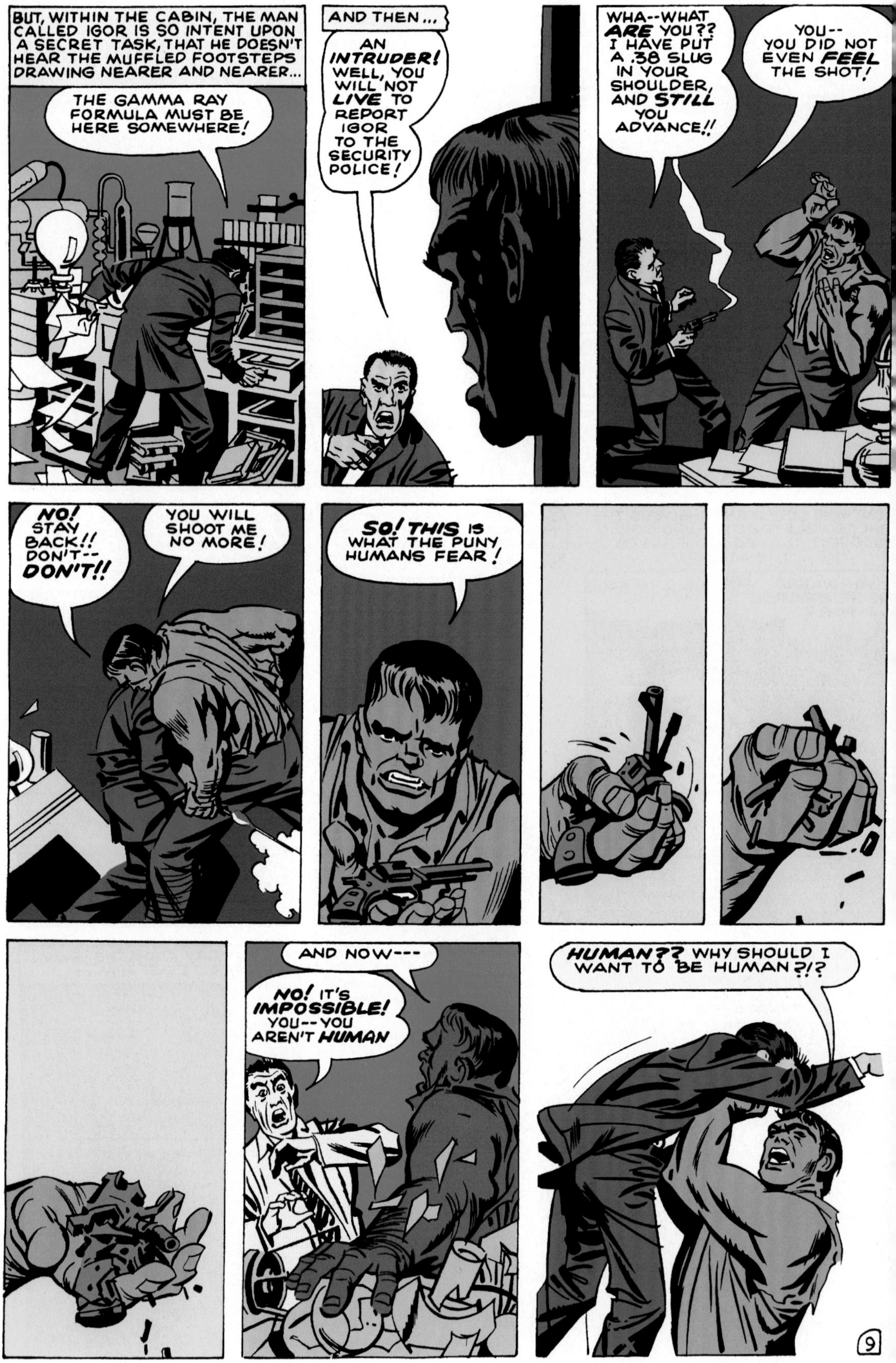
BUT, WITHIN THE CABIN, THE MAN CALLED IGOR IS SO INTENT UPON A SECRET TASK, THAT HE DOESN'T HEAR THE MUFFLED FOOTSTEPS DRAWING NEARER AND NEARER...
THE GAMMA RAY FORMULA MUST BE HERE SOMEWHERE!
AND THEN...
AN INTRUDER! WELL, YOU WILL NOT LIVE TO REPORT IGOR TO THE SECURITY POLICE!
WHA--WHAT ARE YOU?? I HAVE PUT A .38 SLUG IN YOUR SHOULDER, AND STILL YOU ADVANCE!!
YOU-- YOU DID NOT EVEN FEEL THE SHOT!
NO! STAY BACK!! DON'T-- DON'T!!
YOU WILL SHOOT ME NO MORE!
SO! THIS IS WHAT THE PUNY HUMANS FEAR!
AND NOW---
NO! IT'S IMPOSSIBLE! YOU-- YOU AREN'T HUMAN
HUMAN?? WHY SHOULD I WANT TO BE HUMAN?!?

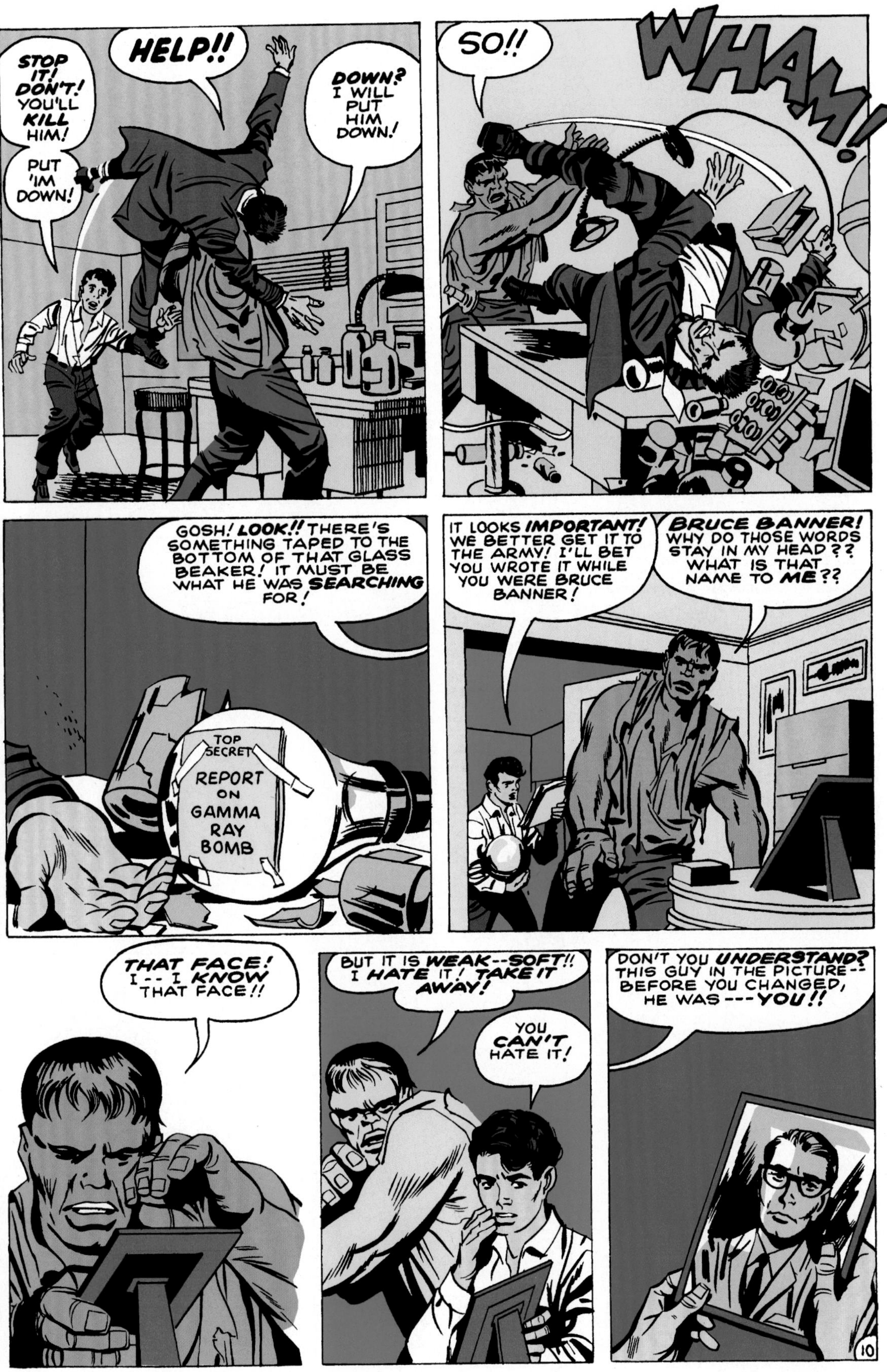
STOP IT! DON'T! YOU'LL KILL HIM!
HELP!!
PUT 'IM DOWN!
DOWN? I WILL PUT HIM DOWN!
SO!!
WHAM!
GOSH! LOOK!! THERE'S SOMETHING TAPED TO THE BOTTOM OF THAT GLASS BEAKER! IT MUST BE WHAT HE WAS SEARCHING FOR!
TOP SECRET
REPORT ON GAMMA RAY BOMB
IT LOOKS IMPORTANT! WE BETTER GET IT TO THE ARMY! I'LL BET YOU WROTE IT WHILE YOU WERE BRUCE BANNER!
BRUCE BANNER! WHY DO THOSE WORDS STAY IN MY HEAD?? WHAT IS THAT NAME TO ME??
THAT FACE! I-- I KNOW THAT FACE!!
BUT IT IS WEAK--SOFT!! I HATE IT! TAKE IT AWAY!
YOU CAN'T HATE IT!
DON'T YOU UNDERSTAND? THIS GUY IN THE PICTURE-- BEFORE YOU CHANGED, HE WAS---YOU!!
10

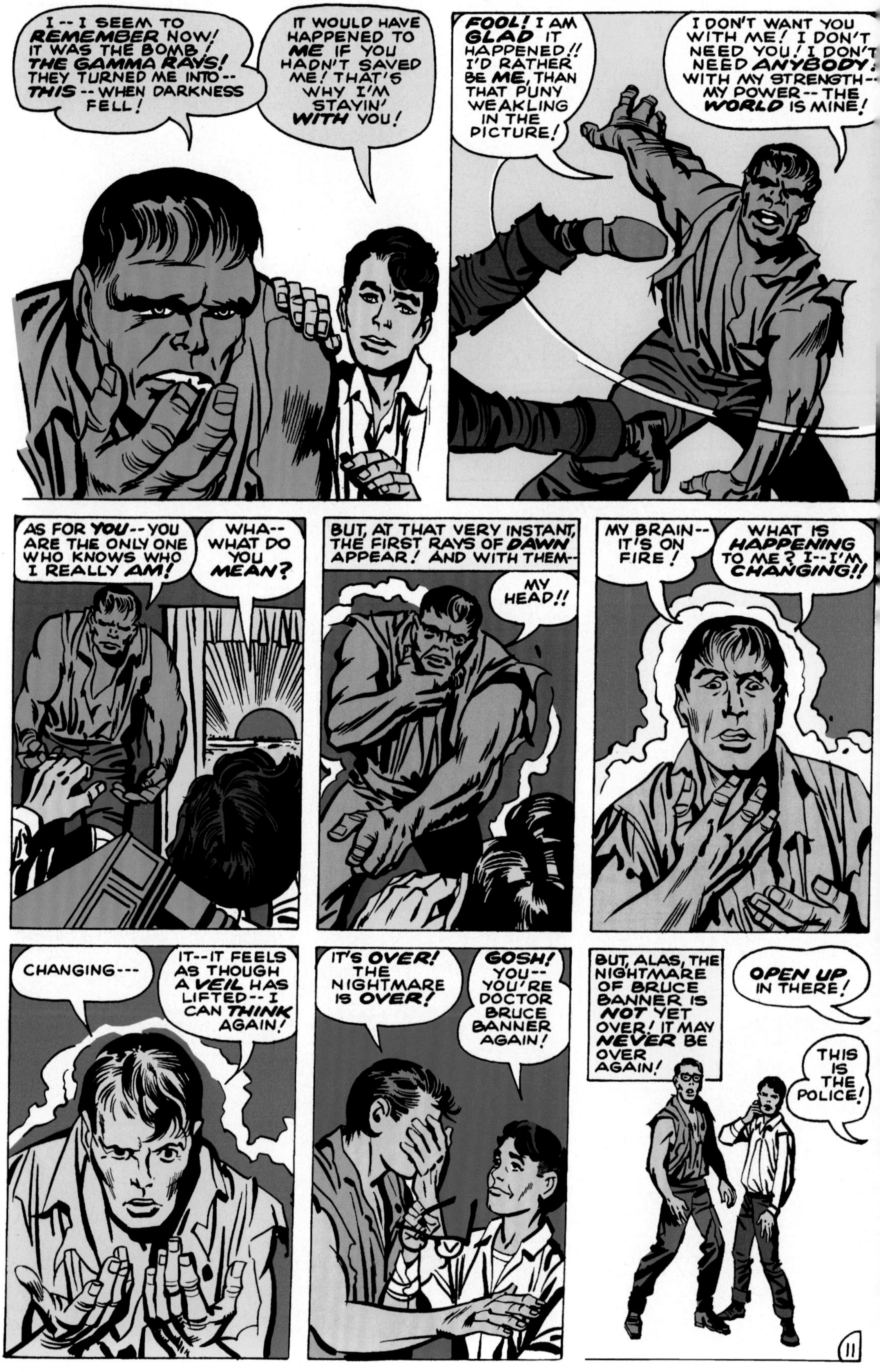

I -- I SEEM TO REMEMBER NOW! IT WAS THE BOMB! THE GAMMA RAYS! THEY TURNED ME INTO -- THIS -- WHEN DARKNESS FELL!
IT WOULD HAVE HAPPENED TO ME IF YOU HADN'T SAVED ME! THAT'S WHY I'M STAYIN' WITH YOU!
FOOL! I AM GLAD IT HAPPENED!! I'D RATHER BE ME, THAN THAT PUNY WEAKLING IN THE PICTURE!
I DON'T WANT YOU WITH ME! I DON'T NEED YOU! I DON'T NEED ANYBODY! WITH MY STRENGTH -- MY POWER -- THE WORLD IS MINE!
AS FOR YOU -- YOU ARE THE ONLY ONE WHO KNOWS WHO I REALLY AM!
WHA-- WHAT DO YOU MEAN?
BUT, AT THAT VERY INSTANT, THE FIRST RAYS OF DAWN APPEAR! AND WITH THEM--
MY HEAD!!
MY BRAIN-- IT'S ON FIRE!
WHAT IS HAPPENING TO ME? I--I'M CHANGING!!
CHANGING---
IT--IT FEELS AS THOUGH A VEIL HAS LIFTED -- I CAN THINK AGAIN!
IT'S OVER! THE NIGHTMARE IS OVER!
GOSH! YOU-- YOU'RE DOCTOR BRUCE BANNER AGAIN!
BUT, ALAS, THE NIGHTMARE OF BRUCE BANNER IS NOT YET OVER! IT MAY NEVER BE OVER AGAIN!
OPEN UP IN THERE!
THIS IS THE POLICE!

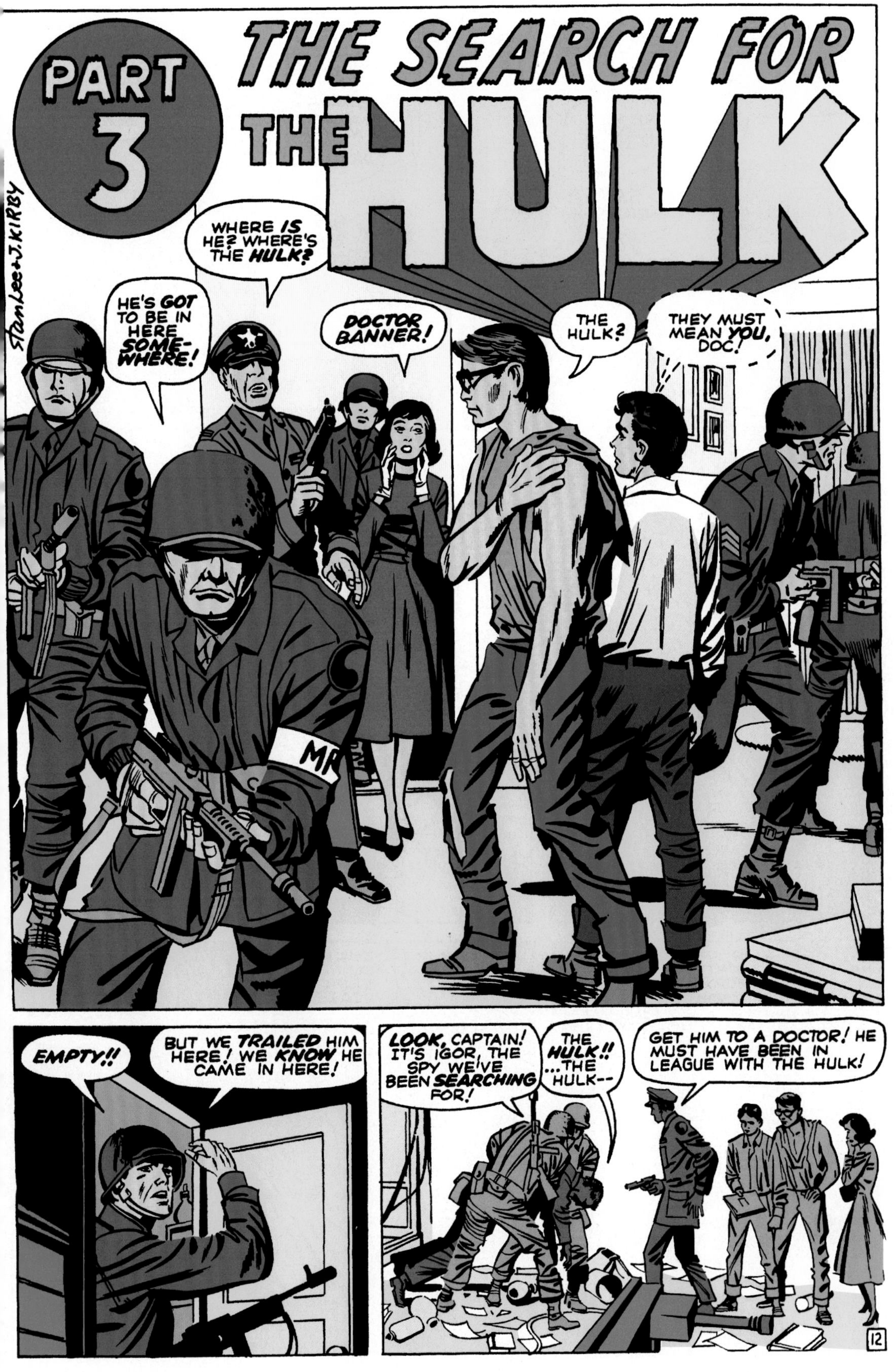
PART 3
THE SEARCH FOR THE HULK
STAN LEE • J. KIRBY
WHERE IS HE? WHERE'S THE HULK?
HE'S GOT TO BE IN HERE SOME-WHERE!
DOCTOR BANNER!
THE HULK?
THEY MUST MEAN YOU, DOC!
MP
EMPTY!!
BUT WE TRAILED HIM HERE! WE KNOW HE CAME IN HERE!
LOOK, CAPTAIN! IT'S IGOR, THE SPY WE'VE BEEN SEARCHING FOR!
THE HULK!! ...THE HULK--
GET HIM TO A DOCTOR! HE MUST HAVE BEEN IN LEAGUE WITH THE HULK!

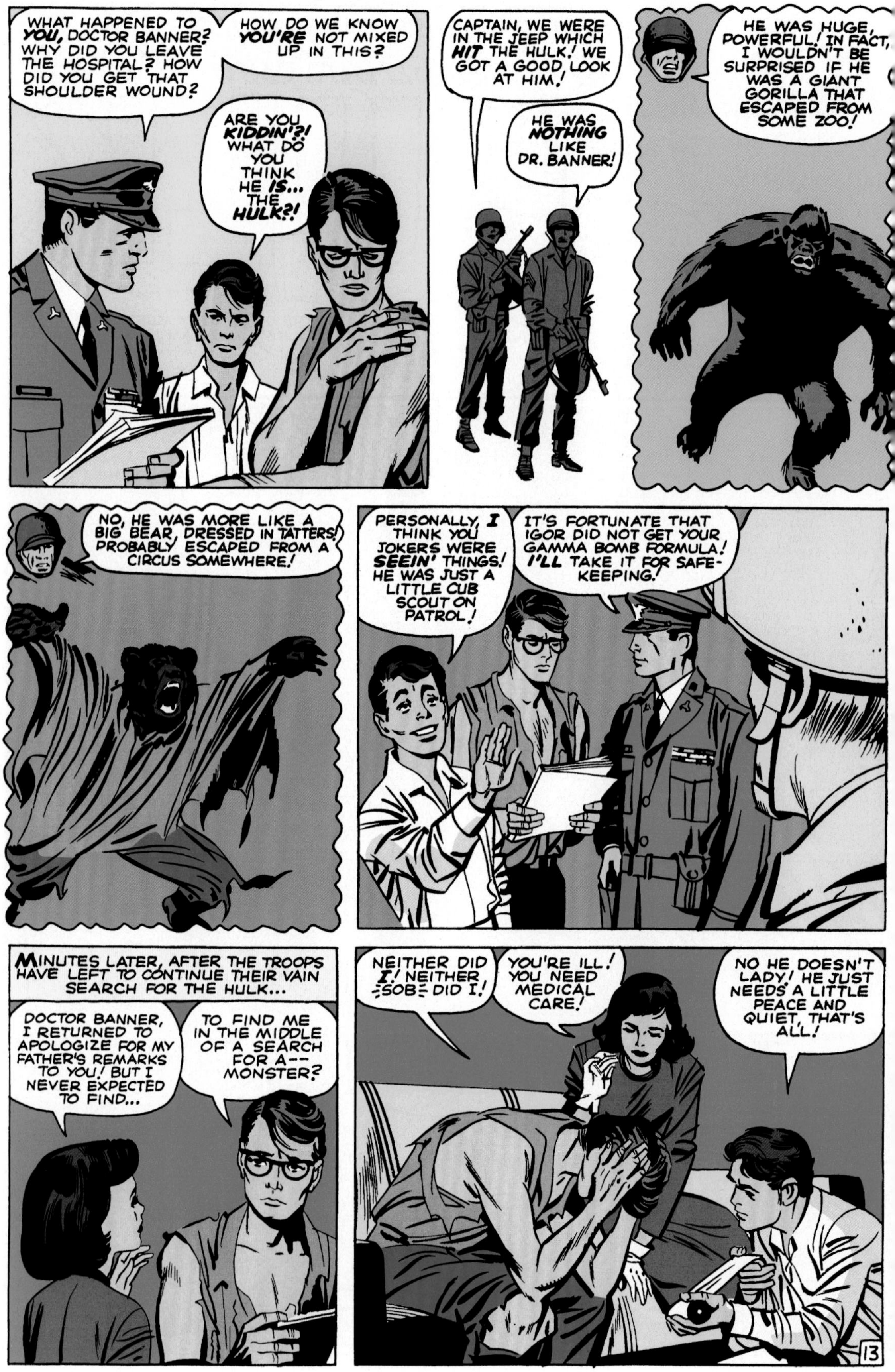

WHAT HAPPENED TO YOU, DOCTOR BANNER? WHY DID YOU LEAVE THE HOSPITAL? HOW DID YOU GET THAT SHOULDER WOUND?
HOW DO WE KNOW YOU'RE NOT MIXED UP IN THIS?
ARE YOU KIDDIN'?! WHAT DO YOU THINK HE IS... THE HULK?!
CAPTAIN, WE WERE IN THE JEEP WHICH HIT THE HULK! WE GOT A GOOD LOOK AT HIM!
HE WAS NOTHING LIKE DR. BANNER!
HE WAS HUGE, POWERFUL! IN FACT, I WOULDN'T BE SURPRISED IF HE WAS A GIANT GORILLA THAT ESCAPED FROM SOME ZOO!
NO, HE WAS MORE LIKE A BIG BEAR, DRESSED IN TATTERS! PROBABLY ESCAPED FROM A CIRCUS SOMEWHERE!
PERSONALLY, I THINK YOU JOKERS WERE SEEIN' THINGS! HE WAS JUST A LITTLE CUB SCOUT ON PATROL!
IT'S FORTUNATE THAT IGOR DID NOT GET YOUR GAMMA BOMB FORMULA! I'LL TAKE IT FOR SAFE-KEEPING!
MINUTES LATER, AFTER THE TROOPS HAVE LEFT TO CONTINUE THEIR VAIN SEARCH FOR THE HULK...
DOCTOR BANNER, I RETURNED TO APOLOGIZE FOR MY FATHER'S REMARKS TO YOU! BUT I NEVER EXPECTED TO FIND...
TO FIND ME IN THE MIDDLE OF A SEARCH FOR A-- MONSTER?
NEITHER DID I! NEITHER -SOB- DID I!
YOU'RE ILL! YOU NEED MEDICAL CARE!
NO HE DOESN'T LADY! HE JUST NEEDS A LITTLE PEACE AND QUIET, THAT'S ALL!
13

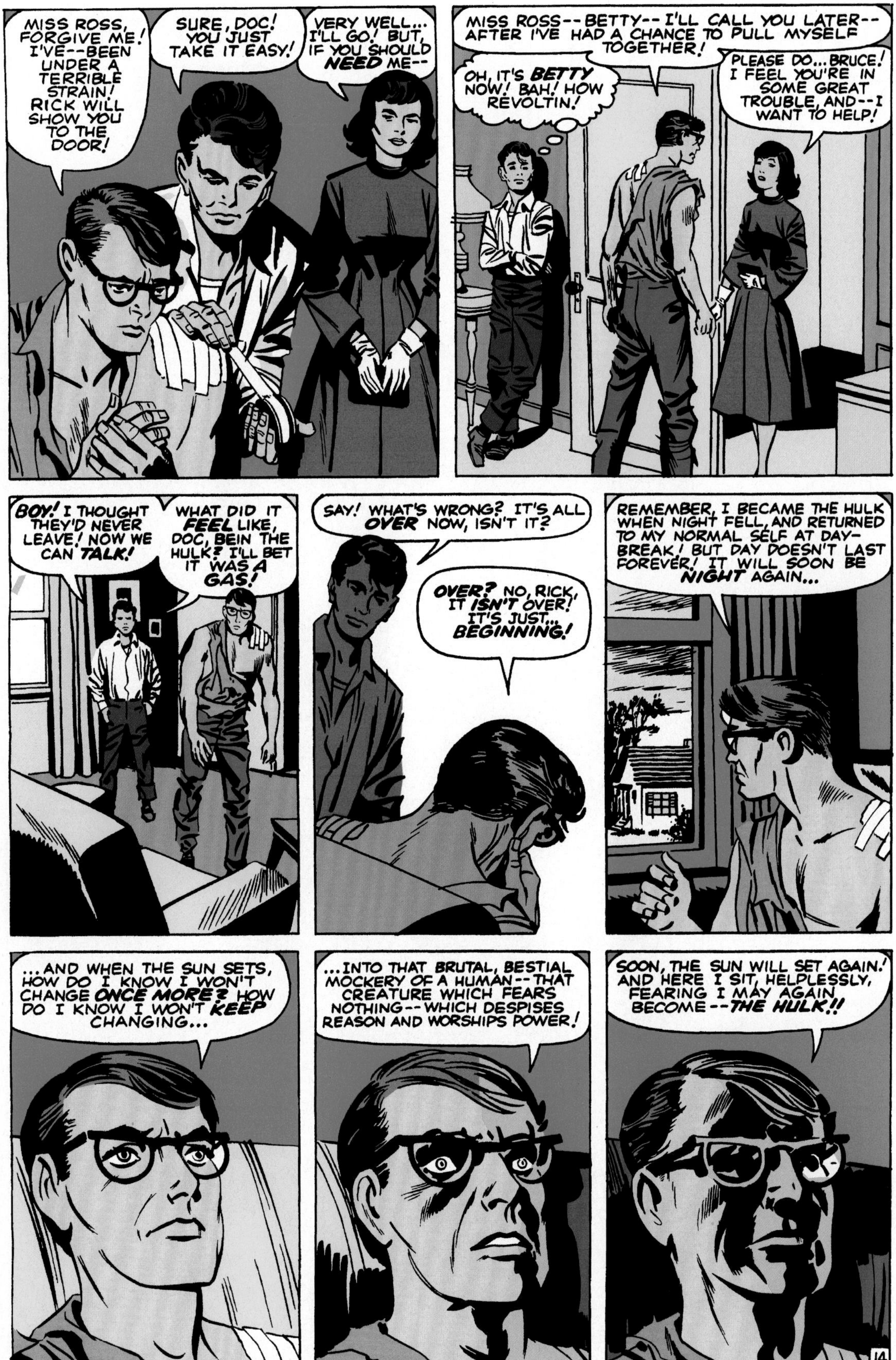
MISS ROSS, FORGIVE ME! I'VE--BEEN UNDER A TERRIBLE STRAIN! RICK WILL SHOW YOU TO THE DOOR!
SURE, DOC! YOU JUST TAKE IT EASY!
VERY WELL... I'LL GO! BUT, IF YOU SHOULD NEED ME--
MISS ROSS--BETTY--I'LL CALL YOU LATER--AFTER I'VE HAD A CHANCE TO PULL MYSELF TOGETHER!
OH, IT'S BETTY NOW! BAH! HOW REVOLTIN'!
PLEASE DO...BRUCE! I FEEL YOU'RE IN SOME GREAT TROUBLE, AND--I WANT TO HELP!
BOY! I THOUGHT THEY'D NEVER LEAVE! NOW WE CAN TALK!
WHAT DID IT FEEL LIKE, DOC, BEIN THE HULK? I'LL BET IT WAS A GAS!
SAY! WHAT'S WRONG? IT'S ALL OVER NOW, ISN'T IT?
OVER? NO, RICK, IT ISN'T OVER! IT'S JUST... BEGINNING!
REMEMBER, I BECAME THE HULK WHEN NIGHT FELL, AND RETURNED TO MY NORMAL SELF AT DAY-BREAK! BUT DAY DOESN'T LAST FOREVER! IT WILL SOON BE NIGHT AGAIN...
...AND WHEN THE SUN SETS, HOW DO I KNOW I WON'T CHANGE ONCE MORE? HOW DO I KNOW I WON'T KEEP CHANGING...
...INTO THAT BRUTAL, BESTIAL MOCKERY OF A HUMAN--THAT CREATURE WHICH FEARS NOTHING--WHICH DESPISES REASON AND WORSHIPS POWER!
SOON, THE SUN WILL SET AGAIN! AND HERE I SIT, HELPLESSLY, FEARING I MAY AGAIN BECOME--THE HULK!!
14

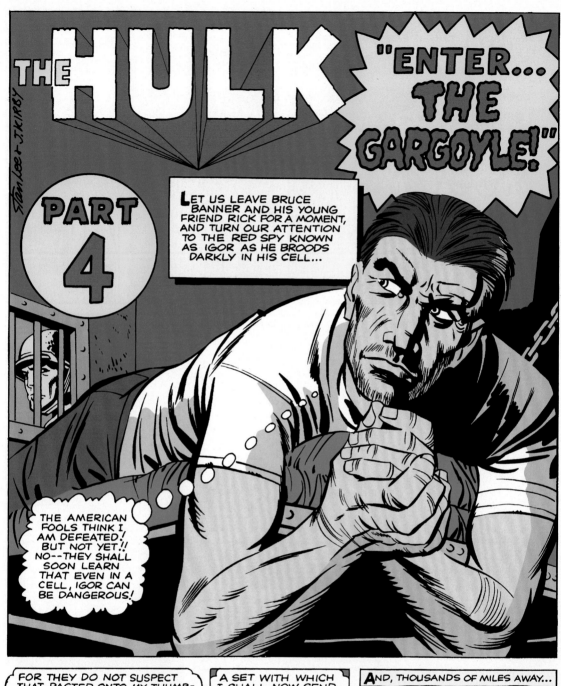

THE HULK

"ENTER... THE GARGOYLE!"

PART 4

LET US LEAVE BRUCE BANNER AND HIS YOUNG FRIEND RICK FOR A MOMENT, AND TURN OUR ATTENTION TO THE RED SPY KNOWN AS IGOR AS HE BROODS DARKLY IN HIS CELL...

THE AMERICAN FOOLS THINK I AM DEFEATED! BUT NOT YET!! NO--THEY SHALL SOON LEARN THAT EVEN IN A CELL, IGOR CAN BE DANGEROUS!

FOR THEY DO NOT SUSPECT THAT PASTED ONTO MY THUMB-NAIL IS A SUB-MINIATURE TRANSISTOR SHORT WAVE SENDING SET!

A SET WITH WHICH I SHALL NOW SEND A SECRET MESSAGE TO BEHIND THE IRON CURTAIN!

AND, THOUSANDS OF MILES AWAY...

COMRADE!! I AM RECEIVING A CODE MESSAGE FROM IGOR!

QUICK! LET ME HAVE IT!

15

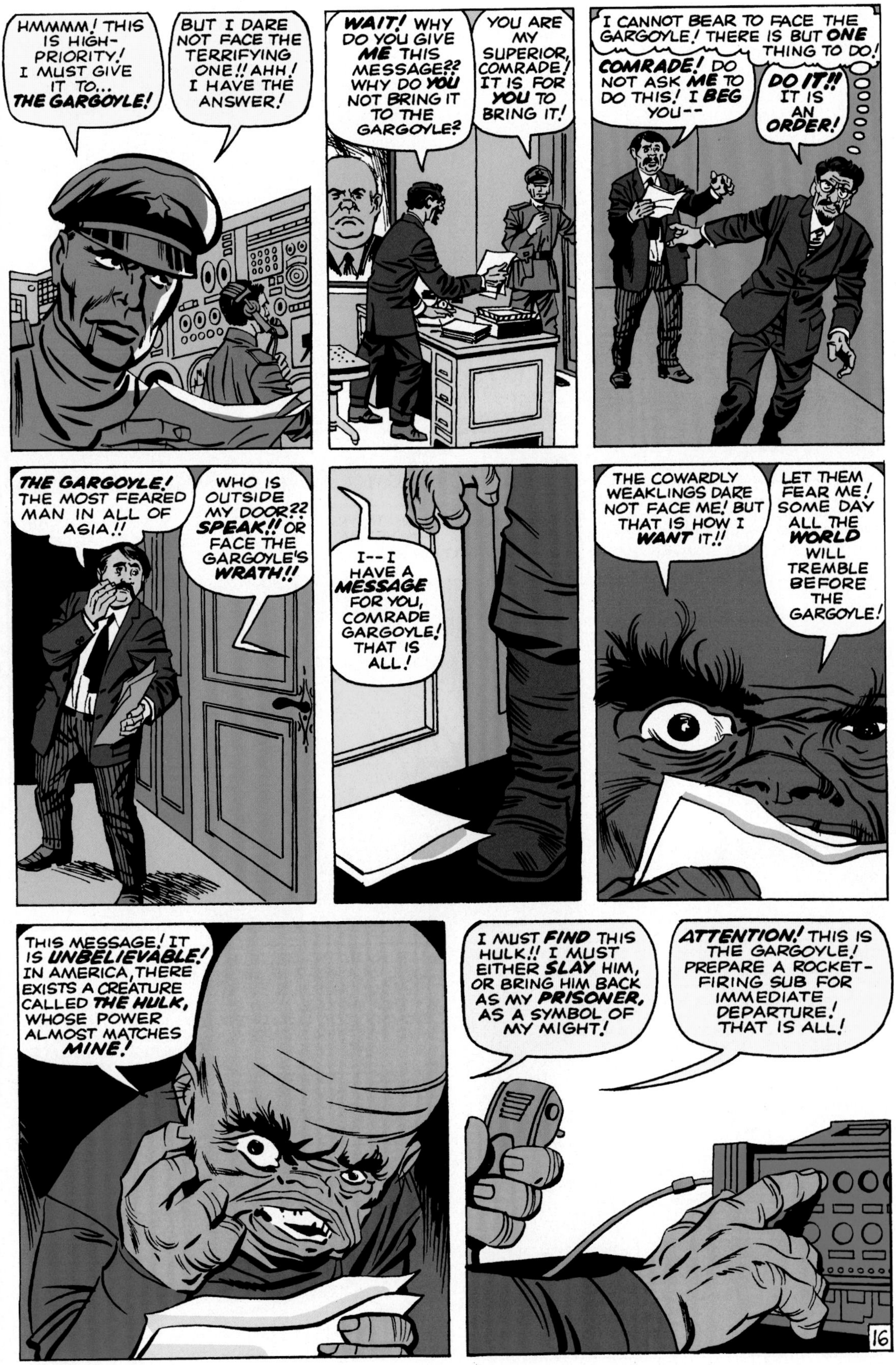
HMMMM! THIS IS HIGH-PRIORITY! I MUST GIVE IT TO... THE GARGOYLE!
BUT I DARE NOT FACE THE TERRIFYING ONE!! AHH! I HAVE THE ANSWER!
WAIT! WHY DO YOU GIVE ME THIS MESSAGE?? WHY DO YOU NOT BRING IT TO THE GARGOYLE?
YOU ARE MY SUPERIOR, COMRADE! IT IS FOR YOU TO BRING IT!
I CANNOT BEAR TO FACE THE GARGOYLE! THERE IS BUT ONE THING TO DO!
COMRADE! DO NOT ASK ME TO DO THIS! I BEG YOU--
DO IT!! IT IS AN ORDER!
THE GARGOYLE! THE MOST FEARED MAN IN ALL OF ASIA!!
WHO IS OUTSIDE MY DOOR?? SPEAK!! OR FACE THE GARGOYLE'S WRATH!!
I--I HAVE A MESSAGE FOR YOU, COMRADE GARGOYLE! THAT IS ALL!
THE COWARDLY WEAKLINGS DARE NOT FACE ME! BUT THAT IS HOW I WANT IT!!
LET THEM FEAR ME! SOME DAY ALL THE WORLD WILL TREMBLE BEFORE THE GARGOYLE!
THIS MESSAGE! IT IS UNBELIEVABLE! IN AMERICA, THERE EXISTS A CREATURE CALLED THE HULK, WHOSE POWER ALMOST MATCHES MINE!
I MUST FIND THIS HULK!! I MUST EITHER SLAY HIM, OR BRING HIM BACK AS MY PRISONER, AS A SYMBOL OF MY MIGHT!
ATTENTION! THIS IS THE GARGOYLE! PREPARE A ROCKET-FIRING SUB FOR IMMEDIATE DEPARTURE! THAT IS ALL!
16

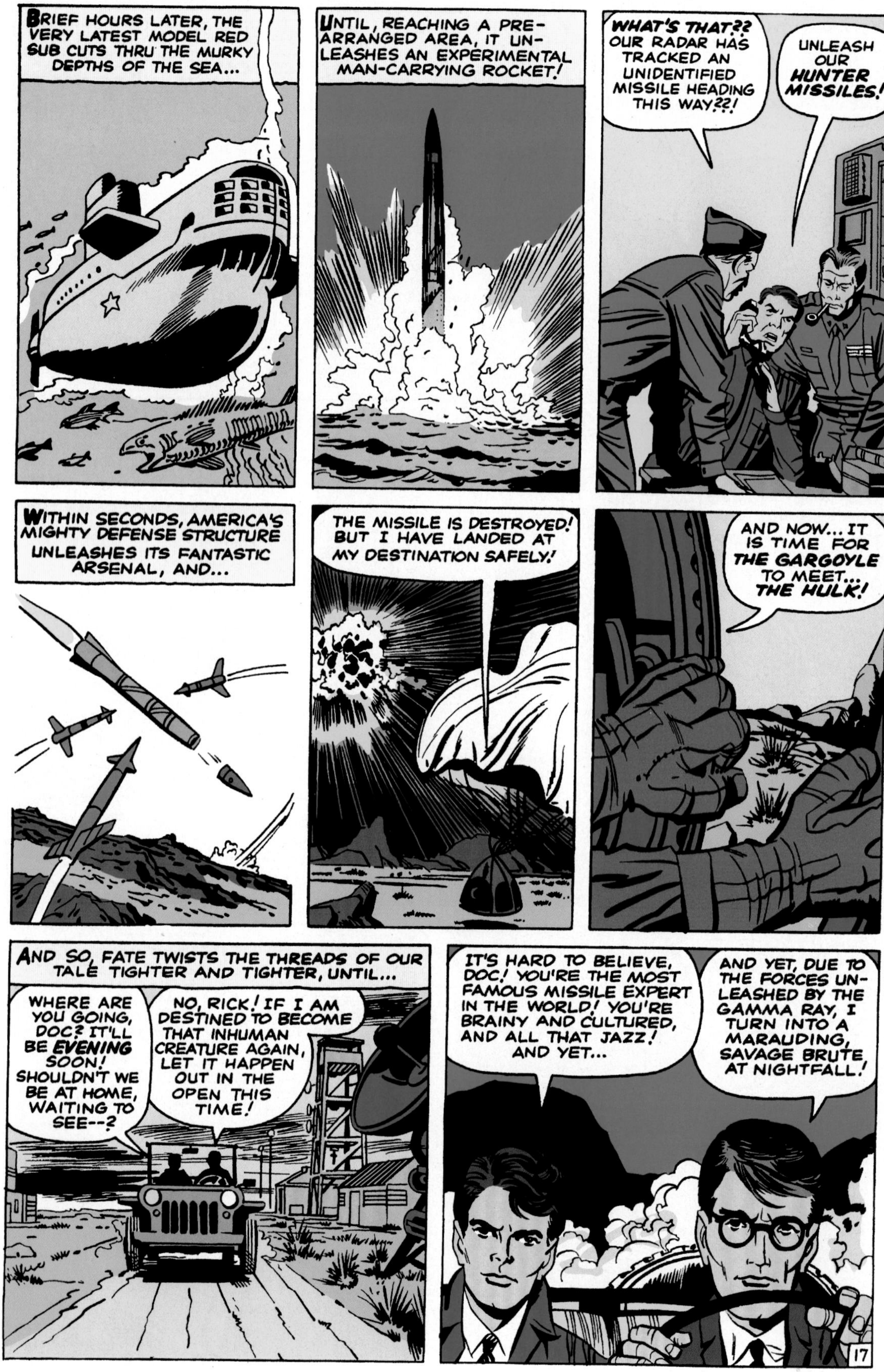

BRIEF HOURS LATER, THE VERY LATEST MODEL RED SUB CUTS THRU THE MURKY DEPTHS OF THE SEA...
UNTIL, REACHING A PRE-ARRANGED AREA, IT UNLEASHES AN EXPERIMENTAL MAN-CARRYING ROCKET!
WHAT'S THAT?? OUR RADAR HAS TRACKED AN UNIDENTIFIED MISSILE HEADING THIS WAY??!
UNLEASH OUR HUNTER MISSILES!
WITHIN SECONDS, AMERICA'S MIGHTY DEFENSE STRUCTURE UNLEASHES ITS FANTASTIC ARSENAL, AND...
THE MISSILE IS DESTROYED! BUT I HAVE LANDED AT MY DESTINATION SAFELY!
AND NOW... IT IS TIME FOR THE GARGOYLE TO MEET... THE HULK!
AND SO, FATE TWISTS THE THREADS OF OUR TALE TIGHTER AND TIGHTER, UNTIL...
WHERE ARE YOU GOING, DOC? IT'LL BE EVENING SOON! SHOULDN'T WE BE AT HOME, WAITING TO SEE--?
NO, RICK! IF I AM DESTINED TO BECOME THAT INHUMAN CREATURE AGAIN, LET IT HAPPEN OUT IN THE OPEN THIS TIME!
IT'S HARD TO BELIEVE, DOC! YOU'RE THE MOST FAMOUS MISSILE EXPERT IN THE WORLD! YOU'RE BRAINY AND CULTURED, AND ALL THAT JAZZ! AND YET...
AND YET, DUE TO THE FORCES UNLEASHED BY THE GAMMA RAY, I TURN INTO A MARAUDING, SAVAGE BRUTE AT NIGHTFALL!
17

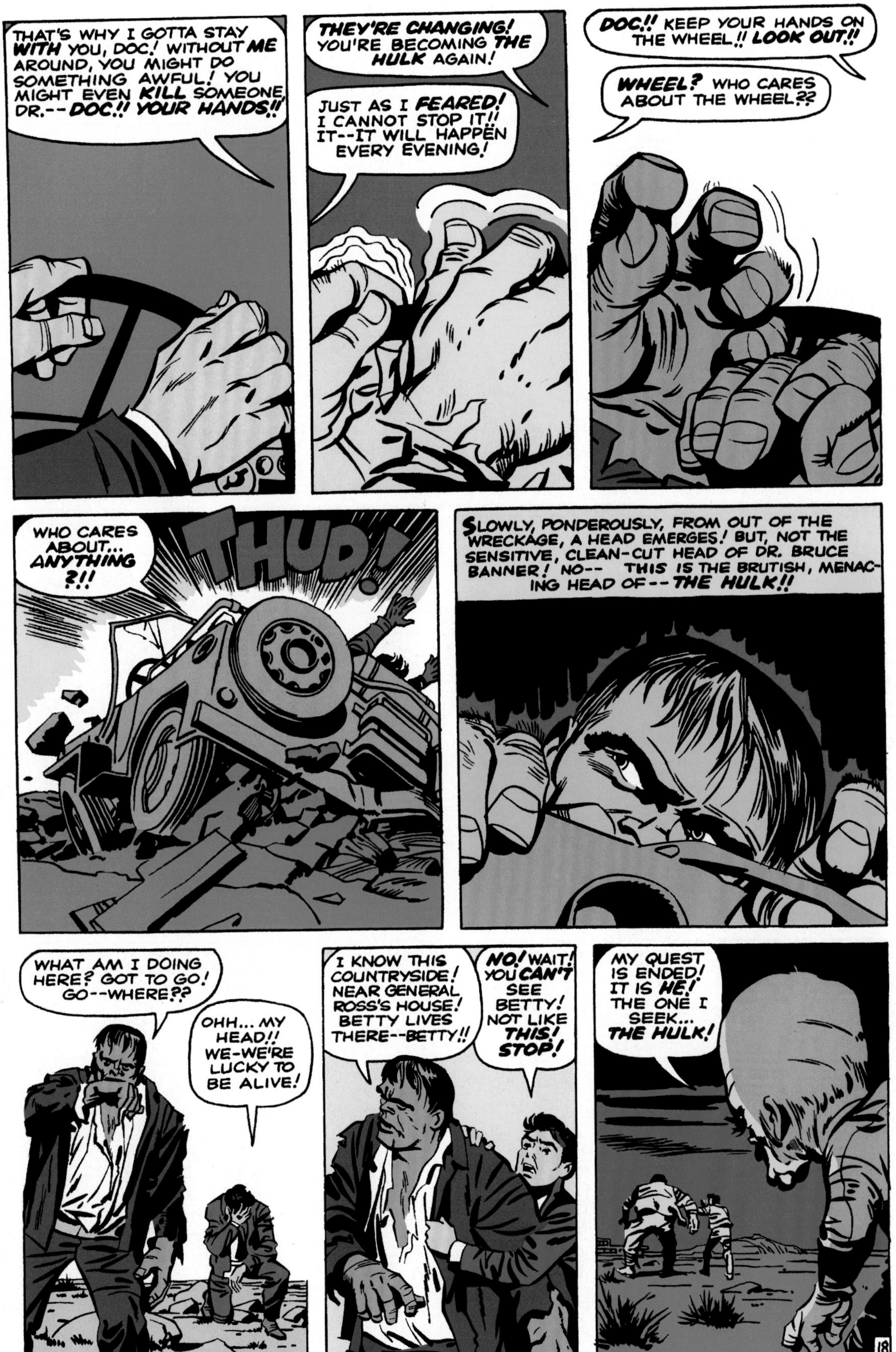

THAT'S WHY I GOTTA STAY WITH YOU, DOC! WITHOUT ME AROUND, YOU MIGHT DO SOMETHING AWFUL! YOU MIGHT EVEN KILL SOMEONE DR.--DOC!! YOUR HANDS!!
THEY'RE CHANGING! YOU'RE BECOMING THE HULK AGAIN!
JUST AS I FEARED! I CANNOT STOP IT!! IT--IT WILL HAPPEN EVERY EVENING!
DOC!! KEEP YOUR HANDS ON THE WHEEL!! LOOK OUT!!
WHEEL? WHO CARES ABOUT THE WHEEL??
WHO CARES ABOUT... ANYTHING ?!!
THUD!
SLOWLY, PONDEROUSLY, FROM OUT OF THE WRECKAGE, A HEAD EMERGES! BUT, NOT THE SENSITIVE, CLEAN-CUT HEAD OF DR. BRUCE BANNER! NO-- THIS IS THE BRUTISH, MENACING HEAD OF--THE HULK!!
WHAT AM I DOING HERE? GOT TO GO! GO--WHERE??
OHH... MY HEAD!! WE-WE'RE LUCKY TO BE ALIVE!
I KNOW THIS COUNTRYSIDE! NEAR GENERAL ROSS'S HOUSE! BETTY LIVES THERE--BETTY!!
NO! WAIT! YOU CAN'T SEE BETTY! NOT LIKE THIS! STOP!
MY QUEST IS ENDED! IT IS HE! THE ONE I SEEK... THE HULK!

MEANWHILE, JUST A SHORT DISTANCE AWAY, BETTY ROSS IS LOST IN HER OWN DISTURBED MUSINGS...

I CAN'T GET BRUCE BANNER OUT OF MY MIND!!

SOMEHOW, I FEEL HE-- NEEDS ME!

WHAT IS IT, GIRL? YOU'VE SEEMED TROUBLED ALL DAY!

OH, DAD...IF ONLY THINGS WERE AS SIMPLE AS IN YOUR DAY, WHEN A CAVALRY CHARGE, OR A SQUAD OF INFANTRYMEN COULD SOLVE ANYTHING!

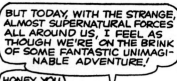

BUT TODAY, WITH THE STRANGE, ALMOST SUPERNATURAL FORCES ALL AROUND US, I FEEL AS THOUGH WE'RE ON THE BRINK OF SOME FANTASTIC UNIMAGINABLE ADVENTURE!

HONEY, YOU JUST NEED A LITTLE FRESH AIR!

DAD'S RIGHT! PERHAPS A WALK IN THE CRISP NIGHT AIR WILL CLEAR MY HEAD--WILL DRIVE THE TROUBLED FACE OF BRUCE BANNER FROM MY THOUGHTS!

AND PERHAPS I CAN TELL MYSELF IT WAS ALL A DREAM-- THERE IS NO HULK!

BUT THERE IS A HULK!! AND DON'T YOU EVER FORGET IT!!

OH-- NO!

FAINTED!! BAH! JUST LIKE ALL WEAK, HELPLESS CREATURES!

HULK-- LET GO OF HER!

YOU'VE GOT TO LEAVE HERE! IF YOU'RE FOUND THIS TIME, THEY'LL--

SHUT UP! NOBODY TELLS THE HULK!

YOU ARE WRONG, MONSTER! TURN AROUND! TURN AND FACE--THE GARGOYLE!

19

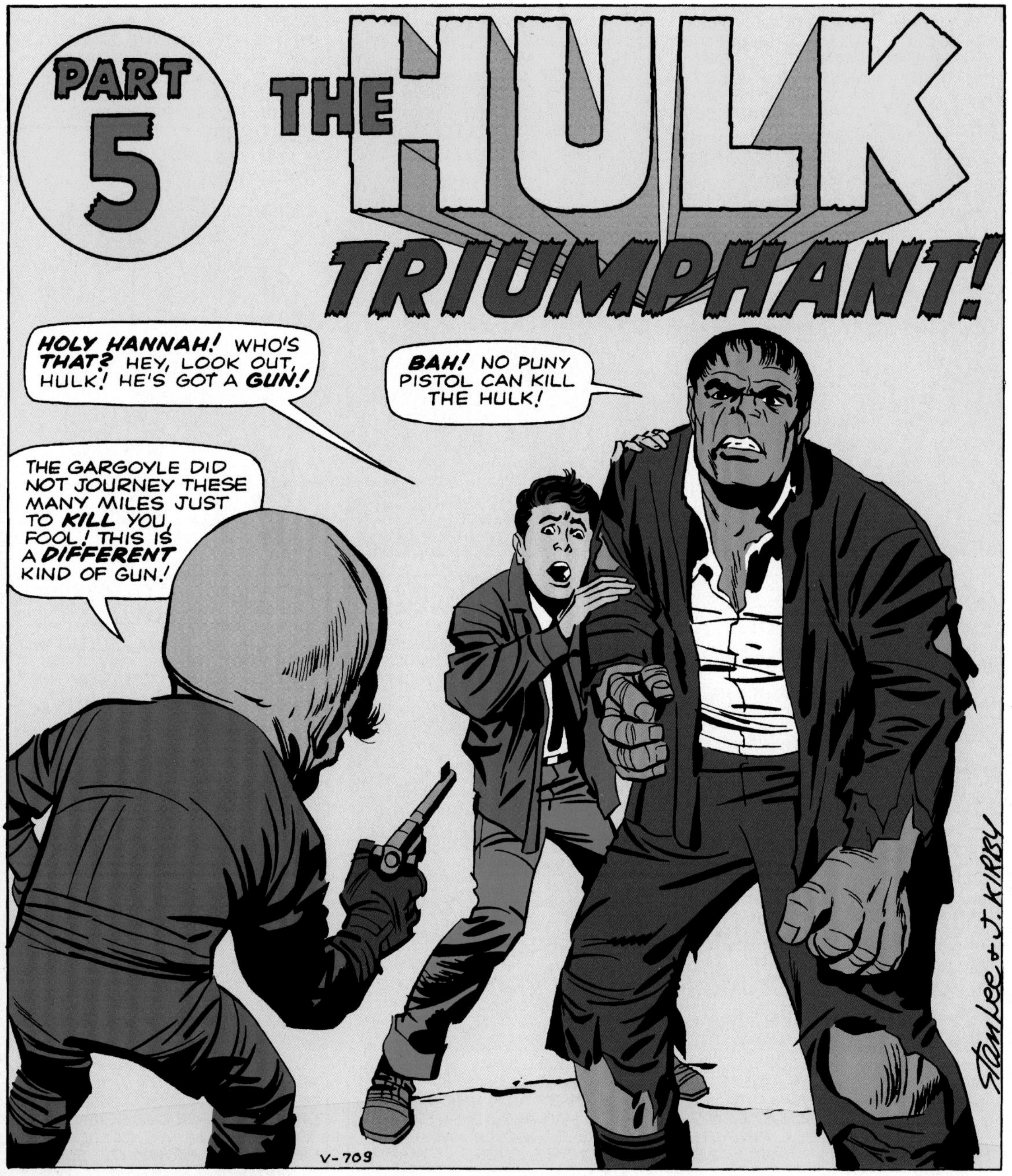
PART 5
THE HULK TRIUMPHANT!
HOLY HANNAH! WHO'S THAT? HEY, LOOK OUT, HULK! HE'S GOT A GUN!
BAH! NO PUNY PISTOL CAN KILL THE HULK!
THE GARGOYLE DID NOT JOURNEY THESE MANY MILES JUST TO KILL YOU, FOOL! THIS IS A DIFFERENT KIND OF GUN!
STAN LEE + J. KIRBY
V-709

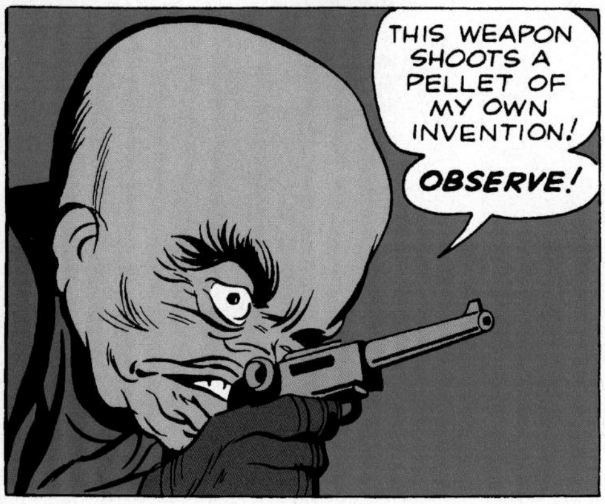
THIS WEAPON SHOOTS A PELLET OF MY OWN INVENTION! OBSERVE!

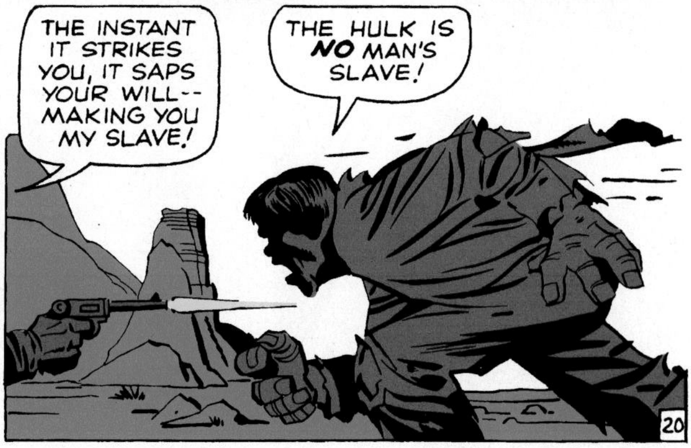
THE INSTANT IT STRIKES YOU, IT SAPS YOUR WILL--MAKING YOU MY SLAVE!
THE HULK IS NO MAN'S SLAVE!

HAH! THE GARGOYLE IS NEVER WRONG!

AND THOUGH *YOU* SEEM TOO UNIMPORTANT TO WASTE ANOTHER PELLET ON, I BELIEVE IN TAKING NO CHANCES!

IT IS *DONE!* BOTH OF YOU... RISE, AND FOLLOW ME!

RISE...

FORTUNATELY, IN THE EXCITEMENT OF THE MOMENT, THE GARGOYLE DOES NOT NOTICE THE UNCONSCIOUS GIRL LYING IN THE SHADOWS BEHIND HIS TWO HELPLESS PRISONERS!

HOW EASY IT IS FOR THE GARGOYLE TO BE VICTORIOUS!

AND MOMENTS LATER...

BETTY! BETTY!

DAD... IT-- IT WAS HORRIBLE!

IT WAS *THE HULK!* HE CAME FROM OUT OF THE DARKNESS! HE--HE WAS *TERRIFYING!*

THERE, THERE, MY DEAR! YOU'RE SAFE NOW!

BUT WHERE DID HE *GO?* WHAT DID HE *WANT?* OR--OR DID I *IMAGINE* THE WHOLE THING?

I'LL *FIND* HIM, BETTY! I *SWEAR* TO YOU, MY CHILD, I'LL FIND HIM AND DESTROY HIM!

AND YET, IN SPITE OF EVERYTHING, THERE WAS SOMETHING... SOMETHING *SAD* ABOUT HIM!! ALMOST AS THOUGH HE WAS SEEKING... HELP!

I'LL FIND HIM! IF IT TAKES AN *ETERNITY,* I'LL FIND THAT MONSTER!

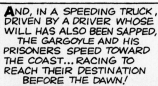

AND, IN A SPEEDING TRUCK, DRIVEN BY A DRIVER WHOSE WILL HAS ALSO BEEN SAPPED, THE GARGOYLE AND HIS PRISONERS SPEED TOWARD THE COAST... RACING TO REACH THEIR DESTINATION BEFORE THE DAWN!

FASTER! *FASTER!*

WHAT A *PRIZE* THE HULK WILL BE.!! WHAT A FANTASTIC SPECIMAN FOR OUR SCIENTISTS TO STUDY! IF WE COULD CREATE AN *ARMY* OF SUCH POWERFUL CREATURES, WE COULD RULE THE EARTH!

21

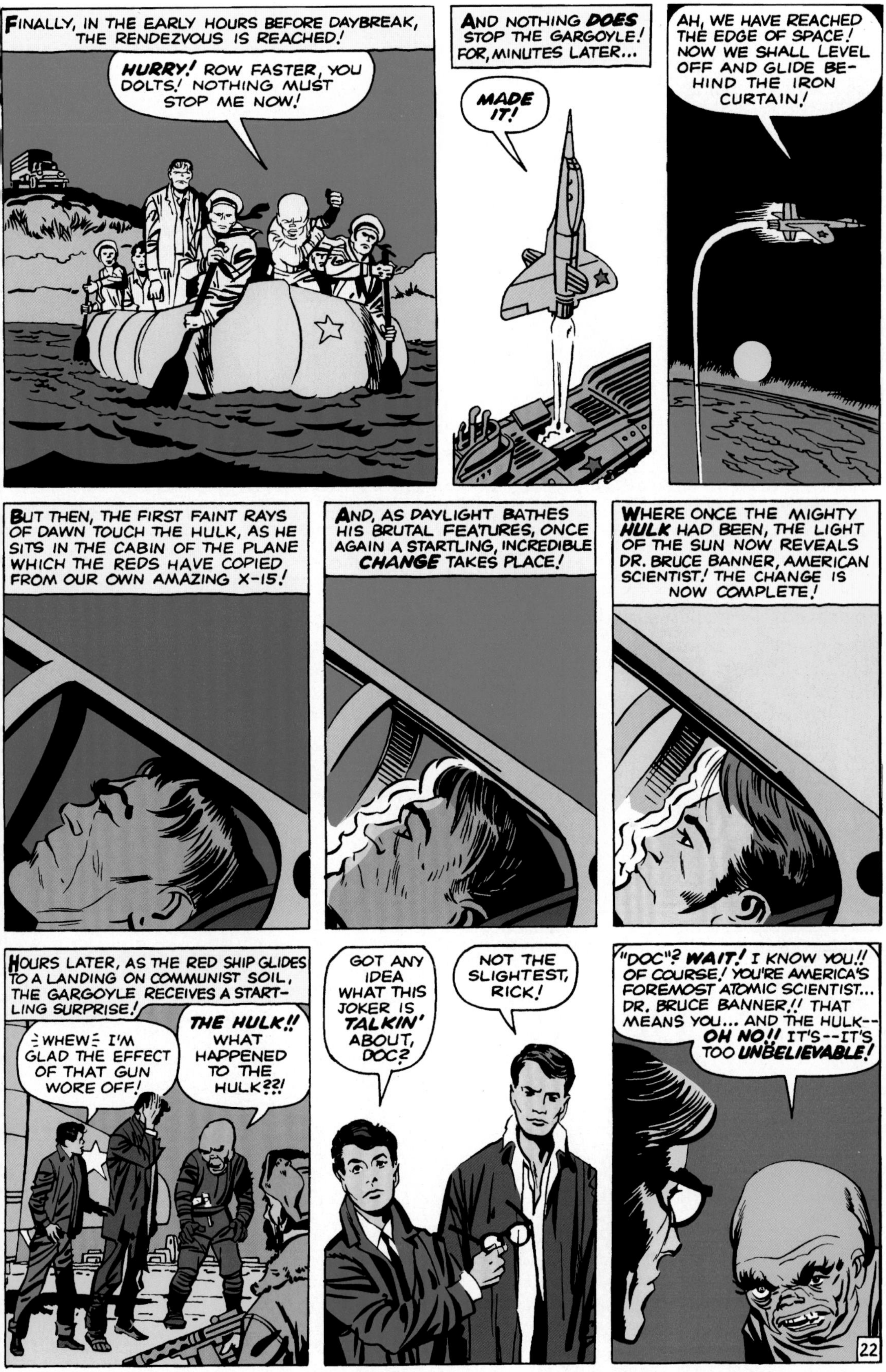
FINALLY, IN THE EARLY HOURS BEFORE DAYBREAK, THE RENDEZVOUS IS REACHED!
HURRY! ROW FASTER, YOU DOLTS! NOTHING MUST STOP ME NOW!
AND NOTHING DOES STOP THE GARGOYLE! FOR, MINUTES LATER...
MADE IT!
AH, WE HAVE REACHED THE EDGE OF SPACE! NOW WE SHALL LEVEL OFF AND GLIDE BEHIND THE IRON CURTAIN!
BUT THEN, THE FIRST FAINT RAYS OF DAWN TOUCH THE HULK, AS HE SITS IN THE CABIN OF THE PLANE WHICH THE REDS HAVE COPIED FROM OUR OWN AMAZING X-15!
AND, AS DAYLIGHT BATHES HIS BRUTAL FEATURES, ONCE AGAIN A STARTLING, INCREDIBLE CHANGE TAKES PLACE!
WHERE ONCE THE MIGHTY HULK HAD BEEN, THE LIGHT OF THE SUN NOW REVEALS DR. BRUCE BANNER, AMERICAN SCIENTIST! THE CHANGE IS NOW COMPLETE!
HOURS LATER, AS THE RED SHIP GLIDES TO A LANDING ON COMMUNIST SOIL, THE GARGOYLE RECEIVES A STARTLING SURPRISE!
-WHEW- I'M GLAD THE EFFECT OF THAT GUN WORE OFF!
THE HULK!! WHAT HAPPENED TO THE HULK??!
GOT ANY IDEA WHAT THIS JOKER IS TALKIN' ABOUT, DOC?
NOT THE SLIGHTEST, RICK!
"DOC"? WAIT! I KNOW YOU!! OF COURSE! YOU'RE AMERICA'S FOREMOST ATOMIC SCIENTIST... DR. BRUCE BANNER!! THAT MEANS YOU... AND THE HULK-- OH NO!! IT'S--IT'S TOO UNBELIEVABLE!
22

UNDER CLOSE GUARD, THE GARGOYLE RUSHES HIS PRISONERS TO HIS SECRET STRONGHOLD, AND THEN...

YOUR SECRET IS A SECRET NO LONGER, BANNER!

I *KNOW* THAT YOU AND THE HULK ARE THE SAME!!

DOC! WHAT DO WE DO *NOW?*

EASY, RICK! IT'S *HIS* PLAY SO FAR!

BUT *WHY?* WHY WOULD YOU *WANT* TO BE A *MONSTER?* YOU MUST BE *INSANE!* IT--IT'S THE MOST HORRIBLE THING IN THE WORLD TO BE A FREAK-- A GARGOYLE! LIKE *ME!*

DOC! HE'S CRYING!

I'D GIVE *ANYTHING* TO BE NORMAL! *ANYTHING!*

SO WOULD I--BUT I AM AS HELPLESS AS YOU!

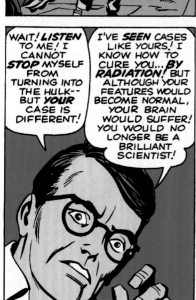

WAIT! *LISTEN* TO ME! I CANNOT *STOP* MYSELF FROM TURNING INTO THE HULK-- BUT *YOUR* CASE IS DIFFERENT!

I'VE *SEEN* CASES LIKE YOURS! I KNOW HOW TO CURE YOU...*BY RADIATION!* BUT ALTHOUGH YOUR FEATURES WOULD BECOME NORMAL, YOUR BRAIN WOULD SUFFER! YOU WOULD NO LONGER BE A BRILLIANT SCIENTIST!

DOC! YOU AIN'T GONNA *HELP* THAT CREEP, ARE YOU??!

QUIET, RICK!

NO MATTER *WHAT* HAPPENS TO ME... EVEN IF I *DIE*... SO LONG AS I COULD DIE AS-- *A MAN!*

THEN, AT A COMMAND FROM THE GARGOYLE, ALL IS MADE READY...

NOW!

AND, WHERE A *GARGOYLE* HAD BEEN LYING...

DOC! IT'S WORKING!

...*A MAN* ARISES!

YOU DID IT!

YOU DID IT!

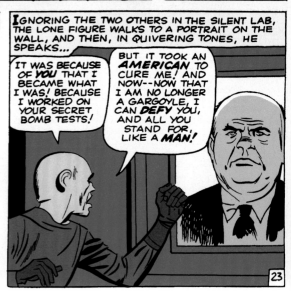

IGNORING THE TWO OTHERS IN THE SILENT LAB, THE LONE FIGURE WALKS TO A PORTRAIT ON THE WALL, AND THEN, IN QUIVERING TONES, HE SPEAKS...

IT WAS BECAUSE OF *YOU* THAT I BECAME WHAT I WAS! BECAUSE I WORKED ON YOUR SECRET BOMB TESTS!

BUT IT TOOK AN *AMERICAN* TO CURE ME! AND NOW--NOW THAT I AM NO LONGER A GARGOYLE, I CAN *DEFY* YOU, AND ALL YOU STAND FOR, LIKE A *MAN!*

23

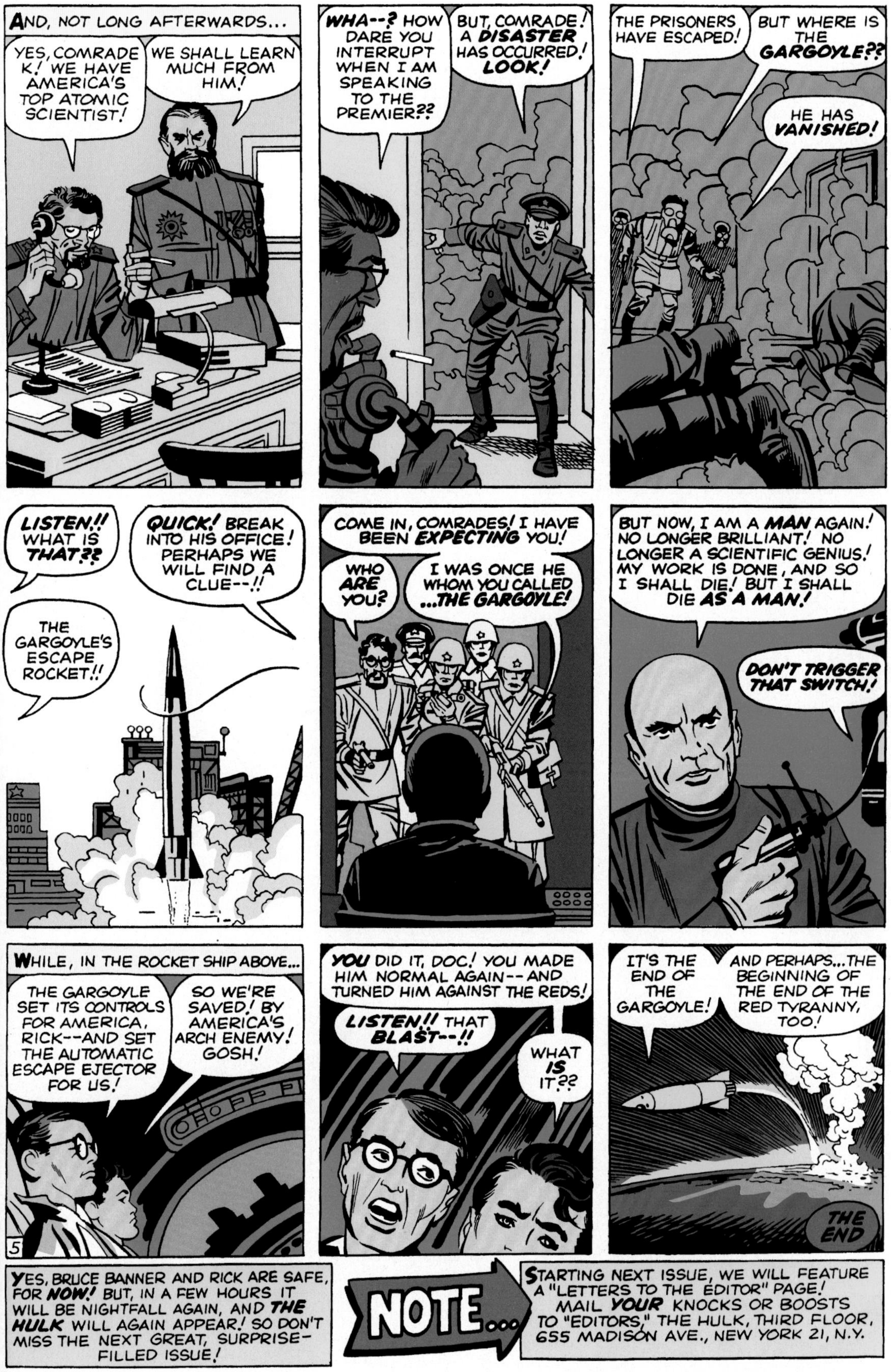
AND, NOT LONG AFTERWARDS...
YES, COMRADE K! WE HAVE AMERICA'S TOP ATOMIC SCIENTIST!
WE SHALL LEARN MUCH FROM HIM!
WHA--? HOW DARE YOU INTERRUPT WHEN I AM SPEAKING TO THE PREMIER??
BUT, COMRADE! A DISASTER HAS OCCURRED! LOOK!
THE PRISONERS HAVE ESCAPED!
BUT WHERE IS THE GARGOYLE??
HE HAS VANISHED!
LISTEN!! WHAT IS THAT??
QUICK! BREAK INTO HIS OFFICE! PERHAPS WE WILL FIND A CLUE--!!
THE GARGOYLE'S ESCAPE ROCKET!!
COME IN, COMRADES! I HAVE BEEN EXPECTING YOU!
WHO ARE YOU?
I WAS ONCE HE WHOM YOU CALLED ...THE GARGOYLE!
BUT NOW, I AM A MAN AGAIN! NO LONGER BRILLIANT! NO LONGER A SCIENTIFIC GENIUS! MY WORK IS DONE, AND SO I SHALL DIE! BUT I SHALL DIE AS A MAN!
DON'T TRIGGER THAT SWITCH!
WHILE, IN THE ROCKET SHIP ABOVE...
THE GARGOYLE SET ITS CONTROLS FOR AMERICA, RICK--AND SET THE AUTOMATIC ESCAPE EJECTOR FOR US!
SO WE'RE SAVED! BY AMERICA'S ARCH ENEMY! GOSH!
5
YOU DID IT, DOC! YOU MADE HIM NORMAL AGAIN--AND TURNED HIM AGAINST THE REDS!
LISTEN!! THAT BLAST--!!
WHAT IS IT??
IT'S THE END OF THE GARGOYLE!
AND PERHAPS...THE BEGINNING OF THE END OF THE RED TYRANNY, TOO!
THE END
YES, BRUCE BANNER AND RICK ARE SAFE, FOR NOW! BUT, IN A FEW HOURS IT WILL BE NIGHTFALL AGAIN, AND THE HULK WILL AGAIN APPEAR! SO DON'T MISS THE NEXT GREAT, SURPRISE-FILLED ISSUE!
NOTE...
STARTING NEXT ISSUE, WE WILL FEATURE A "LETTERS TO THE EDITOR" PAGE! MAIL YOUR KNOCKS OR BOOSTS TO "EDITORS," THE HULK, THIRD FLOOR, 655 MADISON AVE., NEW YORK 21, N.Y.

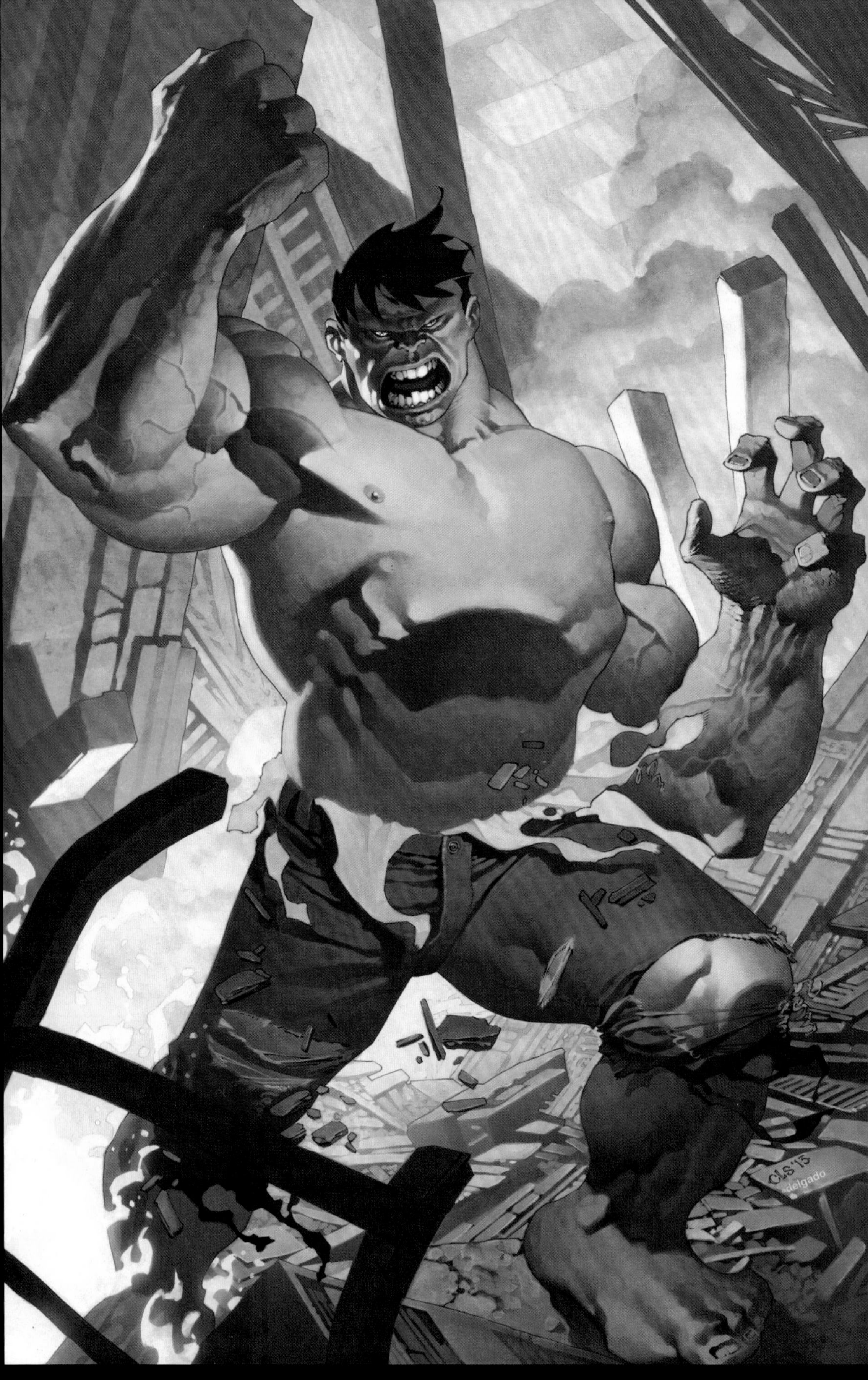
CLS'13
delgado

#1 VARIANT BY CHRIS STEPHENS & EDGAR DELGADO

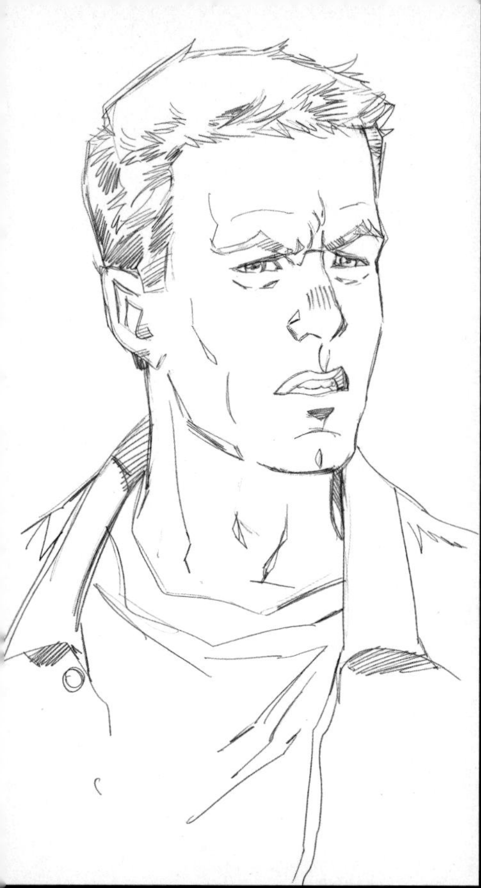

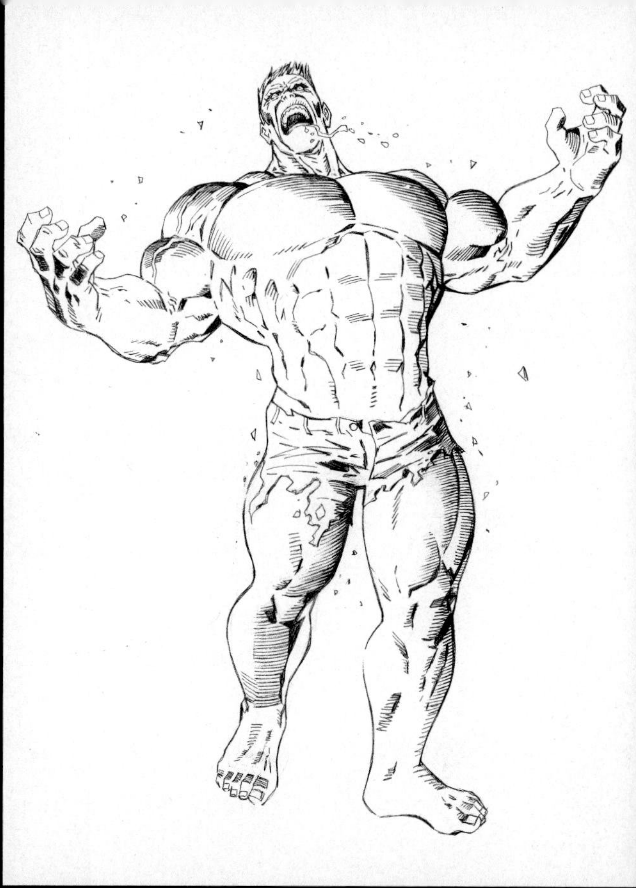

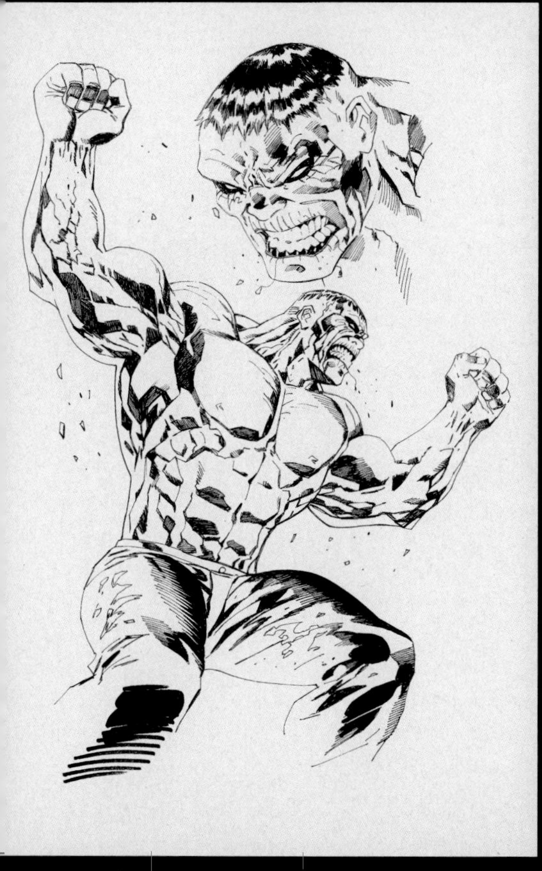

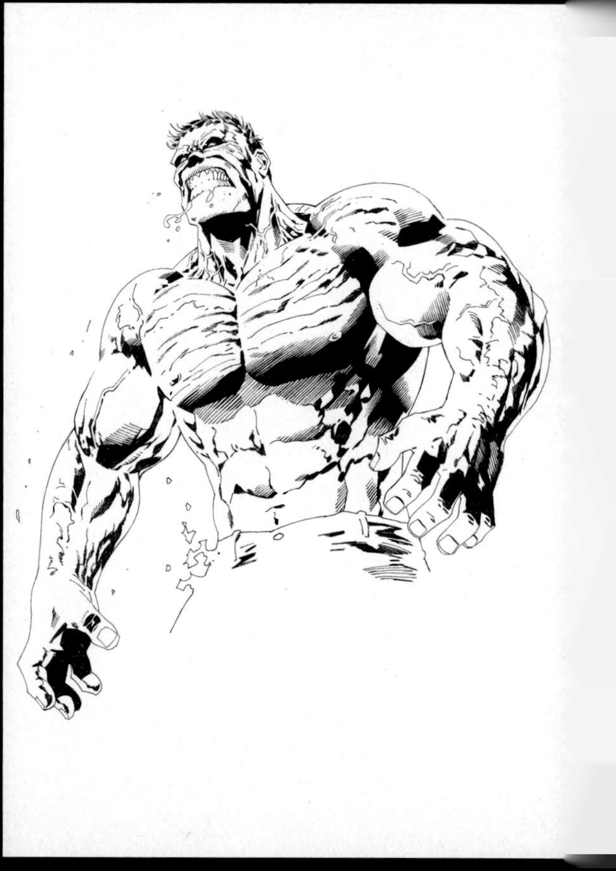

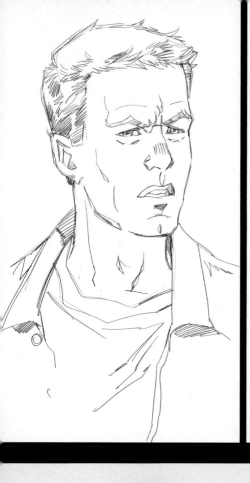

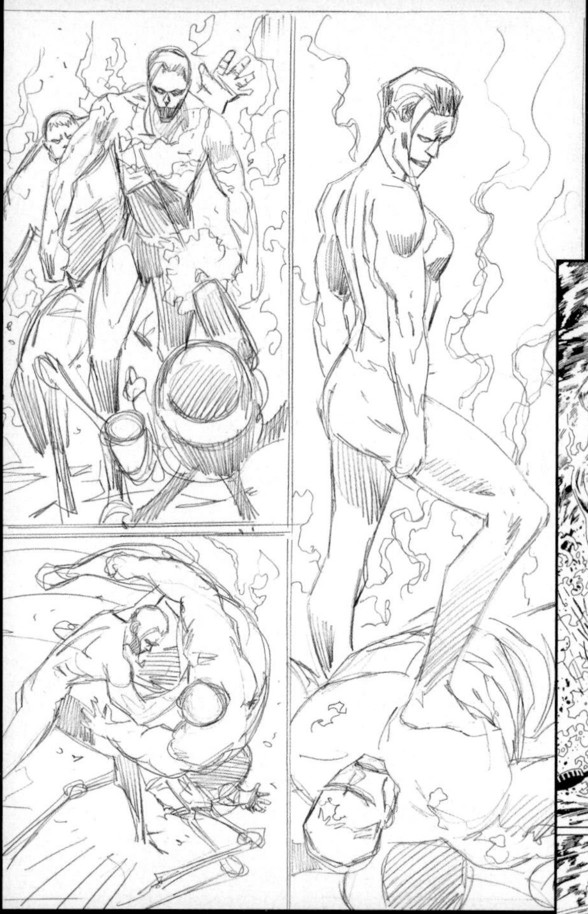

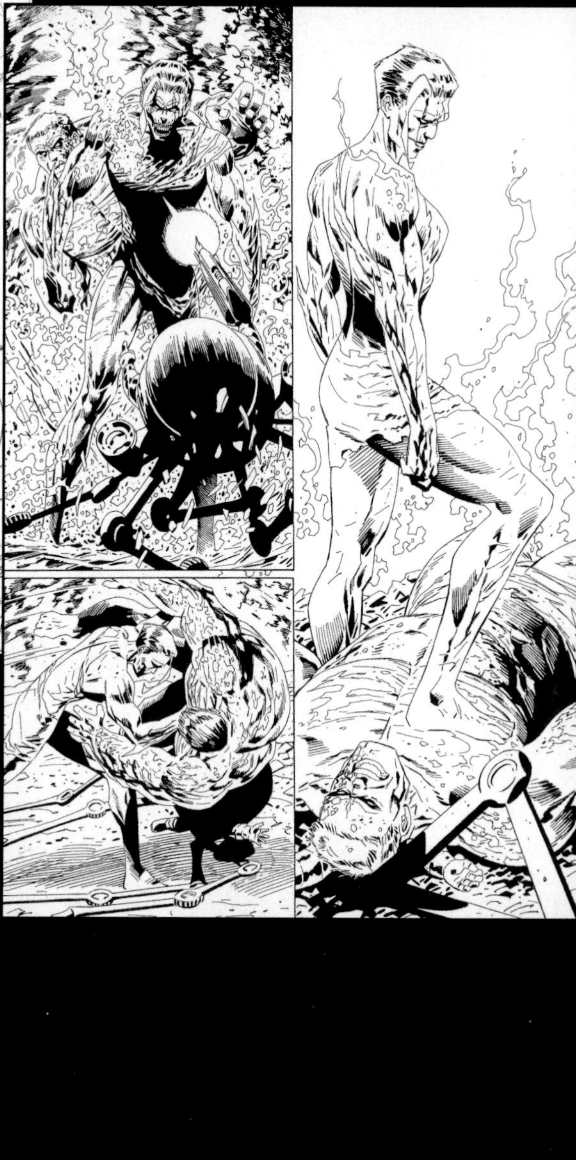

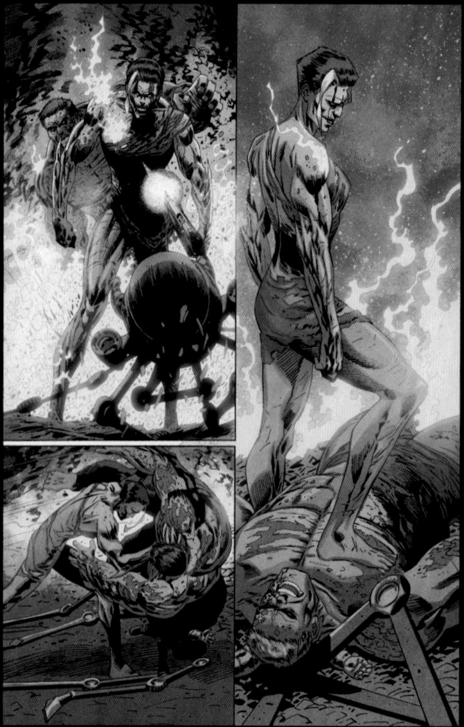

#4 PAGE 12 PENCILS, INKS AND COLOR